COMMUNITY DESIGN
AND THE CULTURE OF CITIES

Community design
and the culture of cities

The crossroad and the wall

EDUARDO E. LOZANO

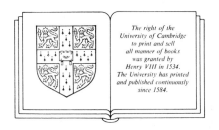

The right of the
University of Cambridge
to print and sell
all manner of books
was granted by
Henry VIII in 1534.
The University has printed
and published continuously
since 1584.

CAMBRIDGE UNIVERSITY PRESS

Cambridge
New York   Port Chester   Melbourne   Sydney

Published by the Press Syndicate of the University of Cambridge
The Pitt Building, Trumpington Street, Cambridge CB2 IRP
40 West 20th Street, New York, NY 10011, USA
10 Stamford Road, Oakleigh, Melbourne 3166, Australia

© Cambridge University Press 1990

First published 1990

Printed in the United States of America

Library of Congress Cataloging-in-Publication Data
Lozano, Eduardo E.
Community design and the culture of cities : the crossroad and the
wall / Eduardo E. Lozano.
p.   cm.
ISBN 0-521-38067-7. – ISBN 0-521-38979-8 (pbk.)
1. City planning.   2. Neighborhoods.   3. Architects and community.
I. Title.
HT166.L69   1990
307.1′216–dc20
                                               90-1431
                                               CIP

British Library Cataloguing in Publication Data
Lozano, Eduardo E.
Community design and the culture of cities : the crossroad
and the wall.
1. Cities. Social planning
I. Title
307.1216

ISBN 0-521-38067-7 hardback
ISBN 0-521-38979-8 paperback

To Elizabeth,
Paula Maria, Julieta, and Florencia

CONTENTS

CONTENTS

viii

PART FOUR
*Which deals with the lessons learned from
traditional settlements and their applications to
community design*

SOURCES OF ILLUSTRATIONS

Alinari/Art Resource: Figs. 2.1 (bottom), 3.13 (left, right, p. 56; bottom, p. 57)

Wayne Andrews/ESTO: Figs. 3.8 (top), 5.8

Archivo General de Indias: Fig. 5.5

J. H. Aronson: Fig. 10.17

Edmund N. Bacon, *Design of Cities* (Viking, 1974): Figs. 2.3 (top, p. 19), 2.6 (top), 2.10, 3.2, 10.6 (bottom), 11.8 (bottom)

Georg Braun, *Civitates Orbis Terrarum* (Cologne, 1576): Fig. 10.4 (top)

British Tourist Authority: Figs. 3.17 (top), 12.4 (top)

California Department of Transportation: Fig. 5.6 (bottom)

Colen Campbell, *Vitruvius Britannicus* (London, 1715): Fig. 6.2 (bottom)

Chicago Architectural Photo Company, David R. Phillips: Fig. 3.14 (p. 58)

Doubleday, a division of Bantam Doubleday Dell Publishing Group, Inc./© 1975 by H. Wentworth Eldredge (ed.), *World Capitals* (1975): Fig. 5.1

Dr. Jonathan Drachman: Figs. 6.1 (top), 10.18 (right, bottom), 12.4b, 12.10 (bottom)

Encyclopaedia Britannica, Inc.: Fig. 7.1

Fondation Le Corbusier: Figs. 2.3 (bottom, p. 19), 2.6 (bottom), 2.8 (bottom), 12.10 (p. 284)

French Government Tourist Office: Figs. 7.2, 10.3 (bottom)

Frederick Gutheim, *Alvar Aalto* (Braziller, 1960): Fig. 11.9

Hedrich–Blessing: Fig. 3.5

Japan Information Center, Consulate General of Japan, New York: Fig. 3.4 (top)

Robert Lautman: Fig. 5.3

Marburg/Art Resource: Fig. 3.13 (top, p. 57), 10.7

Metropolitan Life Insurance Company: Fig. 12.10 (bottom, p. 285)

René Millon: Fig. 3.6

MIT Press/S. E. Rasmussen, *Towns and Buildings* (1969): Figs. 2.9, 3.3, 5.2, 5.7, 8.4 (p. 181), 10.6 (top), 10.13 (right) xii

ACKNOWLEDGMENTS

Several colleagues and friends generously contributed their time to read and comment on early drafts of the manuscript: Professor William Alonso and Professor François Vigier of Harvard University, Professor William Porter of MIT, Ms. Roberta Pappas, Dr. and Mrs. John Stanbury, and Dr. and Mrs. Daniel Drachman. To them I extend my warmest appreciation. I am also indebted to the three readers of Cambridge University Press, who offered valuable insights.

I am especially thankful to my editors, Susan Milmoe, Laura Dobbins, Mary Nevader, and Helen Wheeler, as well as Deborah Menzell, who worked tirelessly to produce this book. Many people and institutions – more than I can mention here – kindly assisted me in assembling the illustrations. The several versions of the book were typed by Karen Arthur and Jane Barnes.

This book has its origins in a variety of sources: my student days at Harvard with José Luis Sert, Fumihiko Maki, Jerzy Soltan, and other great teachers; my research with colleagues and students while I was teaching at Princeton and Harvard. But the main seeds for the book can be found in my professional practice as a planner and architect, in the United States, Latin America, and elsewhere. In my firm, I have worked with partners and associates who have supported me and with whom my ideas have grown and matured.

My family has been a source of strength; my three daughters and especially my wife have always been at my side, supporting and inspiring my efforts.

PROLOGUE

This book is for many people, for those who face a challenging profession or are studying with the feeling that the pearl lies in other shells. But it is directed not only to professionals and academicians. It is for those who love cities; it is for politicians and decision makers who can influence the cultural and socioeconomic forces that affect urban areas; it is for those who are studying history or sociology and are concerned with the future of cities; it is for those who appreciate beauty and have to close their eyes to our environments; it is for those who are struggling for democracy and equality and are seeking ways to create a more human community; it is for those who are shaping new societies and realize that they should not follow the industrialized countries' footsteps; it is for our children and generations of yet unborn children for whom we may leave either a mechanistic world of materialism and exploitation or a civilized community with human, spiritual, and aesthetic values.

Community life should span a continuum of experiences, from climactic urban environments to more intimate, smaller-scale settlements. If community life and urbanity are missing from human experience, there is a serious flaw in society. The purpose of this book is to highlight how community design affects the environment of almost everyone and how community design can fail – indeed, betray – its purpose in societies that ignore urban life. Lovers of cities will understand this book very easily; those who do not know about urbanity and community will be challenged in their beliefs.

Community design should be concerned with the organization of human communities – of entire cities and small towns, of central business districts and suburban areas. I prefer to use the concept of "community" design instead of the better known "urban" design to acknowledge the need to reach villages and small settlements as well as larger urban areas. I also prefer to focus first on "organization" and only later on "form" to stress the systematic basis of community design.

Given the nature of postindustrial society, what is the role of community design? How can the design of human settlements restore the opportunity for choice and exchange that characterizes successful cities? This book is about the sort of community design that will have to come into being within a framework of humane and democratic goals.

If I have tapped many sources and ventured into many fields – sometimes tentatively, always searching for multi-disciplinary bridges – it is because the design of cities and urban areas requires a broad, yet profound understanding of the way cities function. Community design must be based on good technical knowledge, imagination, analytical understanding of the systematic nature of cities, and political commitment to social justice and democracy.

Three major theses are presented in this book: first, that the task of community design is foreign to professional designers, who have lost sight of the accumulated tradition of history; second, that professional designers do not have sufficient insights into the systematic organization of urban areas, and thus lack analytical capacity; and third, that professional designers seem unable to recognize antiurban cultural trends.

The book is organized into four parts. The first is an introduction, dealing with the origin of community design and an initial statement of urban form. The second probes the nature of urban systems, the organization behind urban form and urban processes. The third discusses substantive urban issues, as well as the pervasive influence of antiurban cultural trends. And the fourth returns to urban form, and the rediscovery of lessons from traditional settlements that are applicable to our time.

PART ONE

*Which deals with urban problems today,
community design as a profession, and the
nature of urban form*

CHAPTER I

CITIES TODAY

Cities are civilization; the word "civilization" – related to the Latin *civilitas, civis,* and *civitas* – refers to the culture of cities, places where a heterogeneous mixture of people are concentrated in clusters of meaningful size to exchange – exchange goods, services, and ideas. Cities are not simplistic homogeneous communities with single-minded purposes; those are military camps or company towns, not urban communities. Cities are places where people both compete and cooperate with one another, but they are not merely profit-making corporate entities. And regardless of the differences among their citizens, cities always define their community, as against the outside world; a settlement with internal defense walls cannot be called a true community.

Urbanity is the quality of a civilized community. It is characterized mainly by choice – a civilized community offers its citizens a range of lifestyles – and is expressed in ritualized behaviors of symbolic value. True cities need not be large; it is important to remember that the cities that cradled civilization were small by contemporary standards, and that even today small towns in many parts of the world still display far more urbanity than some vast metropolises. Small settlements can provide opportunities for choice, exchange, and interaction. Indeed, the potential for urbanity in communities of widely different sizes suggests the clear possibility of reshaping postindustrial settlements in physical settings that maximize opportunities for exchange and choice.

If one judges cities today by the universal standards of urbanity and civilization, the conclusions are distressing. Even though affluence is at a peak in history, education is widespread, and there is a tendency to think that we have reached the highest point of civilization, many cities appear to be disintegrating. In industrialized countries, and especially in the United States, the middle and upper classes are abandoning cities to the poor, and large parts of urban areas are slowly becoming live-in ruins. A majority of the affluent population has been resettling in a segregated and dispersed suburbia that is neither urban nor rural and commuting daily to work. Suburban life in a dispersed, homogeneous environment is expressed in routines devoid of symbolism or spontaneity; here is a functional simplification that has reduced personal contact and the exchange aspects of the community and, with them, a sense of belonging. Some wealthy groups have been returning to a few cities – New York, Boston, San Francisco – gentrifying the most desirable areas and, in the process, expelling the poor from them. Whereas traditional cities built external walls against outsiders, cities in industrialized countries have become the first to build internal walls against themselves: The wealthy fear the poor, while the poor just fear.

In some metropolitan areas, glimpses of a postindustrial city have appeared, with the development of exurban centers combining employment and residential uses with automobile transportation. These centers offer an upgraded version of the suburban ideal through a greater variety of land uses, improved recreational facilities, and isolation from the old urban centers; this isolation is reinforced by social segregation and lack of metropolitan transit systems. The new exurban centers are trying to recapture small-town qualities with a very different scale, technology, and values, which explains not only their attraction to many but their structural contradictions as well. In other regions, communities have managed to maintain a small-town atmosphere, because they have been bypassed by economic development; as a result, their young people are leaving for the big cities.

Is the disintegration of cities the fault of designers – architects, urban designers, and city planners? In one sense, clearly it is not. There are limits to what community design can do. Powerful technological and socioeconomic forces have been critical in determining the evolving organization of human settlements – suburbanization of jobs and housing ostensibly resulting from new industrial production and information technologies, new transportation modes and facilities, and conscious public policies. This has resulted in permanent inner-city poverty stemming from declining numbers of entry-level jobs, lower educational quality, and segregation. In another sense, however, designers are at fault.

The failure of community design to recognize these forces and try to (re)create humane physical environments within the new framework has added to the disintegration of cities and increased the sterility of human life. Designers have passively followed trends without seriously questioning their causes and effects, and in this process, they have often aggravated the outcome. That the built form can aggravate social and environmental problems is established by two examples: the high-rise building for family public housing and the auto-oriented shopping-strip area.

Clearly, "better" design is no panacea for the ills of modern society; it is a simplistic approach that disregards the limited capacity of design to correct problems and often leads to attempts at superficial "embellishments" of wrong solutions. But design can, and must, be a tool of change, reorienting physical solutions toward more humane goals and challenging programmatic assumptions that would be at odds with urbanity and better communities. As one of the components of culture, design should have an active role in shaping human settlements, rather than passively echoing other factors. The central thesis of this book is that a community design that builds upon the lessons of the past and is cognizant of the complexity of current realities not only can improve human environments and alleviate social and economic ills, but can also help to reshape cultural goals. These goals must be selected not on the basis of the personal preferences of a single group, but on an understanding of what a civilized pluralistic community should be.

A closer look at the signs of urban disintegration indicates the complexity – and significance – of the job to be done. Community designers face an inherently antiurban society. Fewer choices and deterministic urban routines are signs of the widespread lack of community cohesion and urbanity. Shopping, for example, is now a strictly functional act of purchasing that involves a simple trip from one's home to a shopping center. However, urban shopping was once also a social ritual that included window shopping, promenading, meeting friends informally, and exchanging information. There is still some ritual shopping in a few downtown areas, but the links to community are weakened; many shoppers are suburbanites on an expedition to the city and are thus isolated from the community around them. Similarly, for many people recreation involves, for example, a strictly functional trip to an eight-screen moviehouse in a shopping center. However, true urban recreation was once also a ritual with ancillary stages before and after, in which people met at cafés and restaurants to talk and interact. Spontaneous meetings, exchanges, and unplanned enjoyment of the many activities and spaces of a city are no less important than purchasing goods or watching a movie.

Contributing to this breakup of urban life have been a host of technological developments. Instant communication has eliminated the need for people to go outside – they can watch everything from films to sports events on television and can shop, bank, and work via personal computer. No community remains – no excitement or expectation, no choice or chance – there is only a box that brings the world into the livingroom; the boundaries of reality becomes blurred. Much human contact – which used to take place in streets, plazas, and parks – has become prepackaged; romance has been replaced by singles bars or computer dating services, as another functional task to fulfill. Press conferences on television feed whatever political needs exist, replacing the lively debate that was always the basis for a true democratic community.

The evolution of homo urbanus to homo in cocoon reaches beyond the community to our cosmic relationship with the world around us. Nature is so far removed that many children have never seen a farm and do not know the source of foods; packaged food and pets are nature for millions. This alienation from nature implies more than a lack of information; it is an uprooting from the earth, from the cycles of nature, from life itself. Cities come into being because there was countryside, civilization against wilderness in a majestic play of contrasts. In a fully heated and air-conditioned world, bad weather is merely a nuisance, an obstacle to travel; good weather is simply an opportunity to enjoy a weekend. The seasons have lost their cosmic and ecological meaning; we no longer celebrate the wealth of events related to harvest and climate. It is only when nature shocks us with enough strength to break a glass wall that people notice it, and then usually with grief.

At the same time that technology is becoming more complicated, the new nonurban lifestyle has become an oversimplification of urban life in that the sense of regional identity has been eliminated and many communities are of the same homogeneous quality. Someone can travel around the world and arrive at the same airport and stay in the same hotel anywhere. In every city, suburban areas tend to be increasingly homogeneous, with the result that people do not have contact with different groups, and children grow up with limited social experience. Residential areas are subdivided by class, race, and even age, resulting in monotonous environments, a weak sense of community, and, in many cases, isolation. The pressure of a homogenized lifestyle has forced people to live fantasies of power and success by proxy. Fantasies that compensate for the sterility of life have resulted in the star myth, the elevation of sports and popular music idols to the forefront of culture, as well as the vicarious living of a "fuller" life through television soap operas. The major "landmarks" of other cultures have been diminished: Religion, morality, ethics, and the supernatural are stored in the Saturday-and-Sunday file, and only the short-term heroes of sports and popular music are venerated.

Ours is a culture of short lives. There is no permanence, only cycles of fashion – in clothing as well as in politics, art, and even some sciences. This ephemerality is particularly damaging to community designers, who must deal with settlements that span centuries and not with painted stages. It is even more damaging to society itself, because the culture demands a constant stream of novelty. To feed the fashion cycle, for example, symbols are fast appropriated and then discarded as they fall out of favor with the avant-garde. Comparing U.S. health clubs – one of the latest fashions – with the Roman baths, it is clear that whatever advantage we hold in affluence and technology we lack in social imagination and urbanity.

The degradation of cultural symbols is an indication that there are no visible community hierarchies in the city; urban elites are still elites, but they are no longer urban. Traditionally, elites appropriated power as well as responsibilities; the Medicis in Florence, the pope in Rome, the king in London or Paris, the small lord in a village, the bourgeoisie in a mill town – they were all visible heads of a local hierarchy in a relationship of give and take with their community. Regardless of their tyrannical tendencies, the elites lived in the community and returned to the community part of what they extracted in the form of buildings, art, and institutions. It can be argued that they escaped to rural villas as soon as they could, but these were their second homes and not the true seats of power.

In contrast, the elites of U.S. cities have fled without abandoning power, becoming rural squires with urban power. Their social responsibility flows to charitable foundations – often with tax benefit – without any direct link with communities. These elites have kept their power and continue to

9

extract benefits from the urban system, but they return little in terms of personal presence, taste, or culture. On weekdays they occupy the corporate towers that house their offices, but they do not live in, nor are they committed to, the communities around them, which they seldom see. And thus cities evolve aimlessly in a vacuum lacking community objectives but with constant economic pressures; cities continue to develop, deteriorate, and redevelop with decreasing identity and symbolic values.

Without the patronage of the cultural elite and a truly democratic culture, ephemerality typifies most urban designs; fashions arrive and depart, leaving little more than cultural debris behind. For a few years we trumpeted new towns as a solution, only to build a few oversized subdivisions that were quickly forgotten; urban renewal, reputedly the salvation of cities, resulted in a number of ambitious projects with scarce urban value but with painful relocations for thousands of poor people. Most of the buildings in downtowns have a machine product look, shiny and anonymous as industrial products should be, a boredom of glass and steel blocks that establish no empathy with human beings. Here, as if in giant file cabinets, the country squires of suburbia work in corporations, banks, and government agencies. But some corporations wanted to have their own identity, and soon designers began to appropriate historical architectural symbols and apply them to the huge boxes as superficial decoration, leading to the rapid degradation of those symbols. The social art of architecture has been reduced to another parade of fashions.

The design of cities has suffered from the lack of care of a basically antiurban culture. The private automobile, tool and symbol of individual mobility, has been ruthlessly introduced inside cities with the result that the pedestrian scale and urban pattern have been disrupted by garages and highways. Urban public transit systems are considered marginal, second-rate options. There are, indeed, signs of a suburbanization of central cities, where some urban streets have become high-speed roads and human meeting places do not exist in urban spaces or public halls, but in private "atriums" and "malls" built within corporate headquarters, hotels, and shopping gallerias: atriums and malls built with such conspicuous consumption that one is shocked by the contrast with the nearby slums. This suburbanization of central cities brings with it all the contrived artificiality of the spot-lighted water cascades and manicured trees that appear everywhere as a reminder of nature held captive for consumers' pleasure.

There are signs that the shift of economic activities toward outlying areas is being consolidated. Major highway developments have been under way for some time. New, non-urban "centers," based on automobile transportation and attracting some of the most dynamic sectors of the economy, but lacking the key characteristic of urbanity, are emerging around metropolitan areas. It is as if a subconscious realization that cities are necessary is being distorted by an antiurban culture.

On the one hand, hedonism and banality have resulted in a culture that is negating urban life and the essence of cities. Although power is more concentrated than ever, the "trickling down" of affluence has allowed massive consumerism in the midst of dying traditions. On the other hand, city slums are growing, becoming ghettoes of poor, unemployed welfare clients and poorly paid workers, in striking contrast to the islands of unrestricted affluence. This scenario of the U.S. city is echoed in many Third World countries, where masses of landless peasants are crowding around the cities and elites are fleeing, partly in cultural imitation of their U.S. counterparts and partly in fear of the masses; old, established cities are evolving into metropolises of villages in a historical reversion to primitive ruralism.

Is it possible – indeed, does it make sense – to talk of designing cities within such antiurban cultures? Yes, but not in the conventional sense of producing immediate plans for the immediate problem. Yes, because cities are the base of civilization and communities are the base of society. Yes, because by probing and searching and proposing we might be able not only to produce valid and viable community designs, but also to call attention to the antiurban and anti-human forces at the root of so many of our problems and, in turn, to spur action to redirect these forces. Yes, because the task of building humane communities for the twenty-first century represents a major challenge to society and designers.

CHAPTER 2

TRADITIONS IN
COMMUNITY DESIGN

Or the professional as a newcomer

COMMUNITY DESIGN IN PERSPECTIVE:
A NEW PROFESSION

Professional designers are, historically speaking, newcomers to the problem of designing human settlements. Most urban communities throughout history have been "designed" by nonprofessionals, and most professional designers – architects – have devoted their attention to other matters. Our thesis that the problem of shaping human settlements is foreign to the professional design tradition should explain, at least in part, the inadequacies of architects in dealing with community design.

From a historical perspective, the takeover of community design by professionals is a comparatively recent phenomenon. It began to take place roughly in the last century, depending on the region and culture, and continues in many areas of the world. The most identifiable threshold is the Industrial Revolution in the Western world, which brought about the collapse of the craftsman as a designer and builder; this collapse also affected local decision-making units and small-scale enterprises. Other parts of the world experienced this process in successive decades, and in the Third World, urbanization rather than industrialization has been the major factor of change. The collapse of the preindustrial system permitted the introduction of an ever-growing professional influence in community design. A process of self-consciousness became apparent in all aspects of design, including community design.

Design has developed in all cultures along two parallel traditions, which we shall call "popular" and "professional" (Figure 2.1). These traditions have remained largely isolated from one another and, with some exceptions, have led to different design processes and solutions. The shaping of villages, towns, and cities occurred mostly within the realm of the popular design tradition, as did the design of dwellings. The human habitat was shaped by popular builders. Professional architects, however, concerned themselves with specific buildings and monuments, which represented a small, but highly visible share of the built environment. Their work did not include communal design.

Figure 2.1. The two design traditions. (Top) The popular tradition: Trujillo, a town in Extremadura, Spain. (Bottom) The professional tradition: Palazzo Chiericati, Vicenza, 1550. Andrea Palladio. (Art Resource/Alinari)

A survey of the design literature confirms the separation of the two traditions. Most books on architectural history concentrate on the professional tradition. A few studies consider both traditions in relation to one another, but these were undertaken only after art critics rediscovered the popular tradition.[1] In the past few decades, a series of works have focused on the popular tradition exclusively,[2] and a growing number of articles in professional journals have dealt with popular designs of specific cultures. The rediscovery of popular design has had an impact on professionals, owing mainly to the aesthetic appeal of its formal solutions.

THE POPULAR DESIGN TRADITION

The popular design tradition developed parallel to the professional tradition, though it was almost unrecognized by the professional groups. The popular tradition is an integral part of what anthropologists call "folk cultures."[3] Its design and building activity are rooted in a common stratum of experience and knowledge generated by the local culture, available to most of its members, who, in turn, add their own contributions.

Outstanding design products of the popular tradition are found in many areas and include crafts in addition to buildings. A fascinating craft, still vital today, is rug weaving in the Middle East, where nomads and villagers have competed with urban workshops for centuries. Shepherds weave their magnificent rugs during the winter months when they cannot be in the fields with their herds; the rugs are used by the family, bartered, or sold. The popular production of these masterpieces provides a clue to understanding the capacity of folk cultures.

Community design was once within the exclusive domain of craftsmen and artisans, townsfolk, villagers, and peasants, who were the designers, builders, and users of their own settlements. There was relatively little specialization, and as a result, no clearly identifiable group was responsible for community design; the activity was fairly open to many members of the culture. Design training was acquired through imitation at first and supported by memorization of practical rules (sometimes reinforced by magic or ritual), which defined the "correct" way of doing things; the continuity of traditional solutions was both cause and effect of this type of training. The development of valid and accepted traditions, handed down from generation to generation with only minor changes, was made possible by the high degree of stability typical of these cultures.

Imitation may continue to affect formal solutions long after a technology has changed. A well-known example is the Greek stone temple architecture, which is a formalization of early wood design solutions. Similar cases can be found at any time of history in any culture.

The dwellings and settlements of the popular design tradition belong to specific community typologies (Figure 2.2). These typologies tend to show minor variations at best; there is emphasis on maintaining traditional solutions, and design

Figure 2.2. Popular typologies. (Top) Medieval warehouses, Lüneburg, Hanseatic League. (Winn Swaan) (Left) Medieval houses, Reims. (Right) Town houses, Boston.

success is measured within type parameters. The design prototypes are improved over long periods of time by a slow trial-and-error process, in which successful variations are incorporated into later versions while unsuccessful ones are discarded. Cultural stability and marginal design changes permit an improvement process to take place. This process is observed with interest by the participants, but is perhaps too subtle to be noticed by an outside observer: Minor innovations are, from time to time, introduced by builders and assessed by the community, who, because of the stability of the tradition, are very sensitive to minor changes.

Individual buildings of the popular tradition are elements of the larger community pattern in which they are closely integrated, being largely undifferentiated from neighboring units of similar type. Furthermore, the construction of buildings and communities is carefully timed owing to the scarcity of resources; only the next immediate step is clearly defined, and later stages become improved versions of the first ones, the early experiences being used to good advantage. A capacity to grow and change is a characteristic of these built environments, which are never completed but are always evolving.

Popular designers organize buildings and communities according to the morphological determinants impinging on the problem: activities, access, topography, climate, and resources. The design response takes place through selected variations of the accepted typology, since most morphological determinants are typical of local conditions. Development programs are constituted by the requirements of simple and well-known activities and molded by generations of habit; programmatic specifications often remain implicit because they have become second nature to the members of the local culture. Forms are a cultural response to morphological and programmatic determinants, progressively acquiring symbolic value.

Users are sometimes builders themselves, obviating the need for explicit programming. The roles of designers and builders are always merged, so there is no need to translate the whole package of construction data from one mind to the other. There is close feedback between the process of design and production. Popular designers are essentially interpreters of the culture – cultural agents, in the words of Margaret Mead, who exhibit their individuality only through channels strictly institutionalized by traditional typologies and formalized responses.

The contrast between the two design traditions is sharp. The professional tradition forms the core of officially recorded design history, although its production accounts for a comparatively small percentage of the built environment. It is part of the so-called high culture, in which design work is produced for a client or patron of the arts, a member of the elite of a relatively complex society. Design activity is a result of the individual initiatives of the professional architect, who receives critical feedback from clients, fellow practitioners, and the elite at large. Styles, fashions, fads, academies, schools, and boards are all components of this tradition.

The buildings and built complexes (one hesitates to use the word "communities") of the professional design tradition belong to recognized styles of the high culture. Most buildings are unique, oriented toward elite uses: government (castles, palaces, town halls, parliaments), religion (temples, cathedrals, churches, mosques), specialized public facilities (museums, theaters, exhibition halls), and very few exclusive residences. It is indeed curious to skim any architectural survey and verify that this parade of elite buildings constitutes the "history of architecture," without major reference to the dwellings and communities of masses of people. Until recently, only a small proportion of human habitats were produced by this tradition, and the few settlements that have been designed by professionals are elite oriented, as are Karlsruhe, Brasilia, and Chandigarh – all seats of power exclusively (Figure 2.3).

In this tradition, there is a high degree of specialization within a correspondingly complex society, and identifiable professional groups are responsible for elite-oriented design activities. The high degree of specialization means not only that access to design activity is limited, but also that there is a division of labor among professionals, builders, academicians, and critics.

Until the Industrial Revolution – or the urbanization threshold in the Third World – the high culture was relatively stable, though not to the same degree as the popular culture. It was always subject to the effects of new intellectual ideas, styles, and fashions; the rate of change, however, was nowhere near the rapid change experienced today.

Based on the teaching of abstract rules (stylistic codes) in academic settings, professional design training was, and is, highly institutionalized under the guidance of professionals who, in many cases, specialized as teachers. The rules were, and are, codified in texts that became reference books for design professionals, until a new aesthetic came into prominence. The search for novelty in the storage shelves of history (revivals) was, and still is, considered valid.

The design solutions of this tradition originate in the rules of style but aim at achieving masterpieces, which may force major variations in style and typology. The emphasis is on producing a design that is clearly different from the rest, since the high culture and its professional bodies reward uniqueness. Change is introduced for the sake of the designer's prestige, and innovation is assumed desirable in itself. The sequence of high-culture design styles and typologies is one of cyclical breaks with the status quo and innovations rather than one of smooth improvements; new "solutions" are incorporated as fast as individual designers can develop them. In contrast to the popular trial-and-error process, the professional tradition places relatively less emphasis on the evaluative stage, and fewer experiences are transmitted from one work to the next.

Since the focus of this tradition is on the elite and since innovation is highly regarded, the design products tend to

Figure 2.3. Settlements of the professional tradition. (Below) Karlsruhe, built for the Margrave of Baden Durlach, begun 1709. (Thames and Hudson Ltd.) (Opposite top) Brasilia, built as capital of Brazil, 1957–60. Lucio Costa. (Edmund N. Bacon) (Opposite bottom) Chandigarh, built as capital of the Punjab, India, 1951–6. Le Corbusier. (Fondation Le Corbusier)

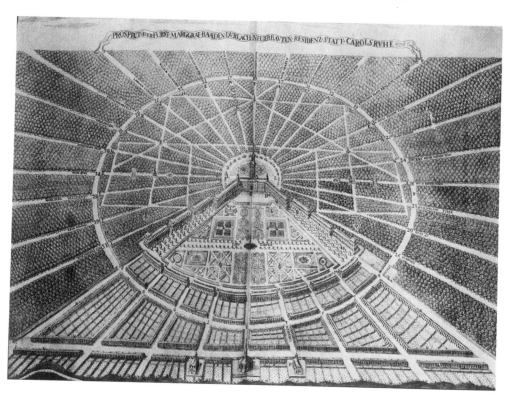

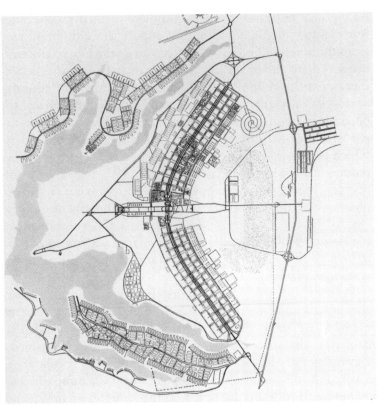

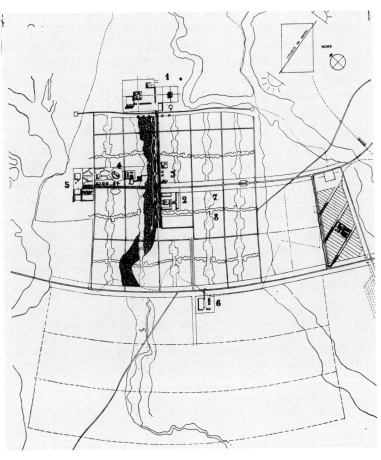

be unique, outstanding, and complete elements. Buildings (mostly for public and elite use) appear to be differentiated from the surrounding urban pattern; even the few settlements produced by this tradition seem distinct from other settlements. Furthermore, buildings and complexes are "comprehensively" designed as a whole, fully determined from the beginning; staging is not a prime consideration owing to the concentration of power and wealth among elite members, which permits the immediate satisfaction of the program and reduces the need for delays. Professional designs are comprehensive and instantaneous, even when time is a factor and phasing actually occurs. Financial constraints may be obstacles to the elite but are seldom accepted as a component of the design problem; thus, though a large project may have to be phased owing to budget limitations, the original design is seldom planned for this event.

Professionally designed environments are organized according to abstract rules, or laws of composition, that is, methods of achieving geometric order relatively independently of the morphological roots of the design problem. Examples are the baroque compositions of Versailles and Karlsruhe and the modern composition of Chandigarh. Development programs are based on the complex requirements of sophisticated, ritualized, and/or technological activities of elite groups. These requirements are explicitly stated in the program, and the design must fulfill specific criteria, such as the court etiquette at Versailles or the bureaucratic rules in Chandigarh and Brasilia.

Professional designers, as mentioned before, are creators of individualized designs who could be considered cultural agents only in the most general way; ostensibly they act as irritants to the culture by provoking waves of change. Furthermore, designers, builders, and developers are differentiated by specialized roles; the act of designing is removed from the act of implementing, with the result that it is necessary to translate ideas into actions across several minds. The specialization of designers and builders and the "noise" implicit in a communication channel between ideas and actions demand a much more refined feedback process than that which exists today.

COEXISTENCE OF THE TWO TRADITIONS

The two design traditions have developed radically different – in many cases opposite – characteristics based on different types of design problems, the popular tradition being concerned with the generation of human habitats and the professional tradition with the design of elite buildings. The two traditions are a manifestation of the dichotomy between high and folk cultures that coexist in society. Though the points of contact between the traditions have been minimal, there are some intriguing instances in which the two merged for extended periods of time.

One outstanding example is the medieval cathedral, which, though laid out by a master architect, integrated the design inputs of journeymen and craftsmen at different levels of detail (Figure 2.4). For example, while the basic location of columns was predetermined by the master architect, each capital was "designed" and sculpted by a different craftsman. As a result, variety was endless within an ordered total structure, and design responsibilities were spread among many of the participants. Local craftsmen did find ways of expressing themselves in an otherwise high-culture building. Indeed, cathedrals have a greater resemblance to cities than to buildings in terms of development time, structural complexity, functional variety, and change.

Another example of contact between the two traditions is the "bastide" towns of Europe, such as Montpazier in France and Freiburg in Switzerland, frontier outposts founded in the Middle Ages by kings and noblemen to protect their borders or to colonize a region (Figure 2.5). Although they were

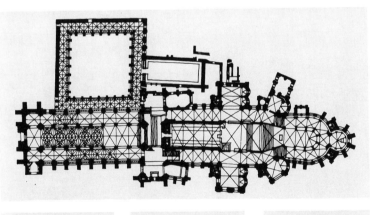

Figure 2.4. The merging of the two traditions: cathedrals. (Top) Canterbury Cathedral, plan, begun 1178. William of Sens. (Winn Swaan) (Bottom) Canterbury Cathedral, column capitals by various craftsmen.

designed by elites and usually built fairly rapidly, their general layouts were formalized versions of communities in the popular tradition, which allowed most of the pattern to be filled in by craftsmen.

Nonetheless, as already stated, the two design traditions have maintained a considerable degree of isolation, resulting in the accumulation of different experiences and, eventually, different attitudes and responses to design problems. Human habitats – towns, villages, and neighborhoods – have been conceived and built under very different assumptions and

Figure 2.5. The merging of the two traditions: bastides. Freiburg, Switzerland, built for the Dukes of Zahringen in the tenth century. (The Swiss National Tourist Office)

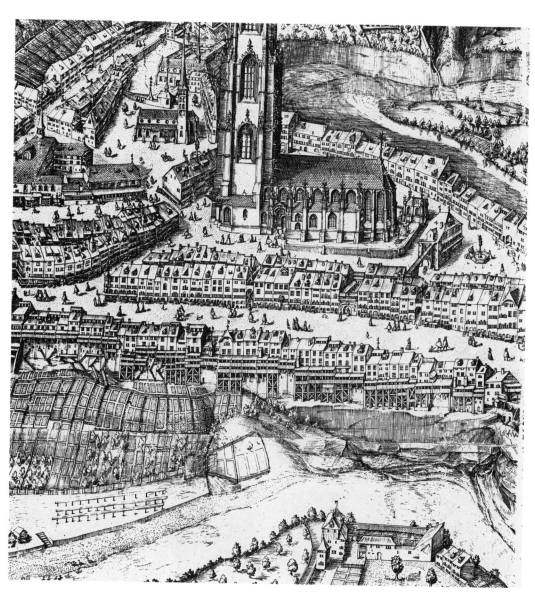

22

processes than elite buildings; the activity of community building has been foreign to professional designers.

The two design traditions coexisted in different cultural strata of the same society for a long time. The break came with the collapse of preindustrial societies – the Industrial Revolution – which led to the disappearance of the popular tradition and the takeover of the task of designing human habitats by the professional tradition. And here lies one root of the community design problem; professionals may be well suited to the design of elite buildings, but they are thoroughly inexperienced in the task of community design.

Regardless of the lack of experience with or even awareness of the issues involved in community design, the professional tradition rapidly adapted itself to the shaping of communities. Large-scale architecture became known as "urbanism," a term and attitude that have extended beyond the original Ecole de Beaux Arts and can be identified as the main source of what is known today as "urban design."

THE MAIN SOURCE: URBANISM

The physical design of urban areas today is the focus of several professional disciplines, which developed from different sources and merged only partially and uneasily. Urban design is a direct descendant of the professional design tradition, in the original Beaux Arts term, "urbanism." The design approach and characteristics of the professional tradition are evident in much of today's urban design practice.

The profession became self-conscious of its newly acquired responsibility in the last century when architects began to take over community designs. The Ecole de Beaux Arts and then the Modern movement saw urbanism as part of the realm of architectural practice and began to undertake the design of large-scale settlements.

Under this concept of urbanism, the physical design of urban areas is an extrapolation of the activity of individual building design, based more often than not on the same compositional rules. Indeed, the application of compositional rules – originating on the scale of buildings – to urban-scale complexes is the basic characteristic of urbanism, regardless of stylistic differences. This extrapolation of composition can be found in "schools" as different as the nineteenth-century Beaux Arts and the twentieth-century Congrès Internationale d'Architecture Moderne (CIAM), although the rules applied are, obviously, different (Figure 2.6). Compositional urban design was widely implemented after World War II, from Mies van der Rohe complexes in Chicago to the urban renewal plans found in every U.S. city.

As an example of this approach, consider one of the earliest and most recurrent "images" in the state of the art: the linear composition for urban organizations, which is clearly derived from the experience of many centuries of professional architectural practice. Linear compositions are a favorite of urban designers; architecturally, they are also commonly found in multibuilding complexes (Figure 2.7). The temple of Karnak is composed along a strict ceremonial axis, on which a series of built elements are sequentially laid in obvious relationship with a procession and ritual. The palace of Versailles faces an axial view that determines direction and symbolism. Although these two examples are borderline cases, since each of them reaches a scale and level of complexity that suggest a precinct, compositional rules are still successfully applied in establishing a layout. Within the aesthetics of each period, compositional rules perform the same task: that of providing a simple, yet powerful spatial idea, upon which a specific design can be developed.

However, the unrestricted application of compositional rules without any regard for the scale and nature of the design problem has resulted in cities designed as if they were buildings. The Linear City is one of the recurrent themes and images of modern urbanism, as is clear from the parade of projects that have been proposed: La Ciudad Lineal of Soria y Mata in 1882, La Cité Linéaire Industrielle of Le Corbusier, as well as Le Corbusier's plans for Algiers and Rio de Janeiro in the 1920s, Hood New Town in 1954, and many others (Figure 2.8). The Linear City was, and to some degree still is, justified on the basis of assumed advantages: It was said to accommodate growth easily, to facilitate a flexible distribution of activities, and to allow for efficient circulation. These claims, however, have never been clearly defined, and in the few cases in which a design has actually been evaluated they have not been confirmed.

Let us take, for example, one of the earliest claims about the efficiency of the Linear City, that commuting between residential and employment areas is minimized. This claim is based on the assumption that the two land uses should be designed as parallel bands so that people can live across the street from their factory or office. In the real world, the search for employment and housing leads to radically different situations, and not even under the most centralized planning

Figure 2.6 (*facing page*). Urbanism by composition. (Top) Prix de Rome, Ecole Nationale des Beaux Arts, 1922. (Edmund N. Bacon) (Bottom) Une ville contemporaine, Le Corbusier, 1922. (Foundation Le Corbusier)

24

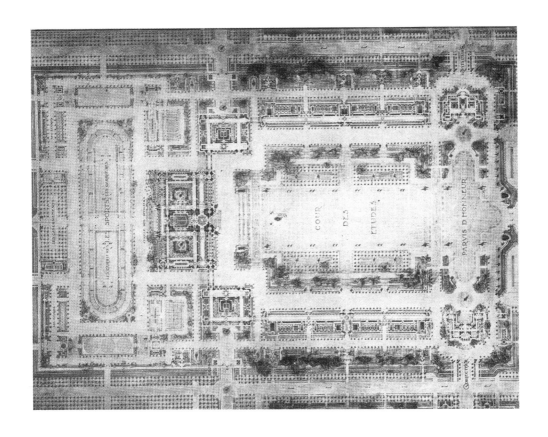

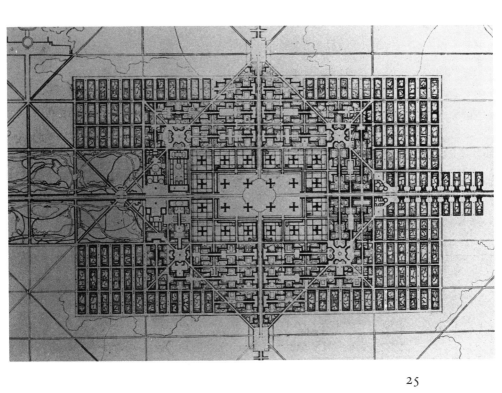

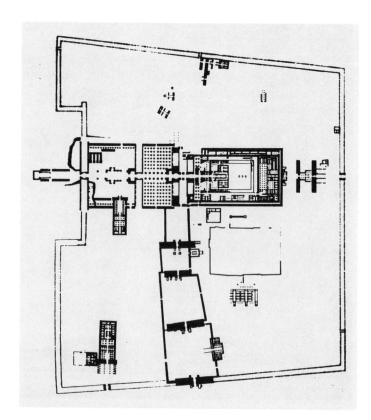

Figure 2.7. Linear composition in architecture. (Top) Temple of Amon, Karnak, 1200 B.C. (Bottom) Versailles palace and gardens, A.D. 1700. (Thames and Hudson Ltd.)

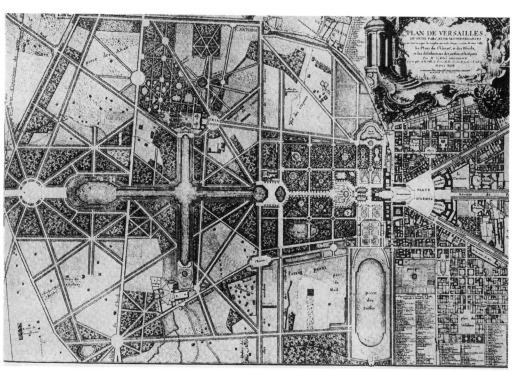

conditions do people live across the street from their jobs – as long as urban choices exist. In other words, this sort of efficiency can occur only in a nonurban environment such as a company town or a military camp. One must seriously question planning objectives that are based on authoritarian conditions in order to achieve efficiency. One must also question whether such schemes of job and house proximity are at all urban in any sense. The relative inexperience of professionals in dealing with community-wide design problems, as well as their lack of analytical insight, lead to mechanistic justifications to support a compositional image.

Urbanism, in merely transposing architectural compositional rules to urban complexes, restricts urban design to the choice of a single powerful compositional idea. This, of course, limits the issues to that of the internal coherence of the composition, but it has little relationship to the objective selection of a physical plan. Most historical precedents for professional urban design involved similar combinations of architectural composition and mechanistic justifications. It is sufficient to mention the many "utopian" designs that appeared in the Renaissance in Italy and northern Europe: formalistic compositions reflecting the simplified image of a

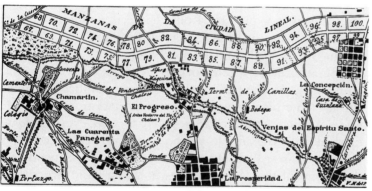

Figure 2.8. The Linear City. (Top) Ciudad Lineal, Madrid, 1882. Arturo Soria y Mata. (Bottom) Cité Linéaire, Rio de Janeiro, 1929. Le Corbusier. (Fondation Le Corbusier)

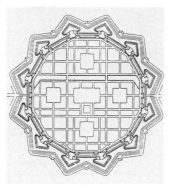

Figure 2.9. Renaissance utopias. (MIT Press) (Left) Vincenzo Scamozzi, ideal city, 1615. (Middle) Buonaiuto Lorini, ideal city, 1592. (Right) Palma Nuova, founded 1593.

community as perceived by a particular architect (Figure 2.9). Basically, urbanism postulates dealing with radically different scales and degrees of complexity in the built environment without changing design approaches and methodologies. But a city is not a large building.

There are historical exceptions to the typical compositional design of urbanism that have found fertile ground centuries later in the urban design explorations that have taken place since the late 1950s. In these exceptional cases, urban designs were not extrapolated from architectural practice but were developed by methods more properly suited to the nature of the design problem. Two of the most remarkable examples are the Sixtus V plan for Rome (sixteenth century) and the Haussman plan for Paris (nineteenth century).

The Sixtus V plan for Rome (Figure 2.10) aimed at establishing an ordered framework in a chaotic city, while facilitating the movement of pilgrims among a number of religious shrines. The plan consisted of transportation links between nodes where the main churches were located; every node was marked with the simple yet powerful vertical accent of an obelisk. This spatial framework was largely independent of the design of the new buildings; it was a basic structure on the urban scale that provided guidance for both physical development and circulation. The plan implied a sound understanding of the technological capabilities and cultural patterns of the time, as well as of the visual and movement implications for the city. It is remarkable that the plan was implemented in the span of two centuries after the death of Sixtus V in 1590, proving to be a true long-range design framework based on its own outstanding merits. Showing few conventional buildings, the plan exerted a critical influence on the long-range development of Rome. Seldom had so little in terms of actual construction had so great an urban "multiplier"

Figure 2.10 (*facing page*). The Sixtus V plan for Rome. (Edmund N. Bacon) (Top) The seven pilgrimage churches of Rome, before Sixtus V, 1575. (Bottom left) The same view with the addition of the new obelisks by Sixtus V, located at the nodes of movement links, 1612. (Bottom right) Transportation links, nodes, and obelisks, 1588.

28

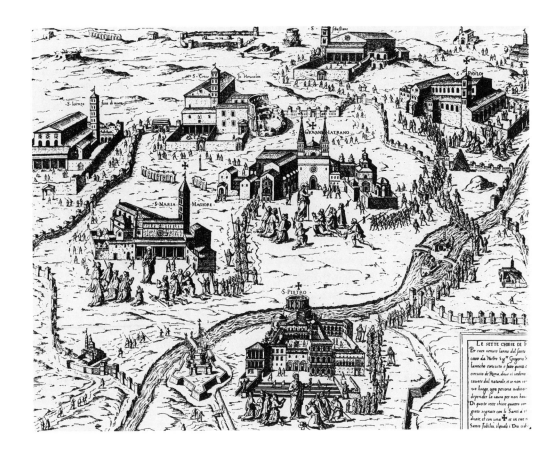

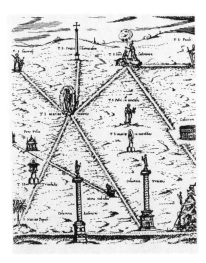

effect over centuries – one of the best indicators of real community design.

The Haussman plan for Paris (Figure 2.11) aimed at introducing order and control in the medieval pattern of the city, by opening new majestic boulevards – a design made up by transportation links and nodes as in the plan of Sixtus V. The difference between the two plans, of course, is that the Paris plan involved changes in the actual built pattern and placed heavy emphasis on the capacity to supress the rebellious working class in the city by changing the urban battlefields from narrow streets to wide boulevards. Some aspects of the Haussman plan can be criticized, such as its socially repressive characteristics or its separation of technical issues from political ones. In retrospect, however, the plan left a permanent imprint on Paris, which, in turn, assimilated the boulevards to such a degree that it would be difficult to imagine the city without them – another clue to a successful community design. Among several innovations, Haussman established façade-control legislation on the boulevards, which has been subject to criticism by most architects trained in the Modern movement. The use of urban façades in the design of the city, the precedent of which was Rue de Rivoli several decades earlier, indicated that the streets were conceived as the façade of the city itself, rather than as mere circulation channels. Façades were no longer only the physical boundaries of the buildings; they had become a living stage for the city, interpreted as an urban theater.

Though part of the official urbanist tradition, these plans originated during times of powerful rulers or public administrators who were probably free of most professional preconceptions. The pope and the prefect of the Seine were pragmatic doers who conceptualized their problem with fresh and sharp eyes, which is probably why they were able to innovate and find design approaches suitable to the task.

It is intriguing that the two exceptions we have just discussed are found in two major world cities, which may owe their inexhaustible magic to the fact that no designer was able to shape them according to a single, simplistic scheme. Furthermore, both plans were implemented over a span of many years, were never really finished, and underwent many alterations. In both cases, the exact details were less important than the "system" proposed – which, of course, would not be possible in a compositional urban design – permitting many different interpretations and alternatives. In both cases, the emphasis on transportation networks and urban nodes

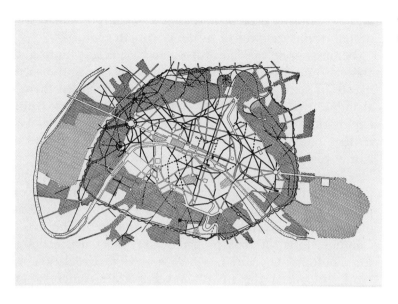

Figure 2.11. The Haussman plan for Paris. (Top) Plan of Haussman "grand travaux" in Paris: boulevards in old quarters (thick black lines) and in undeveloped areas (double lines); new districts (cross-hatching) and public parks (hatching). Prefect of the Seine, 1853–69. (Leonardo Benevolo, *The Origins of Modern Town Planning,* MIT Press, Cambridge, Mass., 1967) (Bottom) Rue de Rivoli, Paris. Percier and Fontaine, architects. An early nineteenth-century precedent with its uniform façades.

was a visionary precedent for the noncompositional urban design of the second half of the twentieth century.

Beginning in the late 1950s, and especially during the 1960s, some urban designers began to recognize the special nature of settlements and urban forms, which led them to abandon the compositional approach. The most fruitful exploration was the use of transportation links and activity nodes, which created an infrastructure to guide future urban development – a direct descendant of the Sixtus V and Haussman plans. Louis Kahn prepared various urban proposals for Philadelphia, stressing street circulation and major garages to control traffic and permit the construction of more rational buildings in the central area. The firm of Candilis, Josic, Woods prepared a series of urban designs for Toulouse–Le Mirail, where a treelike circulation network organized the town, and Frankfurt, where a grid network permitted buildings to fill the blocks progressively. Fumihiko Maki proposed a number of infrastructure concepts and the notion of group form for cities. Other designers, among them the Smithsons, Bakema, and Sert, made contributions as well. These fertile years also saw the birth of a radically different concept, the megastructure, such as the Tokyo plan of Kenzo Tange, in which cities took physical shape on a superhuman scale.

This brief review would not be complete without mention of Broadacre City, proposed by Frank Lloyd Wright in 1934, based on automobile transportation and low-density development. This proposal offered visionary glimpses of today's suburbia and exurban centers. The plans for new towns in the United States in the 1960s and 1970s were closer to Broadacre City – and suburbia – than to the European and Japanese designs; Columbia, Reston, and other new towns were upgraded versions of the standard subdivision. However, there were exceptions to this scenario, such as the creative riverfront plan in San Antonio, Texas, which brought out the best of the interface between river and community.

The 1980s, with their greater conservatism, lower expectations, and public budget limitations, produced plans focused on the private sector, such as Battery Park in New York, as well as the speculative development of exurban centers. Lacking a community viewpoint, they remain a collection of individual projects. But a settlement is not a mere accumulation of elements: The total must be more than the sum of the parts.

The social reform movements that took place in Europe in response to the Industrial Revolution and the utopias spawned by them constitute other sources of urban design. Architects have always been fond of simple and powerful schemes because they have the capacity to convey ideas with a minimum of information.

For most social reformers physical plans are an expression of, and in many cases a catalyst for, new social organizations. The implication of this hypothesis is critical: The hierarchies and relationships of the social organization should be directly expressed in the design of the community which, in turn, should provide suitable shelter for the new society. Since most reform movements tended to favor social organizations of a highly simplified or utopian character, their community designs were equally simple or utopian.

The assumption of a close correspondence between built form and society characterized not only nineteenth-century reform movements, but also some Renaissance utopias – the word "utopia" itself being the title of Sir Thomas More's well-known book. But while many of the fourteenth-, fifteenth-, and sixteenth-century utopian designs were complete geometric abstractions bearing little connection with reality, the forms of Industrial Revolution utopias were subordinated to social schemes. Both influences, that of geometric abstraction and that of social organization as form giver, are found in twentieth-century urban proposals.

Among the many utopias proposed in the nineteenth century, Ebenezer Howard's Garden City was the most influential. One reason for its impact is that it kept social experimentation to a minimum while it stressed the innovations of a new physical system. Howard's notion of achieving the best of both city and countryside was the intellectual cradle of both new towns and suburbia. It was left to British and, later, U.S. architects and planners to give this idea concrete form.

Other utopian proposals that originated in social reform movements were far more controversial than Garden City, because they were based on radically different social organizations. Most radical utopian experiments took place not in Europe, but on the open plains of America, where all kinds of splinter religious sects, sociopolitical reformers, and other visionaries found the opportunity to establish their own Jerusalem on earth. Ironically, most of them advocated an increase in social discipline, internal control, and fixed roles and responsibilities. It seems that, for most of those reformers, the future lay along the path of increasing centralization and authoritarianism. This strain has permeated many contemporary urban designs, where "planning" is sometimes equated with centralized decision making.

But the future of community design cannot follow the path of increasing centralization and authoritarianism – even if this is the path courted by some industrial societies in the late twentieth century – simply because it does not meet the most basic demands for an urban community and its urban form. What that urban form is, and should be, will be explored in the next chapter.

CHAPTER 3

URBAN PATTERNS

Or urban form as a combination of typologies

THE SHAPING OF AN EVOLVING URBAN FORM

Community design focuses on urban form, from cities to villages; its purpose is to "design" community forms, the physical shelter of human settlements. One key concept here is "design," the activity that could, for the moment, be defined as the shaping of built form. Another key concept is "form," the physical result of design and, more generally, the physical characteristic of human settlements.

The nature of urban form and the activity of design are closely intertwined: Form is, to various degrees, a result of design; but design is, to a very large degree, a result of our understanding of urban form. A major cause of the recurrent misdirection of design is the widespread misunderstanding of urban form – hence the urgent need to clarify this concept.

What do we refer to when we talk of urban form or community form? Our first reaction is to consider the physical elements that shelter a community: buildings, streets, and so on. Attempts at defining community form are handicapped by the fact that each definition leaves out important elements and we may have to end up by agreeing that a city is a city, a community is a community. We all seem to know, at least unconsciously, what a city is, what a community is. But do we really agree on these meanings and on the meaning of community form?

I believe that we often betray our subconscious agreement on the nature of cities and communities, and design urban forms according to a disturbed, impoverished, and distorted conscious idea. Designers do not fully understand community form, and continue to consider it an extension of building (architectural) form; indeed, there are many who assume that a continuum exists from urban design to furniture design, with the design process remaining basically the same throughout. The implication is that urban form shares the characteristics of "object form." This is a major misconception. We need a better way to conceptualize community form, based on a clear understanding of its nature.

One characteristic of object form is its boundaries. Buildings are bounded by exterior walls and even property lines; indeed, the boundary definition of a building (its façade) may often be a major design decision. Community forms are quite the opposite, being characterized by loose ends and transitional areas; their major definition is often found at their nucleus. Even in the case of established precincts – such as a university campus or a hospital complex – design considerations must extend beyond their legal limits.

Another characteristic of object form is that it is comprehensively designed in its totality, according to a specific program to meet a set of predetermined uses. Community forms are very much the opposite: They are shaped primarily by disjointed actions guided by controls and incentives; even for those precincts under single ownership, elements that have been designed may not necessarily be built. All along the way, from the establishment of long-term planning guidelines to actual construction, community forms are subject to a range of design interventions. Community design always presupposes phasing over considerable time periods, uncertainty over programming and implementation, and other characteristics seldom found in the design of buildings. For many trained in the design of object form, community design has an elusive quality.

As designers struggle to improve their understanding of community form, many urban areas continue to experience an accelerated rate of change that increases their uniqueness as community forms. The evolution of urban form in the past decades has been dramatic. Major urban centers have grown far larger than at any other time in history, reaching higher levels of complexity. Their dynamism is expressed in rapid social and technological change. Their internal structure has evolved, with larger areas under single (specialized) use and increasing reliance on transportation and communications. Uncertainty about specific details but certainty regarding trends are typical of urban growth.

In contrast, some urban areas, those bypassed by the development sectors, have stagnated, experiencing no growth at all but rather a decrease in sophistication and reduction to a simplistic structure. The world of advanced urban culture has become more spatially selective, concentrated in growing metropolises and leaving behind stagnant regions linked via instant communications. In truth, instant communications are replacing many spatial relationships, greatly weakening the bond of proximity and, in the process, raising serious questions about the nature and meaning of community.

Not everything has changed, however. There are very important elements common to every urban area and community that have remained constants of human settlements. These are, among others, the need for interaction among people individually and in groups, the development of common concerns, and the potential for vitality and uniqueness. The future evolution of urban areas will continue to combine new characteristics with permanent features.

Given the widespread misunderstanding of the nature of urban form, as well as of the morphological factors determining that form, it is essential first to inquire into the nature of urban or community form and then to explore, as is done in the next four chapters, its morphological roots.

URBAN PATTERNS

In community design, unlike the design of buildings, furniture, and other discrete objects subject to boundary definition and individualization, form is not easy to identify. Community design deals with a composite form that is relatively difficult to isolate. This form is the result of aggregations of more or less repetitive elements; we shall refer to such composite forms as patterns. Settlements of any size and type can always be formally synthesized by their patterns: town houses in gridiron blocks, high-rise office structures, academic campuses, suburban estates, and highway retail sprawl are good examples. Patterns often merge into one another, disappear progressively, or, occasionally, end abruptly at urban barriers. Urban form, then, is a result of the bringing together of many elements in a composite totality: the urban pattern (Figure 3.1).

Patterns are the outstanding formal features of urban areas. A pattern can be defined as an elaboration of form that results from a composition of parts, in which a sector suffices as a sample of the rest – or a substantial proportion of the rest. Thus, patterns assume complex characteristics based on their formal elaboration; they also assume some degree of universality, since the total pattern can be represented by a sector. For example, an identifiable area in a city, precinct, or village can be best understood through a typical sector showing circulation, buildings, and open spaces; this typical sector "represents" the formal characteristics found throughout the area and thus acquires some "universality." Patterns have the potential of carrying powerful formal syntheses or visual codes – and hence implications for design guidelines – over a geographic space, independent of the presence (or absence) of boundaries.

These characteristics are substantially different from those of the object form, which can be visually apprehended as a totality but cannot be easily derived from a fragment – a fact that archaeologists reconstructing vases or buildings know all too well. It would seem paradoxical that, although it may be difficult to understand the intricacies of an urban form and its morphological factors, it is relatively easy sensorially, to apprehend its visual code and formal synthesis and to extrapolate from it beyond the known sector. Formally, cities have a greater similarity to rugs and carpets than to other design products, with intricate motifs covering their surfaces and various combinations of patterns complementing one another.

Patterns are the physical expression of an underlying, continuous formal system. Their visual essence lies in the complexity of a number of interrelated motifs, rather than in the total composition, since patterns are fragments or parts of a continuum and not totalities. Patterns can be conceptualized as models of field designs that can be extended (replicated)

Figure 3.1. Urban patterns. (Right) Siena. (Opposite) Manhattan. (U.S. Coast and Geodetic Survey)

38

over geographic space. They are the veritable footprint of a community, reflecting the impact of a society on the earth, through the imposition of their cultural artifacts of shelter and movement.

Clearly, urban patterns do change from one sector of a city to another, according to location in the city and time of development. The commercial high-rise pattern of down-town merges with the dense residential pattern of town houses – two patterns resulting from different land uses and accessibility at different locations. The tight pattern that originated in preautomobile times contrasts with the open pattern typical of the automobile era – two patterns resulting

from two periods of development. In this way, an urban area is truly a tapestry of patterns, each corresponding to specific morphological factors – location, technology, culture, and so on.

Furthermore, patterns tend not to reflect the will of a single designer, but rather composite wills – like the inherited wills involved in the traditional design of carpets or the pluralistic wills that have shaped so many human habitats. Indeed, patterns are true community forms.

How is one to gain an initial formal understanding of urban patterns? Quite often, complex forms can first be grasped through the identification of their range of formal outcomes.

Let us identify the "formal extremes" that patterns can take, which we shall call dualities because they tend to appear as nominal opposites. Urban patterns, complex community forms that they are, can be conceptually understood through a series of dualities – not unlike the series of X-ray images used by geologists to study rock structures, which when put together enable them to grasp the totality of a crystal. The world is full of dualities that, when understood, are seen not as irreconcilable opposites, but as complements representing the complex nature of a realm of the universe.

I have selected three dualities for examination here, not only for their descriptive quality, but because of their operational value for designers: unbuilt space versus built form, continuous events versus discrete events, and repetitive elements versus unique elements.

Unbuilt space–built form duality. This duality recognizes that urban patterns integrate built structures enclosing space for some use together with unbuilt areas used as open space or circulation. It provides the basic gestalt of urban areas, with figure-and-background images (Figure 3.2). Compare traditional urban blocks solidly built among urban streets with large nineteenth-century apartment buildings around central courtyards and with twentieth-century isolated apartment structures typical of modern urbanism. In the last case, for example, the street is no longer spatially defined as in the two earlier cases, but is simply a traffic channel. Spatial concepts and definitions, environmental qualities, microclimate and health conditions, and other aspects of urban life can be thrown into relief by examining this relatively simple duality of unbuilt space versus built form.

This duality is related, though not fully equivalent, to the distinction between public and private realms in cities. Although most unbuilt space – open space and circulation – can be considered public, some open space can be private, as in institutional cloisters or residential courtyards. Also, enclosed space can be public or enjoy some sort of semipublic status, as in the case of churches, museums, department stores, and even street-covered arcades. The famous sixteenth-century Nolli plan of Rome, in which the chosen gestalt was between public and private realms – whether open or enclosed – is an excellent example of the partial overlap of these two dualities (Figure 3.3).

Between enclosed buildings and open spaces there are many intermediate possibilities: buildings lacking one wall, such as Greek stoas; buildings with a roof supported by free standing columns, such as the arcades of Bologna; a space open to the sky and surrounded by walls, such as a stadium;

Figure 3.2. Unbuilt space–built form duality: Venice. (Edmund N. Bacon)

a plaza with a few vertical elements, such as San Marco. The discrete nature of the transition between the built form and open space does not mean that the catalogue of solutions is limited; on the contrary, the combinations, permutations, and innovations are practically inexhaustible. In addition, there is a continuum between the public and private realms, which often overlap one another.

The unbuilt space–built form duality follows two basic traditions. One is Western, in which built form defines enclosed open space; the other is Eastern, which deals with the space within which the built form is immersed. That these spatial concepts are intimately related to aesthetic and philosophical concepts is apparent in the difference between European and Chinese or Japanese painting. One of the few places where the two traditions merge is the haunting religious area of the Piazza del Duomo in Pisa, where a solid wall of buildings barely annotates an enormous open field within which the cathedral, campanile, baptistry, and campo santo are located, as objects in a special (and rarified) space (Figure 3.4).

The two concepts of spatial definition developed with multiple variations until the Modern movement, which treated the built form as an independent element in a non-spatial vacuum (Figure 3.5). This lack of conceptualization of urban space resulted in its degradation to a remnant without formal will and thus made it confusing and banal. The failure to recognize the potential dialogue between built form and unbuilt space is reflected in an im-

Figure 3.3. Public and private realms: Nolli plan of Rome, 1748. (MIT Press)

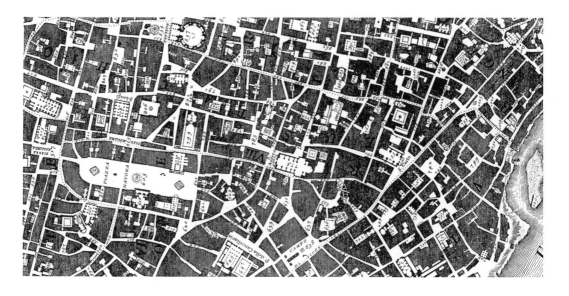

Figure 3.4. The Eastern
and Western traditions.
(Top) Horyuji Temple,
Nara, Japan, 607. (Japan
Information Center,
Consulate General of
Japan, New York)
(Bottom) Piazza del
Duomo, Pisa, 1063–1278.
Baptistry, cathedral,
campanile.

poverishment of community patterns. Designers, however, are not the only ones at fault. Institutional forces have a major role in establishing the "private" and "public" realms of society and ultimately in shaping the built form and open space; economics, law, and culture are reflected in the definition of those realms. The paucity of the public realm in U.S. cities today may be explained by the priorities of this society, which relegates "public goods" to second-class status.

The design implications of this duality are many. A reinterpretation of the two spatial traditions of the East and West could lead to new conceptual positions. For example, the notion of built elements set in space, which is in turn surrounded by built elements, can be understood vis-à-vis the concept of spatial recursion. A well-known analogy is that of Russian dolls; an architectural analogy is the Minotaur Palace in Knossos. Another implication of the duality is that the interface between built form and open space could lead to the creation of community "doors" and that the interface between private and public realms could lead to the creation of community "filters," which allow different levels of privacy. Not only could various built forms and unbuilt spaces be modulated, but their interfaces could be exalted to passageways in a community.

Figure 3.5. The Modern movement: a nonspatial vacuum. Illinois Institute of Technology, Chicago, 1940. Mies Van der Rohe. (Hedrich-Blessing)

Continuous–discrete events duality. This duality recognizes that urban patterns are made up of two quantitatively different kinds of elements: Some are interconnected and extend virtually over the whole area; others are discrete. This geometric difference is extended to implicit qualitative differences in the two types of events. The first can be characterized as continuous forms – networks – weaving through a community, and the second as sets of discrete forms aggregated within or adjacent to the networks – infillings. Communities are structured by continuous networks within which an infill of discrete events takes place. The combination of networks and infillings results in a total pattern (Figure 3.6).

Urban networks are identified primarily with transportation and other city infrastructures, which by nature must be

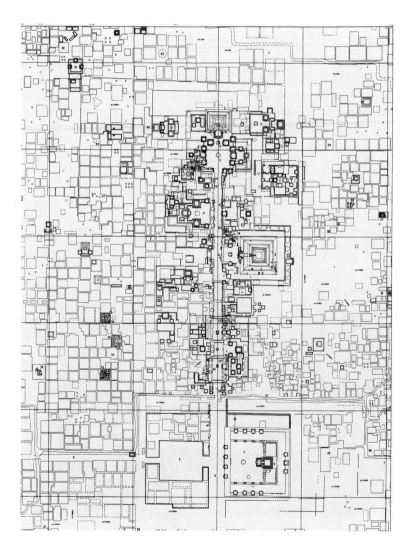

Figure 3.6. Continuous–discrete events duality: Teotihuacán, A.D. 0–400. (Modified copy of 1968 map © 1968, 1988 René Millon)

45

continuous throughout the pattern. Streets, roads, avenues, boulevards, canals, highways, aqueducts, rail lines, and high-tension lines are all continuous networks that structure urban areas in one way or another, and in so doing they have more than just a utilitarian function; they become outstanding visual elements of the urban pattern. Buildings have occasionally played the same role, ranging from defensive walls in the Middle Ages to the megastructures of the 1960s. But in most cases, buildings, from cathedrals to houses, garages to skyscrapers, as well as most open spaces, are all infillings within the network structure, defining the three-dimensional architectural quality of a place (Figure 3.7).

The interface areas between networks and infillings constitute the most alive zones – similar to tidal ponds – of the man-made environment. Human beings are not truly participants in community life until they are on foot; the interface between transportation networks and infillings is the place where people shift from being passive riders to being active pedestrians (Figure 3.8). For this reason, the design of these interfaces – subway stations, bus stops, train terminals, garages, sidewalks, and docks – is critical for the vitality of social and economic life in urban areas, as well as for their aesthetic expression.

And yet one of the most obvious failures of urban design has been the improper handling of these interfaces, as wit-

Figure 3.7. Urban networks and infillings: Ponte Vecchio, Florence.

nessed by the grim "garage stage" experienced between highways and buildings; downtown buildings may be designed
for conspicuous consumption, but their garage arrival and
transfer to pedestrian modes often exist in marginal environments. Here lies one of the most fertile areas for creativity
in community design today; it includes a whole range of

Figure 3.8. Interface
between riders and
pedestrians. (Top)
Pennsylvania Station, New
York City, 1910. McKim,
Mead, and White. (Wayne
Andrews) (Bottom) San
Marco *molo*, Venice.

interface possibilities. The "gates" to an urban community should appear at those points where riders become pedestrians; these are highly strategic areas where intense and special uses tend to become concentrated and where pedestrian networks acquire special significance.

The distinction between continuous and discrete events is not absolute, however. Size and scale may affect this distinction since what appears to be discrete on a metropolitan scale may seem continuous on a neighborhood scale. For example, rows of party-wall town houses, which are discrete elements on an urban scale, can be seen as continuous events on a neighborhood scale. Should every town house be seen as an individual infill in the block? Should the block be seen as community infill in the neighborhood, or even as a continuous element spreading over the pattern? All these interpretations are probably valid and overlapping, showing the multiple roles that urban elements play.

Repetitive–unique events duality. This duality recognizes that urban patterns are made up largely of a limited number of relatively undifferentiated types of elements that repeat and combine. Relatively special elements appear from time to time, either isolated or clustered, forming unique islands in the midst of the undifferentiated elements. This is one of the most hermetic of the dualities, because it implies that the image of a city can be created by the visual repetition of undifferentiated elements as well as by unique elements (Figure 3.9).

Notre Dame de Paris is a powerful image and symbol for that city, but the repetitive elements of the city's urban pattern – apartment buildings, hotels, and offices – represent it as much as does its unique cathedral. Perhaps it is the combination of repetitive urban elements – on the Left Bank, in Le Marais, in the 16me Arrondisement – rather than any one image, that constitutes the final and irreducible image of Paris.

Repetitive elements are the true urban form givers, sheltering the community's activities and expressing its way of life and culture. Unique elements are the expression of either a very specialized activity or, more likely, the apex and more symbolic layers of the community hierarchy. Human habitats and workplaces are repetitive elements, but temples, palaces, town halls, parliaments, universities, opera houses, and museums are unique and highly visible in each community.

In preindustrial traditional societies, repetitive buildings

Figure 3.9 (*facing page*). Repetitive–unique events duality. (Top) Florence with Palazzo Vecchio and Duomo. (Bottom) Moulay Idriss, Morocco, with mosque.

49

such as dwellings vary according to regions, whereas unique buildings are universal. Repetitive buildings, although roughly the same within an urban area, tend to change drastically among regions and cultures; unique buildings, although special in their urban area, tend to repeat themselves across regions and even cultures. The wide regional variety of human dwelling types found in the cities, towns, and villages of Europe (Figure 3.10) stands in contrast to the minor stylistic variations of similar unique buildings – for example, Gothic churches – that exist across the continent (Figure 3.11).

This apparent paradox has its roots in the different sources of designs of the repetitive and unique elements. The former are bounded by scarce resources, whereas the latter often belong to powerful institutions that demand, and can afford,

Figure 3.10. Regionalism of repetitive elements: dwellings. (Top) Castelo de Vide, Portugal. (Bernard Rudofsky) (Bottom) Rouen, France. (Opposite top) Prejmer, Rumania. (Bernard Rudofsky) (Opposite bottom) Mykonos, Greece.

a pervasive image of "international" symbolism, as was discussed in Chapter 2 in terms of the popular and professional traditions. The attachment of repetitive elements to land and local culture, which become regional expressions, as well as the universal character of unique elements, are critical to the understanding of community forms.

Probably no other duality has been so misunderstood. To consider an obvious example, skyscrapers built in downtown areas for the purpose of housing the managerial activities of

corporations often indulge the egocentric corporate identity. Corporate headquarters vie with one another to attract the most attention – in the process unraveling the urban pattern (Figure 3.12).

The jumble of pseudo-unique corporate office buildings in city centers shows a lamentable lack of understanding of "uniqueness." A corporate workplace is a repetitive building type making up the majority of downtown urban patterns; it is not meant to be unique. Whenever the design of skyscrapers becomes a competition among corporations, the re-

Figure 3.11. Universality of unique elements: churches. (Top) Amiens Cathedral, France. (Bottom) Ely Cathedral, England. (Opposite top) Paris Cathedral, France. (Opposite bottom) Milano Cathedral, Italy.

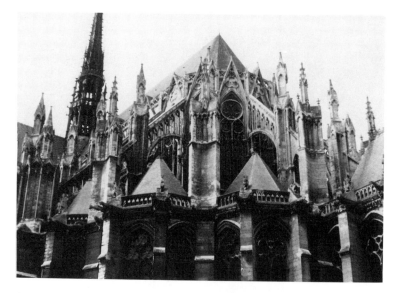

sult is pointless escalation, confusion, and the breakdown of the urban pattern. Clearly, there is a lack of design awareness in those who foster such antiurban competition, but the problem goes further; there is a lack of cultural bonding, which prevents a consensus from being reached on what should be unique. Downtowns are becoming turf for unbridled competition among built symbols of the most powerful corporations and institutions.

The implications of this duality for community design are widespread. For example, the design of a parking system repetitive throughout an urban area must be conceptually different from the design of a garage serving a unique facility – the latter should be the "gate" to that building. Designers must distinguish between routine parking areas and arrival points at special destinations.

The most critical issue related to this duality is that of assigning the special status of uniqueness to some structures, institutions, and uses and not to others, particularly in times of cultural disintegration, as well as distinguishing the various scales of different buildings in the context of the community.

Combination of dualities. Dualities represent ranges of formal outcomes in urban patterns, taken one parameter at a time. In reality, patterns synthesize the various dualities in a single form. The following are possible combinations and examples:

Unbuilt space, continuous, repetitive   Urban streets

Figure 3.12. Confusion of pseudo-unique buildings: downtown Boston.

54

Unbuilt space, continuous, unique	Champs Elysées
Unbuilt space, discrete, repetitive	Neighborhood plazas
Unbuilt space, discrete, unique	Piazza San Marco
Built form, continuous, repetitive	Arcades
Built form, continuous, unique	Defense walls
Built form, discrete, repetitive	Office buildings
Built form, discrete, unique	Chartres Cathedral

Dualities have a considerable capacity to account for a wide range of urban elements and to provide designers with an operational tool for manipulating urban patterns. And no matter how varied, they are all part of the taxonomy of urban patterns and belong to what we may call urban types.

URBAN TYPOLOGIES

Urban patterns are formed, as already discussed, by repetitive elements within which unique elements occur. Hence, these patterns have strong similarities and can be grouped conceptually into what we call typologies. The many similarities among certain urban structures, facilities, and spaces suggest a "family resemblance" among them.

This family resemblance can be found among network elements such as streets and infill elements such as buildings, among unbuilt spaces such as plazas and built forms such as urban blocks, and even among unique buildings and spaces. Some typologies are universal, others are bounded by culture, and yet others are clearly local. In other words, all elements in urban patterns can be, to various degrees, typical (Figure 3.13). As with other community design concepts, the concept of typology is relative, and the recognition of a type often depends on the scale of analysis.

Some definitions are in order. "Type" is defined as the general form, structure, or character distinguishing a particular kind, group, or class of beings or objects – hence a model after which something is made. "Prototype" and "archetype" are practically interchangeable concepts, indicating the first or primary type of any thing, the original from which copies are made. "Stereotype" is defined as something continued or constantly repeated without change; it can be applied to the case of an obsolete or ill-adjusted type.

The definition of "type" is based on the recognition of the essence of an object as well as on the possibility of reproducing that essence in another object. It should be clear that typologies do not mean reproducible casts, to be molded one after another on an assembly line. The essence of a typology is made up of a combination of key characteristics of the elements in the typology, as well as by the range of variations that the elements can experience without losing their affiliation with the typology. A typology is not merely reproduced; its essence is selected, and a design is based on this essence. A typology, then, has a built-in capacity to show optional variations of the initial object (prototype or archetype). I am talking deliberately about essence and not standards, to convey the idea (and ideal) of a type without the constraints of catalogue models. Thus, any and all specific designs of a type must be variations, options, and interpretations of that type, with perhaps a few of them being closer than the others to the ideal. Clearly, the more abstract the essence of a type is, the wider the range – and the richer the variation – of a typology will be.

Urban types are basically types of spatial organizations in

Figure 3.13. Urban types – the palazzo. Florentine fifteenth-century types: (Left) Palazzo Rucellai, 1451. Leon Battista Alberti. (Alinari/ Art Resource) (Right) Palazzo Medici–Riccardi, 1460. Michelozzo Michelozzo. (Alinari/Art Resource) Venetian sixteenth-century types: (Opposite top) Palazzo Vendramin-Calergi, 1509. (Marburg/Art Resource) (Opposite bottom) Palazzo Corner Ca'Grande, 1537. Jacopo Sansovino. (Alinari/Art Resource)

settlements. However, additional cultural factors introduce the aspect of style. Gridiron blocks with row houses, central plazas, and roadside developments are ubiquitous patterns translated into various styles; but radial boulevard patterns, for instance, are typical of baroque urbanism.

How do typologies come into being? The concept is simple: Built elements that face the same (or very similar) sets of requirements and constraints will, in all likelihood, end up generating one typology as the best solution to these con-

ditions. It is possible to imagine more than one good solution, but since human behavior tends to follow early successes, the result is often that a single typology emerges as the dominant one.

In the development of a typology, several periods can be distinguished. At a given point, socioeconomic, cultural, and technological conditions may all come together to foster a new typology. For example, the Industrial Revolution and the subsequent development of industrial corporations led to the creation of large pools of administrative personnel working together in central cities served by streetcars and, later, subway systems. The introduction of iron and, eventually, steel structures, as well as the invention of the elevator, made it possible to build tight clusters of high-rise office buildings in central areas. Later, the development of air-conditioning systems eliminated the constraints on the size of those buildings imposed by the need for natural ventilation.

In the initial "search" period, several attempts may result in dead-end solutions and eventual historical curiosities. But

Figure 3.14. Development of urban types: office buildings. (Right) Search period: Guaranty Building, Buffalo, New York, 1894–5. Adler and Sullivan. (Chicago Architectural Photo. Co., David R. Phillips) (Opposite top) Formalization period: Rockefeller Center, New York City, 1931–55. (Rockefeller Center. ©The Rockefeller Group, Inc.) (Opposite bottom) Conflict period: New England Life Building, Boston, 1987. Philip Johnson.

fairly soon, an efficient mainstream solution is found and followed during the "formalization" period (Figure 3.14, p. 58).

During the formalization period, the typology comes closer to being a standard to be imitated, although there are always variations, since each case must be adapted to particular conditions and requirements. During this period the concept of typology acquires more clarity: A typology is an ideal model, made up of the composite characteristics of the built pattern, that satisfies a common set of requirements, constraints, and conditions (Figure 3.14, p. 59, top).

Later, during the "conflict and change" period, new requirements and constraints may emerge, forcing the modification of the stereotype or the generation of new types. It is in this period that most environmental problems may arise, especially at the interface between facility and community (Figure 3.14, p. 59, bottom). For example, the increasing number of private automobiles commuting to downtown patterns belonging to preautomobile typologies has not yet been satisfactorily dealt with, leading to overcrowding of city streets and the ad hoc creation of the marginal "garage stage" between building and highway.

Here the problem originates in the disruption of the relationship between office buildings (built, discrete, repetitive events) and urban streets (unbuilt, continuous, repetitive events) by the nonmarginal change of conditions and the decline of urban types into obsolete stereotypes. The vital interface zone where people can regain their role as pedestrians is under serious stress and is the first to suffer environmental problems.

This social process of typology selection has many important implications for community design. It is critical for designers to understand at which stage the process is operating – that is, are we comfortably designing urban patterns with stable formalized typologies, or are we facing stereotypes riddled with internal conflicts, or are we already searching for a more valid prototype? Can the problems found in the existing typology be solved simply through improvement and refinement, or are they major conflicts that demand a new approach? These questions will be discussed in the remaining chapters. For the time being, let us say that recognizing the relative value of a typology is among the early critical steps in community design.

The actual sociocultural process of generating, selecting, and refining built types is affected by the multiple factors and

actors that participate in the development of communities.
Common determinants that affect a typology include the physical urban structure, municipal services, zoning and codes, technology, financial and tax structures, alternative investments, cultural beliefs, microclimate, and many others. Specific project requirements that affect a typology include the program – which is itself biased by cultural beliefs – the organization of the development entity, land and construction costs, demand markets, soil conditions, competition, and others. These determinants and requirements apply as much to a family building a house as to a developer building a suburban subdivision, to a corporation building its world headquarters or a speculative office building, to a public agency undertaking the redevelopment of some central city area, or to private investors assembling a downtown project. Technology, economic systems, social institutions – in a word, culture – are the social factors that, together with natural factors (such as microclimate, soil, and bodies of water), shape the patterns of human settlements.

Technology, especially since the nineteenth century, has had an increasingly important effect in the shaping of urban typologies, including the critical areas of urban transportation – public transit, commuter rail, buses, and trolleys, as well as private automobiles along with highways and parking garages – building structures, mechanical systems, vertical circulation, instant communications, and, most recently, information processing. But quite often, built types herald later technological advances; some of the first skyscrapers in Chicago were built with load-bearing masonry walls.

Culture is the prime mover in the development of urban typologies. Technology, as one of the cultural components of society, is a facilitator in that it enables the members of society to do certain things, though it does not influence what it is they want to do. The central city skyscraper, for example, is a product of both technology and a cultural trend that encourages certain patterns of social behavior and, ultimately, certain events. Tall office buildings exist, in part, because there is a pervasive trend toward concentrating greater economic power in fewer corporations, which cluster together with other financial institutions and use their headquarters to project a corporate image. The development objective of profit maximization in speculative office buildings, in turn, increases land values proportionally to the capacity to obtain larger yields by building huge structures – thanks to technological advances.

The environmental, social, and visual conflicts caused by the increasing size of office buildings in old central cities represents, to a large degree, a self-fulfilling prophecy brought about by speculative expectations and profit-maximizing practices, and made possible by technology. Furthermore, the lack of community design guidelines and controls in central cities is explained by an institutional framework in which private objectives are consistently given priority over public concerns.

Thus, an economic system that pushes land values to their maximum potential without regard for environmental, social, or visual consequences; an institutional system that assigns top priority to private property and the fulfillment of its objectives while relegating the public realm to a secondary role; and a legal system that zones the city according to private objectives but fails to provide a high-quality public infrastructure – are all major cultural factors in the shaping of downtown patterns in U.S. cities.

Cultural factors have always affected urban typologies. In the Middle Ages, the high cost of transportation, the uncertainty of life beyond defensive walls, growing trade opportunities within a feudalistic system, and the universal institution of the church led to the generic medieval urban typology. It was a tightly clustered pattern, with marketplace and trade streets, often two centers of power (political and religious), and myriad social institutions such as a hospital, asylum, orphanage and school near the church, and cloister. The twentieth-century search for an expression of the socialist city is a search for an urban pattern suitable for a changing society with new institutions, economic system, and laws.

Conditions change, cultures evolve, and urban typologies become obsolete stereotypes riddled with internal contradictions of increasing severity. The insertion of huge office buildings into the urban network of central cities, in what was a pattern suited for smaller building types, is environmentally disastrous. The street system, with intersections at every urban block and without strategic parking facilities, cannot cope with the traffic; the sidewalks are badly linked to subway stations and garages; parcels are too small and streets often too narrow. Office workers are situated in artificially lighted and ventilated spaces, often without windows, and then walk through windswept streets in permanent shadow.

Economics and technology may continue to foster the expansion of such obsolete patterns, and institutions may be unable (or unwilling) to control their negative effects. Designers, as agents of cultural change, and citizens at the forefront of the most progressive sectors of society should recognize the need for new design solutions and bold actions. The need for community design is more apparent now than ever; the development of urban typologies and community design must go hand in hand in order to provide urban solutions that acknowledge the public realm's needs and concerns.

Culture, building program, and technology shape typologies. Can we say that there is a deterministic relationship among these factors and types? Certainly not. In some cases, when efficiency is the overwhelming concern, changes in conditions surely change the built type; the old four- and five-story industrial buildings became obsolete as soon as the assembly line and truck transportation came into being, to be replaced by the well-known one-story plant of today. However, in most cases there is much more flexibility. The less technologically related a structure's function is, the more permanent its type can be, changing only because of tastes or costs, as in housing; the solution to sheltering a family can be a suburban house, a central apartment, an old town house, a renovated mill, or one of many other structures. A hospital, however, may face recurrent cycles of obsolescence in technical areas, such as intensive care.

Often, old types built for some specific users can be successfully adapted to other users, indicating that programs and types are not locked in a one-to-one relationship; instead, programs determine types through cultural interpretations. Examples can be found at any level in any region: The typical Italian neighborhood of the North End in Boston was formerly the home of earlier immigrants whose lifestyle was different from that of the current Italian population. The basilica of Hagia Sophia, built by Constantine to be the center of Eastern Orthodox Christianity, was taken by the Turks and immediately converted to the Mosque of Istanbul, after which all other Turkish mosques have been patterned (Figure 3.15). The basilicas, in turn, were adapted from a Roman type of legal court building by early Christians, who used them as temples. Are these cases of cultural lag or adaptation, of program or type flexibility, or something different?

There is a subtle relationship among culture, technology, program, and typology – subtler than we have been able to ascertain up to now with our deterministic biases. Perhaps typologies are ideal expressions of very general requirements of a culture – built shells or spaces that are designed to satisfy deep needs other than specific programs and that are viable at a subliminal level. One of the main roles of typologies may be to shape cultural symbols. Both the Byzantines and the Turks needed impressive halls to exhibit the religious glory of their empires: Hagia Sophia, the most unique element in the pattern, provided a magnificent edifice with a celestial dome that transcended differences in beliefs and rituals. The town houses found in so many cities of the United States and England are a fine example of related types ideally adapted to the urban network, conventional construction technology, and activities on a human scale; they were built as single-family homes, but now they serve as, among other things, apartments, offices, and clinics (Figure 3.16, top).

This rediscovery of older typologies started in the United States in the last decade; it is a pity that in so many countries of the Third World similarly viable (and valuable) typologies such as the courtyard house or patio house, so well adapted to climate and culture, are being systematically demolished to make room for imitations of foreign types (Figure 3.16, bottom).

One of the trends most damaging to environmental richness is the cultural homogenization of urban typologies in many areas of the world. This phenomenon is well known to travelers, who find that hotels built in recent decades do not reflect regional differences, so that one cannot tell whether one is in Cairo, New York, Singapore, or Mexico, unless one leaves the hotel. Technology, of course, makes possible large climate-controlled shells anywhere, but it is the cultural dependency of many Third World countries that bears a major responsibility for this environmental impoverishment.

Typically, human habitats have been rooted in the land and the local culture; it is only recently that we have come to see the same apartment blocks all over the world, from New York to Caracas to Paris. As was discussed earlier in this chapter, it was the unique elements in cities that belonged to the same universal typologies across different regions. Universality was restricted to the apex of the community hierarchy. It is only now that we see repetitive elements such as office buildings being elevated to the status of the universal, betraying their transnational character.

As already mentioned, some typologies are local, while others are universal. The wide difference in the residential typologies of human habitats indicates that local conditions impose heavy constraints on people: Microclimate, defense,

Figure 3.15 (*facing page*). Adaptation of urban types: the basilica. (Turkish Culture and Information Office) (Top) Basilica of Hagia Sophia, Constantinople (now Istanbul), 532–7. (Bottom) Sultan Ahmet Mosque, Constantinople, 1609–17.

construction materials, and topography account for the majority of the differences among habitat typologies. However, the widespread use of one unique typology in very different regions means that local conditions were not as important to those in power and that the universality of the unique type was, and is, both possible and desirable. In the past, churches, kings, and municipalities had the capacity to pay for the "proper" type. Today, the differences between local and universal typologies are blurred; power tends to be concentrated in large, anonymous corporations without religious or political links with the community, and climate and culture can

Figure 3.16. Urban types: dwellings. (Top) Town house: Boston. (Bottom) Courthouse: Marrakesh. (Musée de l'homme, L. Vogel)

be overcome by technology. Thus homogeneity, with its by-products of anonymity, gigantism, and lack of meaning, pervades urban areas in many countries.

This cultural homogeneity has often been justified as being the result of powerful forces that are transforming the world into a so-called global village, with fewer and fewer differences among regions. I have a very different outlook. Cultural homogeneity is a result of the increasing absorption of the world in the markets of the industrialized countries – primarily the United States – and the reshaping of regions and local cultures to fit the needs of the world economic metropolis. This reshaping includes the manipulation of what is considered the "good life" and thus the generation of "perceived needs" by local markets (and cultures).

Around the world, the good life is seen as benefiting from the replacement of local goods with foreign ones, resulting in a Hieronymus Bosch–like collage of Coca Cola and hamburgers, blue jeans and permanent press, Chevrolets and highways, glass skyscrapers and suburban developments – the glutton's paradise. Local production is eliminated, local lifestyles are forgotten. And in the process regions become "culturally addicted" to expensive, and often wasteful, foreign technologies and capital.

Hidden behind homogeneous programs that disregard regional differences are often cultural assumptions about the role of typologies in urban areas – and their cultural contexts. Designers must penetrate these assumptions and examine their validity. Is the transportation system planned to be hopelessly dependent on high-energy consumption? Are housing types divorced from microclimate, lifestyle, and local building techniques? Is the commercial center zoned and built following obsolete, or foreign, patterns? Designers must clarify the distinction between urban elements that belong to local (regional) typologies and those that belong to more universal types. Designers are entrusted with this task by default, because, crucial though it is, this distinction is seldom recognized by society at large. By focusing on the right combination of localism and universality, designers will be able to produce far more responsive designs and also to (re)create new urban typologies suitable to time and place.

URBAN AGGREGATIONS AND COMBINATIONS

An urban area is a community form. This form is not the result of a composition, as in painting and some architecture;

nor is it the result of blind aggregation. Community form is the result of a process in which different urban elements are combined into coherent patterns. Thus, it is possible to identify both the urban elements that combine to form communities and their laws of aggregation. Community design can be viewed as a giant game, with pieces and rules that guide their moves on the land and in space. Elements belong to the realm of unbuilt spaces or built forms, of continuous or discrete elements, of repetitive or unique facilities. The combination of these elements follows morphological laws – laws related to the nature of the urban form that guide the development process. These laws will be discussed in Chapters 4 through 6. For the time being, let us state their existence as a hypothesis.

From this point of view, community design can be interpreted as dealing with decisions at two levels: at the level of urban elements and at the level of aggregation. However, this definition of the problem neglects many of its complexities. Many urban elements do combine into increasingly larger intermediate aggregations – from the dwelling unit to the apartment building to the urban block to the precinct to the neighborhood – but others do not.

As the size of urban areas increases, new laws of aggregation apply. Some elements appear and combine only as exceptions to previous intermediate aggregations – in response to the size and specialized needs of those aggregations. Community facilities and transportation systems are clear examples of new players introduced into the urban game by the emergence of new laws as aggregation proceeds. For example, a general hospital or a rapid-transit system appears only above a certain community size. Thus, different elements appear after the first stages of urban combination, provoking a qualitative change in the pattern type. Simply put, larger means more complex.

The qualitative change that takes place as urban aggregations grow offers opportunities to guide urban development through the manipulation of new elements appearing in larger areas. For example, the control of urban transportation is an effective, indirect design strategy.

Excellent examples of the combination of built typologies are the patterns of the two Cambridge universities – in Cambridge, England, and Cambridge, Massachusetts (Figure 3.17). Both are organized around clear, though not deterministic, gestalts of built form and open space. Though there are some differences – at Cambridge University there are

Figure 3.17 (*facing page*). Urban types: universities. (Top) Cambridge University, England. (British Tourist Authority) (Bottom) Harvard University, Cambridge, Massachusetts. (Brad Washburn/*Harvard Magazine*)

closed quadrangles, whereas at Harvard there are more open yards – the two are fairly similar. In both, the combination of built wings and open spaces establishes a true relationship of mutual definition. Do the buildings define the open spaces, or do the open spaces define the buildings? Both questions must be answered in the affirmative. The two patterns are also a good example of how practically the same academic typology can show small but critical variations, forming in both cases a repetitive pattern that provides room for additional buildings within clear community design parameters. And beyond a certain number of quads, unique elements begin to appear, such as the magnificent Christ Church in Cambridge, a jewel properly set up in a quad with the academic wings in the background.

Community patterns are the result of continuous combinatorial processes of various urban typologies following laws of aggregation that originate in morphological forces. The importance of the latter forces has been increased by the acceleration and magnitude of the urban development process, which has changed settlements from relatively static, simple, and atomistic units to dynamic, multiple, and integrated complexes. It is time to open up the surface of urban form and study its underlying morphology, the systems that organize urban settlements.

PART TWO

Which deals with the systematic nature of urban form, the effects of time processes on cities and the built environment, and the relationship between size and form

CHAPTER 4

BELOW THE URBAN SURFACE

Or how urban systems, organized in complex hierarchies, are the roots of urban form

URBAN SYSTEMS

We have defined community form as resulting from the combination of various typologies of urban patterns. We have interpreted patterns in terms of their underlying morphology. We know that the forces shaping community forms originate in pervasive processes that have been studied in separate disciplines such as urban economics and sociology. Thus, we can conceptualize the existence of a "nature" of urban areas and their organization in space as an irreducible and underlying characteristic of urban form.

Conventional studies of human settlements by separate disciplines must be integrated into a totality. Community designers deal with totalities; their plans have myriad effects beyond the immediate area of concern. My aim is to focus on the physical-spatial form of settlements, to search for universal characteristics, constraints, laws, and determinants inherent in community forms. This will improve our understanding of urban problems and the reasons for the failure of so many design "solutions"; it will also highlight viable design paths. The raison d'être of community forms lies hidden below its surface.

Social scientists have for some time recognized the systematic nature of urban complexes. Human communities – cities, towns, villages, neighborhoods – are interrelated entities with underlying regularities that, in the eyes of many social scientists, have attained the status of laws. These laws do not determine outcomes; rather they describe regularities that organize the apparent randomness of history – people, time, and space. The notion that urban complexes are indeed systems is far reaching and brings into question the conventional understanding of urban problems and solutions. Often, apparent problems are really "syndromes of underlying disease mechanisms."[1] Without a systematic understanding of them and their interrelationships, "solutions" themselves have unintended, unforeseen, and sometimes disastrous consequences.

The concept of systems originated before the Second World War in the field of communications but was developed in earnest in military applications during the 1940s and especially the 1950s. It eventually expanded into new fields – systems engineering, systems analysis, systems theory, information theory, operations research, management systems, and mathematical modeling – which applied interdisciplinary knowledge from other branches of science to the solving of complex problems. These fields have attracted scientists and scholars from a variety of disciplines; among those relevant to our concerns we might mention Ludwig von Bertalanffy (biology; originator of general systems theory), Howard T. Odum (ecology), Lancelot Law Whyte (systems and form), Kenneth Boulding (economics), Herbert Simon (organization), Joseph Needham and Julian Huxley (biology), Magorah Maruyama and Norbert Wiener (cybernetics), Russell Ackoff (operations research), Britton Harris (mathematical modeling), and Brian Berry (regional science).

A system can be defined as "a group of parts whose interaction facilitates the performance of the parts into an organized whole with characteristic overall responses"[2] or as "a set of interrelated worlds and activities linked together to accomplish a desired end."[3] Basic to the notion of systems are the concepts of interrelationship and interaction, which tie together a particular universe for a purpose.

The notion of systems is diametrically opposed to the instinctive approach of most designers, who tend to see descriptively rather than structurally. Understanding the systematic nature of urban complexes requires a true change in mental attitude, but it would allow for a far more powerful and effective intervention by designers that would upset conventional solutions, interpretations of urban crises, and meanings of urban order.

The orthodox statements of some urban problems, if set within a systematic framework, seem plainly incoherent. For example, one of the most intractable urban problems in the United States is that of its ghettoes: large, dilapidated areas populated by blacks and other minorities, riddled with poverty, unemployment, crime, and poor health. The conven-

74

tional view is that of a self-contained problem leading to conventional "solutions" such as providing welfare assistance and public housing. But these "solutions" have consistently failed: The numbers of slum units and impoverished, malnourished, and unemployed people, as well as infant mortality, are increasing. How can we reconcile this conventional formulation of the problems in U.S. ghettoes if a city is defined as a system of interrelated and interacting parts joined together with the aim of achieving desired ends?

From a systematic viewpoint, the ghetto population is implicitly treated as – and behaves as – "surplus" population without any active role in the urban community; high rates of unemployment and poverty testify to this. High rates of morbidity and illiteracy are witness to the indifference with which ghetto dwellers are treated. The negative effects of crime and vandalism extend to the rest of the metropolitan area. The problem of ghettoes, then, should be broadly reformulated as one in which metropolitan areas have made no room for the poor and minorities within the established urban system. The conventional solution of providing welfare "benefits" – such as appalling public housing – is nothing more than an attempt to ameliorate the pain and frustration of ghetto dwellers and thereby avert violent disruptions that affect the rest of the city – the functioning part of the system – but does not begin to address the structural problem of bringing the poor and minorities into the urban system.

Downtown revitalization is another "solution" that fails because of a lack of understanding of the systems underlying changes in urban form. With the suburbanization of the middle class, the settling of minorities in deteriorating housing in central cities, and a pervasive shift in consumer preferences toward suburban shopping malls, many central areas have become wastelands. The typical solution has been to "beautify" Main Street, add garages, and subsidize merchants. The result has been that most of these downtowns are now beautified wastelands, because the urban system has abandoned them. There is simply no reason for their existence under current cultural conditions.

In many instances, urban problems are a manifestation of partial disruptions in the system that demand a "repair" solution to bring the system back to its original state. In other instances, urban problems may be symptoms of increasing incoherence within the system – of an organization that is no longer able to satisfy emergent goals because they are in increasing conflict with the system. In those cases, a "repair" solution would do no more than buy time, and the only way to bring about a viable new system would be to rearrange it structurally.

SELF-ORGANIZATION AND SELF-REGULATION

One of the essential characteristics of systems, including urban systems, is that they have their own internal corrective mechanisms that trigger processes aimed at solving their problems. The behavior of most urban systems "is governed by the dynamic structure of the system," and "outcomes are latent in the dynamic structure of the systems we have or we may adopt: they will inexorably emerge."[4] Thus, design solutions must be attuned to the internal corrective processes of urban systems.

The corrective mechanisms of an urban system are qualitatively adapted to its needs and may range from marginal to radical processes. They are to a large degree determined by "natural laws governing the behavior of large interacting systems; laws that can be aimed at self-regulating the system or self-organizing the system."[5] In the case of self-regulation, it is possible, by repairing disruptions, to bring the system back to its original state. The case of self-organization is different, since radical changes are necessary to achieve a system that is more stable than the original one.

The self-regulation of an urban system is an integral part of a community's behavior, involving different actors and factors. For example, families make decisions to sell, buy, or rent dwellings. The residential real estate market is affected by each of these decisions and, in turn, affects the decisions of other families, encouraging or discouraging groups to move and developers to build, renovate, buy, or sell property. Municipalities improve streets and utilities, rezone areas, change their tax revenues, and adjust the provision of services such as public schools, which again affect the decisions of families to sell, buy, or rent dwellings. Institutional, business, and social entities generate a host of adjustments from within the community, resulting in the routine systematic processes normally found in urban areas. In aggregate, the effects of these marginal changes, each of which is intended to correct a marginal problem, may sometimes be less than optimal. Occasionally, self-organization may take place, in which case major changes in the urban structure and in the relationships among urban components can lead to an entirely different urban system. For example, the trend toward large-scale areal specialization has radically altered the U.S. metropolis since World War II with the creation of extensive areas of homogeneous land use, such as middle-class residential suburbia. Depending on the forces behind changes, they may result in only short-term stability because of new conflicts within the system, leading to the need for further self-organization intended to provide longer-term stability.

Self-regulation and self-organization are relatively inter-dependent processes that originate in the system itself. But the interaction between them is not always smooth. When normal adjustments fail to solve community needs, the community may appear either to face a challenging opportunity or to have come to a dead end. Crises and conflicts create stress in the community, and, like minor earthquakes sig-naling some larger activity beneath the surface, they are symptoms of future radical change and impending self-or-ganization in the urban system.

An understanding of the operation of these processes in an urban system does not lead to easy answers, only to appro-priate responses attuned to the system's internal corrective mechanisms. As already mentioned, laws guiding the behav-ior of communities and urban form do not dictate determin-istic outcomes, but a subtle order of regularities. Community designers must recognize these regularities but, at the same time, allow for uncertainty in the specifics. They must also recognize the implications of different responses, encouraging changes with positive effects and alerting the community to those with negative effects. The behavior of urban systems over time is the result of partial disequilibria that generate self-regulating or self-organizing responses. To control the uncertainty and guide the system toward stability is the role of planning, but we may never achieve this. It may be that improvement will be achieved only through disequilibrium.

To take an example, there has been, for some time, an obvious disequilibrium between supply and demand in the housing market in most U.S. cities, which can be defined as a lack of residential options for low-income groups and a narrowing of options for middle-income groups. The cor-rection of this disequilibrium, through the combined effect of a large number of public and private actions, results in identifiable changes – most marginal and routine, others re-quiring structural reorganization. Some of these changes – subsidized interest rate programs, housing cooperatives and land banks, for example – may have positive effects and should receive support and encouragement. But some of the changes may have negative effects. Implicitly, the social "solution" to housing the poor has been the provision of slums; this determines the spread of urban deterioration, a slumlord real estate industry, and unacceptable living conditions. The provision of dwellings for moderate and middle-income groups through the private market has led to the development of low-quality units on cheap land far from employment centers and public transportation, which requires long and costly commuting trips. Changes such as these should be strongly opposed. Opposition should take the form of generating options with positive effects consistent with the laws underlying urban systems – even if this means implementing radical changes, that is, self-organization.

I consider planning and design activities valid agents of change. They are among the mechanisms for regulating and organizing human settlements. Urban planning and community design are internal factors in the urban system; they are intrinsic to the social, political, and economic subsystems of the city. This point of view is extremely important, because it locates planners and designers, mentally, within the system, not outside of it. Professionals are not detached experts overseeing problems with unbiased perspectives and dealing solely with fragments of reality. Community design is one of the several social mechanisms by which the system controls itself.

Recognizing the existence of self-regulating and self-organizing processes is a precondition for a successful design intervention. The ultimate responsibility of community designers is to decide, in each case, whether to work with self-regulating processes, and thus to correct and improve – in effect to maintain the existing path – or to join the forces leading toward a new organization through radical changes.

URBAN COMPLEXITY

Planners and designers must immerse themselves in the urban system in order to understand it thoroughly, but the more they probe the system, the more complex it appears. The feeling of those attempting to penetrate and study urban areas is that "the more they know, the more they don't know." Because of their increasing specialization and size, contemporary cities are far more complex than they were, say, a few decades ago. "The large metropolitan settlement is indeed the locus of a wide variety of activities, and it does indeed comprise a more complex network of functional inter-dependencies than any one man can comprehend."[6]

As an example of urban complexity, consider the design of a residential area in an urban community. Planners must account for such factors as location in the metropolis, accessibility, land use mix and adjacencies, densities, open space, population, social trends, dwelling unit types and variations, site design, cost levels, and fiscal impact; these, in turn, must be disaggregated and their interrelationships considered and evaluated.

Complexity originates in the "richness" of a system, with the multiplicity of its parts – individuals, families, groups, neighborhoods, institutions, government agencies, private corporations, stores, industrial plants, services – and the "high and highly differentiated level of interaction between the parts."[7] It is defined by the "number of possible connections between component different parts of the system."[8] The level of interaction is related to the level of development of the urban area, including such factors as cost and time of overcoming distance, as well as incentive and need to contact other individuals.

Given two different centers of equal size, the more developed one will be more complex, because its transportation system will involve less cost and time per mile, and because there will be a greater need for interaction among its increasingly specialized activities, which will result in more benefits to the city as a whole. Urban complexity is thus both the cause and the effect of the level of development in a community; more highly developed cities (say, postindustrial metropolises) are far more complex than less developed ones (traditional cities, for instance). Urban communities in the Third World are less complex than those in industrialized countries; lower complexity, however, does not mean that urban problems are less challenging.

There is also a relationship between complexity and urban size, by which larger urban centers demand more complex systems in order to be viable. Although I will discuss the effects of size on urban form in Chapter 6, let me mention that as urban areas grow, new elements – from ring belts to rapid transit, from government centers to cultural centers – emerge. This means that bigger areas are not merely quantitatively larger than smaller ones; qualitatively different elements appear at specific size thresholds, precluding linear growth. The existence of such noncontinuous behavior in urban systems – thresholds, limits, nonlinearity – adds to their complexity.[9] The level of complexity in an urban area grows much faster than its size; other things being equal, a center twice the size of another is several times more complex. In theory and practice, complexity grows exponentially with size.

URBAN SPECIALIZATION

The tendency of urban development is toward greater complexity. Larger cities, lower costs and less time to overcome distance, and more incentives or needs to link with other individuals all add up to richer, more differentiated and more complex systems. This is the result of a universal, complementary process that accompanies economic development, or, as it is known in the industrialized world, the process of specialization and interdependency.

Cities spatially reflect development through increasing specialization and interdependency. The process of sectoral specialization involves the differentiation of socioeconomic units adapted to narrower functions within the urban system; each unit tends to cluster with similar units, resulting in locational specialization. In turn, specialization depends on interaction, leading to a rapid increase in the need, and the convenience, of linking those specialized units with complementary units throughout the urban area and beyond. The efficiency of the specialization process is complemented by the efficiency of clustering, that is, the economies of concentration. The so-called technological process in economics, a combination of specialization and concentration that increases the size of the unit of production,[10] extends to cities, where specialization and concentration increase with increased complexity.[11] Cities reflect, and in turn influence, the socioeconomic processes of development in space through the specialization and, thus, homogenization of increasingly larger areas.

Although in every settlement in history there has been some clustering of homogeneous activities, the industrial city has a typical pattern of extensive homogeneous land use. Similar economic areas tend to cluster together – the financial districts, the jewelry districts, and so on – to their mutual benefit. The same is observed in noneconomic activities, such as health care, in which there are clusters of "hospital precincts." One phenomenon with more far-reaching effects is the tendency for residential land uses to cluster in socially homogeneous districts, as discussed in subsequent chapters. In these patterns, formed by sizable differentiated and specialized areas, no one area is self-sufficient, and interaction is essential for the survival of the urban system. Increasing land use homogeneity in large districts, the trademark of the industrial city, forces complex transportation systems to satisfy its growing interaction requirements.

It is precisely the internal restructuring resulting from the increased areal specialization and interaction of urban development that accounts for a major difference between industrialized cities and those of underdeveloped regions. Despite the fact that some metropolises in the Third World may have huge populations, their structural – one can almost say qualitative – difference with industrialized cities is what determines a radically different level of complexity. Many of these cities are still an aggregation of nonspecialized and fairly autonomous settlements, suggesting that they cannot be considered (integrated) urban systems, that their level of complexity is much lower than that of industrialized cities, and that they could be better described as a cluster of villages and towns around a traditional urban core.

Planning approaches based on the experience of industrialized cities, which can be fairly misguided on their own turf, when applied to Third World communities are doubly wrong. Many cities in underdeveloped countries must be considered protourban systems that are currently undergoing painful crises of self-organization. Important political and socioeconomic issues are often not being satisfactorily answered, and in many cases, internal obstacles are preventing a successful search for a viable system, thus perpetuating the sense of constant crisis.

One of the most critical questions is whether Third World cities will follow the path of those in developed countries. This question leads to an even more fundamental issue: Are urban development and its process of specialization universal? Areal specialization, homogeneity, and interdependence, as spatial expressions of the socioeconomic system, are influenced by the institutional framework in which they exist. In the industrialized Western countries, these processes have been adapted to the characteristics of the capitalist culture and its institutions; it is conceivable that they would vary in other institutional frameworks. Although we say that there are universal laws governing urban development, the specific pattern in different regions of the world will differ according to the institutional framework of each culture. The Third World's search for a more viable path must include a search for urban development patterns better adapted to their emerging institutions; specialization and interdependency will certainly occur, but their specific patterns are still to be found.

There are additional reasons for my skepticism concerning a deterministic urban development process. Analysis of the process of specialization indicates that urban development in industrialized countries is not without flaws and, I propose, may even lead to a dead end in the long run. The specialized urban system, as we know it, particularly in the United States, may contain the seeds of its potential own destruction, and thus of radical change, because of the danger of overspecialization.

It is obvious that cities specializing in a single economic activity face a constant risk: Economic failure of this activity may cause the collapse of the whole community. Detroit is only one sad example of many such cities in the industrial rust belt of the United States. The recurrent failures of company towns and the boom-and-bust cycles of narrowly specialized communities are clear examples of the dangers of overspecialization on a regional scale. Successful cities, in the long run, have a resilient economic base, thanks to their reliance on a broad range of activities, especially in the growing service sector.

A more subtle, though equally pervasive, problem exists in cities on the urban scale. As a result of increasing areal specialization and growing concentration of activities, they face the constant risk of partial breakdowns – from rapid-transit strikes to power failures – that can lead to dangerous and unmanageable situations, breakdowns that in less specialized cities are no more than bothersome events.

What are considered "successful" urban areas in industrialized countries are becoming more and more like giant corporations: Enormous metropolises are undergoing increasing internal division of functions: "The technological and institutional transformers are becoming more complex, more concentrated, more specialized, and more vulnerable to breakdown."[12] The development of these cities is based on a single objective – profit – which is sometimes disguised as or confused with "efficiency"; few social costs are ever taken into account. The tendency is toward overspecialized systems, which are known for their efficiency (read profitability) within a strictly defined and stable environment, but which are also known for their inability to adapt, to change, and to accommodate new conditions. The self-proclaimed efficiency and standard of living that these cities offer to part of their urban population must be reconciled with the increasing risk of technical and social breakdowns and deterioration of the environment.

Overspecialization may result in the need to restructure the system (self-organization) so that it is less efficient but more reliable. Underspecialization, however, may indicate an underdeveloped system. Urban overspecialization requires community designs with more highly integrated patterns and a greater mix of activities aimed at obtaining a more resilient urban system – a system that may appear to be less efficient but that is more adaptable to changing conditions, as is detailed in Chapter 7. Underspecialization requires learning from the mistakes of the industrialized world and applying that knowledge to the search for viable paths of development. Urban development must reconcile the need for urban specialization with the need for resiliency.

THE WHOLE AND THE PARTS AND THE COMPLEXITY OF SPACE

The complexity of urban areas requires that the total system be considered in the analysis, planning, and design of any of its components. Solutions developed within a limited framework often fail. An obvious example of the consequences of ignoring the totality and concentrating on one part is found in transportation planning. Most new highways are congested from "day one," although demand projections may show much lower volumes. What is generally lacking is the realization that drivers in the region immediately change travel patterns when the new road opens, and these continue to change until all advantages are equalized and the new highway is as congested as the old roads. Even more important is the fact that transportation planners often fail (or are unable) to consider land use changes as an efficient tool for improving travel conditions.

In general, it is possible to identify a problem in area A, only to find the structural causes for this problem in area B and to discover that the best way to implement a solution is by making changes in area C. This means that the sectorial definitions and spatial boundaries of the problem should be widened to account for the myriad effects and linkages impinging on it.

The fact that urban complexes are systems is itself an indication that one cannot select a part for analysis or action without also including the relevant effects of other parts on that part. There are two broad approaches to this issue. One

83

is to focus on the component parts; the other is to consider the totality. The first position can be summarized as reductionism; that is, "a whole can be understood completely if you understand its parts, and the nature of their sum"; the second position can be characterized as holism; that is, "the whole is greater than the sum of the parts."[13] However, for our purposes, neither position is fully adequate: Feedback from the general to the particular and from the particular to the general is probably the wisest path, since knowledge cannot be found exclusively in either the whole or the parts by themselves.[14] Maintaining a balance between the whole and the parts is critical for the urban planner and community designer.

The urban problem is the totality; we find consistently that the issues extend beyond the boundaries of the study area. It is the increasingly complex interrelationships in advanced urban systems that force the universalization of the problem. One of the major causes of the complexity of urban areas is that they are spatially defined; each element has a position in space that can be established only in relation to the other elements in the system. The most important advantage of holism is the ability to deal with the positional value of the elements in space, establishing a framework for the total urban system. Urban areas are spatial systems composed of parts whose values are not absolute but relative.

Population, income, and employment data; houses and workplaces; land uses and densities – all have a limited capacity to define an urban system until they appear distributed in space. Two office centers of equal size would be radically different if one were downtown and the other on a suburban highway. The logic of wholes deals not only with sectorial relationships, but also with other, more suitable logical units defined by the following characteristics.[15] In holistic systems, the parts do not interconnect by virtue of inherent qualities, but by virtue of their position in the system; the relationships of these parts cannot be ordered lineally. Furthermore, parts do not become members of the system because of their intrinsic qualities, but because of their distribution within the system. Relative location in space is crucial to understanding the urban system.

Indeed, urban systems can be defined only because of the positional value of their elements. Location in space, for a long time the concern of designers with limited analytical capacity to assess it and often a low priority for socially oriented planners, is indispensable for understanding urban systems. The components of such systems are not significantly connected with one another except in reference to the whole: The nature of dwellings and workplaces, for example, depends to a large degree on their relationship, which is radically different in industrial metropoles and small agriculturally based towns. The reality of the whole complex system in space is the core of community design.

URBAN HIERARCHIES

The recognition that urban communities are holistic, complex systems in space provides a framework within which information and experience can be organized. But unless a system has an internal hierarchical order, we are left with ever-expanding and partially defined wholes, taxing our ability to understand them. To face the complexity of a large urban system would overwhelm our analytical capacity. Intuitively, it is apparent that some urban factors have priority over others. For example, the decision to locate a residential area at a certain site eliminates the option of using some building types: Single-family homes on a lot are implicitly excluded from consideration in central city locations. Urban systems are hierarchically ordered in a way that greatly facilitates our analysis and understanding.

Hierarchy is the basic structural order of complex systems with pervasive and universal laws of organization. As Herbert Simon stated, "Complexity frequently takes the form of hierarchy, and hierarchic systems have some common properties that are independent of their specific context. Hierarchy is one of the central structural schemes that the architect of complexity uses."[16] According to Lancelot Law Whyte, "hierarchical structure is the basic feature common to matter and mind."[17] Hierarchies permeate most of our universe, including cities, urban complexes, and buildings, as well as socioeconomic organizations and urban sectors such as education and health.

Hierarchies provide a conceptual framework for probing, and dealing with, the complexity of an urban system, because they organize its constituent subsystems into a totality. Hence, hierarchies allow us to prioritize subsystems without missing the totality. Urban hierarchies are spatial systems with distinguishable levels. Each level is related to at least one other level, while a unit at any level is composed of parts each of which is a unit at the next (smaller) level.[18] Levels are identifiable subsets composed of parts characterized by

85

the same status,[19] that is, similarly related to other levels. Thus, hierarchies show the "natural" way to disaggregate a whole into its constituent parts, or subsystems, as well as the relationships between the "lower" and "upper" subsystems, which are based not on coercion but on logic.

Each level of a hierarchy is connected by asymmetrical relationships to other levels.[20] Parts and levels are organized directionally in specific ways: Each one influences some other component and is influenced, in turn, by yet another component; each one is subordinated to some component, but subordinates yet another. Examples of "directed" relationships abound: Basic employment influences the location of residential uses, which influences the location of retail uses, which influences the location of more residential uses, and so on. Pedestrian access and circulation influence the location of new buildings in precincts, which influences the access and internal circulation of buildings, and so on.

The law of asymmetrical relationships defines the type of urban hierarchy and thus many of the characteristics of an urban area. For example, we can recognize the levels corresponding to the physical realm – dwellings, blocks, precincts – and to the social realm – families, groups, classes – as well as the lateral connections between entities of the same status. The simpler the lateral connections are, the poorer the system is: A highly segregated settlement with only one class or group of very similar families inhabiting very similar dwellings is one example. The more complex the lateral connections are, the richer the system is: An example is a heterogeneous settlement with various classes or groups where a variety of households live in a variety of buildings. Furthermore, we can recognize pairs of levels, connected by asymmetrical relationships of influence and subordination, which may become urban typologies – for example, the town house and the rectangular block, the rapid-transit station and surrounding commercial development.

The notion of hierarchy helps us to see urban elements from different angles, since "a member of a spatial hierarchy [can] be regarded from three points of view – firstly from that of its membership of a level, secondly from that of its entering into the constitution of a member of the next higher level, thirdly from that of its analysis into an assemblage of members of a lower level."[21] For example, a commercial center can be considered as a component of the metropolitan retail subsystem, as a center in itself, or as comprising a number of stores and shops. It is at the same time a unit competing with other units, an aggregate formed by individual stores, and a part of the retail sector of the city; it is a service center to area residents, a business for its owners, a workplace for its employees, a buyer for wholesale distributors, a real estate investment, part of the city tax base, a factor affecting surrounding property values, a place to which people travel, a cause of congestion and possible public investments in streets, highways, and mass transit, and a place for social encounters. It is clear why Lancelot Law Whyte restated the well-known dictum "The whole is more than the sum of the parts" as "The system is different from the mere aggregation of the parts," since each part "may possess . . . different properties when several of them are arranged in an ordered system by appropriate asymmetrical relations."[22]

Though hierarchy is an objective notion, it has acquired pejorative connotations. Often, it is misunderstood to mean a rigidly controlled organization in which authority flows uncontested from top to bottom. The degree of authoritarianism or democracy in an organization is reflected in its hierarchy. Tree structures, for example, are the typical organization of a closed, authoritarian system, whereas more highly developed and complex networks reflect an open, pluralistic system, with many channels and options linking the elements. Thus, the concept of hierarchy does not, by definition, imply an authoritarian or rigid organization; it could allow for a highly democratic and flexible organization by introducing order to complexity.

Understanding urban areas as hierarchical systems allows community designers to select the minimum whole necessary for study, by choosing or discarding other levels, parts, and relationships, based on their relative impact on the problem area; it allows them to formulate an efficient definition of a relevant whole. Hierarchy is truly the grammar of urban order.

CHAPTER 5

CITIES IN EVOLUTION

*Or how growth and change guide urban
form in time*

A DYNAMIC VIEW OF URBAN AREAS

In the past two centuries or so, human settlements have
undergone radical changes to a degree unequaled since their
appearance in the second millennium B.C., and they are still
experiencing continuous waves of change (Figure 5.1). The
radical nature of these changes can be easily perceived by
comparing the preindustrial city with today's urban settlements: size, structure, and function show basic differences
(Figure 5.2). The evolution of urban systems continues; cities,
urban complexes, and precincts are not static organizations,
but have a critical dynamic dimension. Even buildings, quite
often selected to give an image of stability, have a dynamic
dimension. The effect of time on urban systems is as important as that of space. Urban areas are systems that literally
transform themselves over time in a manner that can be compared to the series of individual still photographs that make
up a film sequence.

When seen from a dynamic perspective, urban areas experience a kaleidoscopic transformation, involving several
processes over time – growth, change, reconcentration, dispersion, aging, reconstruction, and many others – that,
though identifiable for analytical purposes, interact with and
influence each other continuously. "Form is simply a short
time-slice of a single spatio-temporal entity."[1] Planners and
designers must understand the time dimension and learn from
the internal processes that govern growth and change in the
built environment.

The effects of time in urban areas involve complex processes and are closely related to physical and social factors.
The number and variety of these factors are enormous: from
interest rates to oil prices, from air-conditioning technology

to fashions, from academic registration levels to population immigration. Many study fields – among them economics, demography, finance, and building and transportation technology – are involved and have received specific attention. My interest, however, is to examine the combined effects of these factors, as they result in specific dynamic processes with intrinsic regularities, constraints, and fundamental laws for urban form.

The first step in examining the dynamic effects of time in urban areas is to consider the processes of growth and change. It is becoming clear that the boundary between growth and change is taxonomic only and that these processes interact very closely. Within each of them, a number of distinct sub-processes can be identified. Growth can be characterized as qualitative when a new functional complex is added to a system – as in the development of a new university campus in a city. Growth can also be characterized as quantitative when existing complexes are expanded through the repetition of similar units or structures – as in the construction of new buildings on an existing university campus. Growth can be marginal, that is, proportionally small compared with the total organization – as in the construction of a few houses in a city or a shed to a building. Growth can also be nonmar-

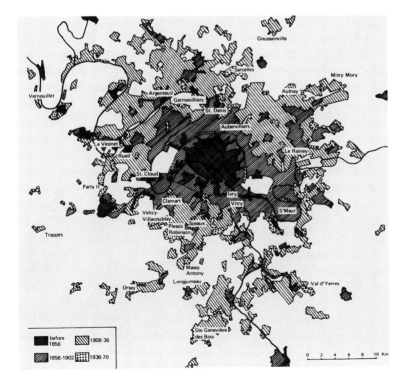

Figure 5.1. Urban growth: the industrial city. Paris, 1856–1970. (Jean Bastie: Doubleday/H. Wentworth Eldredge)

ginal, that is, proportionally large compared with the total organization – as in the construction of a large residential subdivision or a large module of a building.

The recognition of these growth processes could assist in the analysis of urban dynamics, as long as one is not caught in taxonomic rigidity. We must take into account their varied nature and not be satisfied with mere classification: For example, a nonmarginal expansion could result in a qualitative addition as well, such as the severalfold increases experienced by a small college with the addition of new graduate and professional schools.

Growth could reflect increases in urban activity and population without immediate physical implications. Increases in manufacturing production, retail sales, or services are all non-physical manifestations of growth that would affect the urban system and might eventually result in physical growth. Immigration to an urban area could also take place without physical expansion if vacant dwellings or surplus space within dwellings were used. Thus, growth can occur without an expansion in area or in number of buildings through the intensification of the use of existing space and the creation of higher population densities. Furthermore, we can distinguish areal growth – as in the urbanization of rural land – and building growth – as in the redevelopment of an urban sector (the latter could also be described as a change in the area).

Finally, we can talk of negative growth, a phenomenon common to depressed areas where people and activities leave empty structures; this is a process involving regrouping, redistribution, reuse, recycling, and, in some cases, aban-

Figure 5.2. Urban growth: the preindustrial city. (S. E. Rasmussen, *Towns and Buildings,* MIT Press, 1969) (Left) Paris, early Middle Ages. (Right) Paris, 1180–1225. (Opposite top) Paris, 1370. (Opposite bottom) Paris, 1676.

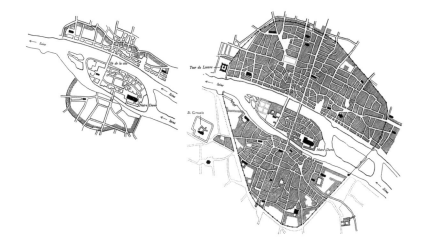

donment – in other words, internal change in the urban organization.

A wide range of physical changes take place in urban areas: aging, maintenance, repair, rebuilding, reuse, preservation, abandonment, demolition, redevelopment, and redistribution, among others. Some are caused exclusively by the effects of time, some by additional sociocultural factors that deserve close attention.

These changes are visible in most urban areas in the world but are most prominent in U.S. cities, whose very nature is one of social, generational, seasonal, and daily changes. The overspecialization of urban land use in extensive, homogeneous residential and work areas causes daily changes in the population distribution and utilization of facilities that in-

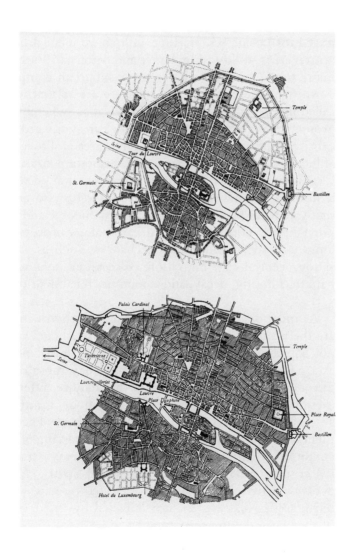

volve commuting and the abandonment of suburbia by workers after 8 a.m. and of downtowns after 5 p.m. Climate causes seasonal changes in the use of open spaces and recreational facilities, in energy consumption from heating, lighting, and air-conditioning, in institutional routines (those of schools and theaters), and in community life in general.

Human generational change follows family formation and development; it includes shifts in income and lifestyle, as well as additions and losses of family members. In the U.S. city, this means a typical housing cycle for a middle-class family, starting with a small apartment, followed by a first house, a larger house, an apartment after the children leave home for college or work, a retirement house, and, finally, a nursing facility. For many working-class people this sequence is simplified by a lack of options, and for the poor, a slum or public housing is the only alternative. Parallel sequences can be traced for businesses, starting with cheap incubator space in central areas, followed by larger and better facilities, and, for many firms, ending with extensive suburban compounds.

Most of these processes of change are related to the so-called urban ecology typical of U.S. cities, whereby affluent groups keep shifting their residential areas toward the suburban periphery of the metropolitan area, followed by less affluent groups, who occupy the deteriorating housing stock. Occasionally, the reverse of this phenomenon occurs – gentrification – whereby affluent groups return to an area to renovate it, displacing the existing low-income and minority populations. Throughout the urban ecology process there are long-term social and land use changes, such as suburbanization, central-city migration, succession in a segregated pattern, filtering, decay, and sometimes rehabilitation (Figure 5.3).

As mentioned, the many processes of growth and change are the result of a variety of factors. Growth and change do not happen only because there is a deterministic need, such as a population increase. Technology may cause change by introducing new work processes that require different facilities or by introducing new transportation or communication systems that permit dispersion over the land. The environment may cause change by requiring better living or working conditions or limits to growth. Culture may cause change by creating needs based on perceived status. As society evolves, growth and change are affected by new values and technologies that are, in turn, affected by the development of the urban culture over time.

But are all these factors ad hoc? Must we take every occasion of growth and change as an isolated event understood only as a function of the factors that ostensibly cause it? Are there regularities or universal laws intrinsic to these dynamic processes? Certainly there are, and these laws can help planners and designers to establish whether the growth of an urban complex is desirable, whether change is wasteful, or whether obsolescence can be prevented. Planners and designers have been accumulating experience based on specific project data; we must generalize from this experience. In this way, policies, programs, and plans can be better anticipated, problems avoided, and better designs obtained. The recognition and application of laws underlying the processes of urban growth and change are the subjects of this chapter.

THE PROCESS AND LAWS OF GROWTH

The process of urban growth has at least two sources. One is the social system composed of the population, economic activities, and organizations; the other is the physical–spatial system of the built environment. Each influences the other;

Figure 5.3. Urban change: The U.S. metropolis. Washington, D.C. (Robert Lautman)

the physical plant of cities has a profound effect on population, economic activities, and organizations, but the building process can take place only as a result of human decisions. For this reason, the urban system combines growth in discrete steps – as buildings do – and the uncertainty typical of social systems.

Cities not only grow at the whim of exogenous factors – economic, institutional, or otherwise – but are also subject to internal systematic laws that regulate growth and its effects on the total organization. Similarly, buildings grow according to internal laws, beyond the pressure of exogenous factors such as programs and market demand. Growth is common to all systems, including social organizations and man-made environments; all of them show regularities in their development, indicating the existence of underlying laws that control that development. In order to illustrate the regularities that underlie most, if not all, growth in social and built organizations, I will present two examples at two extremes: of the regional and the building scale.

The first example illustrates the consistency of regional-scale development in the United States.[2] It is based on a study of the so-called index of population potential, a field quantity that measures accessibility at a given location of a given population. Over a period of 180 years, the mean population potential grew as a constant power of the total population, with an extremely high correlation. The same relationship was found between the growth of urban population and total population. That is, the mean potential of total population and the urban fraction of the population was linearly related between the years 1790 and 1970, "a constant quantity hidden within a growing population, a quantity which relates the proportion of the population which lives in cities of 2,500 persons or more to the average accessibility to the population as a whole."[3] This result suggests that there is an internal control mechanism that regulates the increase in demographic concentration, which in turn regulates the formation of the urban component. In a dynamic view, "there is a striking convergence of nearly all regional values with time, especially since 1880; . . . the differing initial conditions were steadily overruled by changing regional specialization and the integrating factors of improving transportation and communication technology."[4] Equally suggestive regularities are found in the population rank (by size) and the spacing of cities on the land, for example. The movement of people in the economic space in search of jobs and other opportunities is not random but results in systematic regularities, high-lighting the capacity of urban systems for self-regulation through time and space.

The second example illustrates the phenomenon of growth at the level of the building complex. A study of British hospitals shows remarkable regularities in their growth, regardless of capacity and year of construction.[5] In a plot of the expansion of floor space over time, each hospital shows the S-shaped curve so well known in statistics. We know that the S-shaped curve also describes the growth of animals, plants, and human beings, of certain populations of humans and animals, and of organizations: It is a universal growth curve that describes systems' self-regulating laws. In this study, the first period of time reflects a slow rate of growth, indicating that the new hospital is performing satisfactorily. In the second period the growth rate accelerates dramatically owing to the increasing inadequacy of older facilities; approximately 100 percent of the original floor area is added in this period of rapid expansion. The third period shows a leveling around the thirtieth year of the complex, indicating that the original nucleus capacity for expansion has been reached; leveling takes place at approximately 110 percent expansion of the original floor space.

These two examples of observed regularities in urban organization and built form reflect the existence of underlying laws of growth. These laws are derived from the laws of generic systems: the principle of nucleation and the principle of equal advantage. As will be seen, each law can be related to the two previous examples.

Principle of nucleation. Quite often, community designs are produced as a "totality," as if human settlements were constituted by similar elements that could be assembled like children's blocks. But in urban systems, some elements appear first, forming a nucleus, around which other elements later develop. The first universal law of growth is the principle of nucleation or critical mass, which succinctly states that "any structure has a minimum size, which is its nucleus."[6] Once the nucleus is formed, additions can be made to the structure. The formation of the nucleus itself involves issues that are quite different from those related to the growth of established structures. One issue is the existence of minimum initial size, or critical mass; this is especially important if the nucleus has an innovative character. Another issue is that the nucleus need not be homogeneous with the structure around it; indeed, in most cases it is not, since heterogeneous nucleation has the necessary complexity to start a sustained growth process.

Specks of dust are the nuclei around which raindrops are formed; grains of sand act as irritants that trigger the oyster's deposition of layers of nacre, which results in pearls. (It is interesting that impurities are often behind the process of growth in nature.) In the example of hospital complexes, the initial program forms the nucleus of the future institution, which is completed by successive additions and expansions.

The most immediate value of applying the law of nucleation to the urban development process lies in the qualitative insights it offers, insights that are crucial for (re)directing planning and design processes. For example, new towns in the United States in the 1960s and 1970s started with nothing more than typical subdivisions. Later stages simply repeated more of the same, complemented in some cases by shopping centers. These towns were developed with the sole objective of profiting the entrepreneur and were populated by families searching for what they thought to be the best house. There was no complex minimum mass, no heterogeneous nucleus, such as a set of institutions or activities. These oversized subdivisions never became viable communities, in part because they lacked a legitimate nucleus. They were never more than large-scale real estate ventures and lacked the variety of objectives that could have created a nucleus (Figure 5.4). Had urban policymakers of the 1960s understood the systematic nature of cities and recognized, among other factors, the law of nucleation, their programs would have had a far different outcome – or may not have been undertaken at all.

A comparison of new towns with most early American settlements is striking. Although the newcomers to this continent were motivated in part by economic interests, their goals also included national and religious expansion, individual and community freedom, and even a thirst for discovery and adventure. The foundation of their settlements, guided mostly by the laws of Indies set up by the Spanish Crown, clearly established a minimum nucleus within a community hierarchy, around which growth could and did occur (Figure 5.5). The results, considering the relative scarcity of resources and the magnitude of the enterprise, cannot but be considered awesome.

In the case of new towns, the shopping center was planned to be developed during the mature stages of settlement and not at the beginning, because of limited cash flow. It was thought that, at these later stages, the larger residential population would have formed a market large enough to justify a number of retail activities; the settlement was just an investment. However, this is very different from a real community. A settlement should be planned with a vision, with a heterogeneous nucleus carrying the seeds for future development.

Principle of equal advantage. The second universal law of growth is the principle of equal advantage, which, in general terms, governs the distribution of elements of a structure among the various parts of the structure.[7] This principle states that the units of a system tend to flow toward locations of greater advantage.

This law is related to several phenomena with implications for community design. First, it is related to the phenomenon of flows assignation within a system. Second, it is related to the phenomenon of functional substitution and regeneration,

Figure 5.4. U.S. new towns. Columbia, Maryland. (Northway Photographics Inc., William S. Pearson, Jr.)

in which, if one organ in an organization is missing, there is a tendency for other organs to take over its function. Third, it is related to the phenomenon of loose ends being the growth points of systems – another indication that full stability is incompatible with growth. In the regional location of urban populations in the United States, as mentioned earlier in this chapter, the internal mechanisms regulating population distribution follow the principle of equal advantage.

The implications of this law for community design are numerous and profound. As one example, traffic flow congestion tends to afflict every new highway as soon as it is completed. According to the principle of equal advantage, drivers tend to seek the better routes, resulting in the ultimate equalization of advantages throughout the highway system. This suggests that trying to solve traffic problems by the addition of more highways on the basis of deterministic estimates is, as we mentioned in Chapter 4, fruitless. It is necessary to assess the total system, including the various transportation channels and modes as well as the activities causing people to travel, that is, the land use distribution.

Figure 5.5. Laws of Indies towns: Lima, Central area, 1687. (Archives of Indies)

Ignorance of the principle of equal advantage is a major factor in explaining permanent traffic congestion regardless of the public works projects undertaken.

As another example, one specifically related to the functional substitution aspect of the principle, the excessive provision of overspecialized facilities weakens the vitality of urban areas and reduces their ability to improvise and substitute. In order to ensure a safety margin against overspecialization, flexibility in the tasks and roles assigned to the components of the urban system, as well as imaginative improvisation should be encouraged. The vitality of street markets – that is, streets that function as food retail areas – the imagination of children creating their own play environment, the awesomeness of concerts and plays in churches, the earthy quality of religious services in secular places, the beauty of work taking place in full view of a community, and the joy of recreation within a work environment must all be regained. Let us be very wary of a precise and exact allocation of every function to every facility; that is antithetical to urbanity.

The complexities of the internal laws of growth can be summarized in the so-called D'Arcy Thompson principle: "At any moment, the form of any object, organism, or organization is the result of its laws of growth up to that moment."[8] The mutual constraints imposed by the form of an organization and the process of growth are a supremely important parameter for designers, since "growth creates form, but form limits growth."[9]

CHANGE AND EVOLUTION

If there is one characteristic that differentiates today's cities from those of the past, it is their rate of change. It is not only that urban structures and activities are changing; the fact that they do so at an accelerated rate is most important. Indeed, everything around us seems to be changing rapidly: social mores, scientific concepts, lifestyles, and fashions. Urban organizations are also changing rapidly, experiencing continuous waves of physical, technical, administrative, and financial innovation.

The key source of change is, as already discussed, the internal rearrangement of a system experiencing growth. Examples are the emergence of specialized transportation facilities and single-use business centers as urban areas grow and of exurban centers as metropolitan areas expand. But the most pervasive process of change is a complex one that includes succession, downgrading, and renewal.

Succession, downgrading, renewal. In the United States, cities experience a complex process of change that is based on the continuous expansion of residential zones and the invasion of one group's area by another group. This process involves a constant series of changes in land use and population, with more affluent groups moving toward the periphery, followed by less affluent groups, and the handing down, or "filtering," of buildings from the departing higher-income group to the lower-income newcomers. In some areas, filtering results in the abandonment of extensive zones, such as the South Bronx, which revert to a state of urban ruins. This process, identified as succession, is characterized by the paradox that "the occupancy of the land by one use tends to make it unsuitable for further occupancy by that use."[10] The reason for this paradox is that this type of urban ecology is based on a constant process of downgrading; lower-income groups follow higher-income groups, accompanied by the deterioration of previously well-maintained neighborhoods.

In the past decade, the opposite version of this process, "gentrification," has been evident in such cities as New York, San Francisco, Boston, and a few others; middle- and upper-middle-class people are displacing the poor inhabitants of some central city neighborhoods and rehabilitating their deteriorating town houses, forming enclaves of affluence adjacent to slums. Though physical deterioration is reversed, a high social cost is imposed on poor families forced to move to other slums.

Thus, growth may result, under given conditions, in a wasteful and damaging process of change. The problem, of course, is not inherent in growth as such, but originates in the cultural values of society. Planning requires an understanding of the negative effects of change in urban areas and the ability to anticipate the impact of change throughout a metropolitan area.

Only a combination of actions can ameliorate the negative effects of change in urban areas. The aim of design policy must be to disengage project areas from the downgrading sequence and to buttress them from every angle: rehabilitation of buildings, development of needed community facilities, creation of neighborhood organizations, improvement of public transportation, and generation of employment. Clearly, there will be financial obstacles – from absentee landowners who refuse to cooperate, to banks that refuse loans, to city halls that refuse to decentralize authority. In the long range, we must eliminate social and racial discrimination and neighborhood segregation, which lead to the damaging process of succession and deterioration – nothing less than a revolutionary change.

Timed development and time lags. Because technological innovations are often timed with shifts in social tastes, settlement patterns can be dated. The historical background of a city is very important for understanding its particular structure, as well as for probing the systematic complexities that result in physical patterns. An example is the change in urban densities with the advent of the automobile, which is also reflected in locational patterns and building types; older cities dating from preautomobile eras have different urban structures and behave differently, even today, than do cities built after the invention of the automobile. "Older cities have somewhat higher average densities, and their densities respond more to increases in size than is the case for cities a major portion of whose growth has taken place since the inception of the automobile age."[1] As the size of a population increases, a self-organization process takes place that involves a compensatory change in density and area. Typically, older cities responded to population growth by increasing central density levels, and they continued to do so long after the introduction of the automobile (Figure 5.6).

In contrast, settlements that have been automobile oriented since their inception lack a "nucleus" – in other words, their growth has not followed the principle of nucleation. Their inability to generate centers is reflected in their diffuse pattern and homogeneously low densities; these settlements are condemned to roadside sprawl. Perhaps affluent residents may, as in the case of Houston, pay for an artificial center, but it seems that these settlements cannot recover something they never had.

The existence of time lags in urban systems adds complexity to the development process, since the characteristics of the urban structure at a given time period are not directly related to contemporary technology but may also have origins in the technology of earlier periods. Urban characteristics defined during previous periods tend to remain, influencing later patterns of change. The physical plant of buildings and street systems developed before the automobile age still make up the pattern of many central cities, a pattern

Figure 5.6. Pre- and
postautomobile cities:
(Top) New York City.
(Port Authority of New
York and New Jersey)
(Bottom) Los Angeles.
(California Department of
Transportation)

that limits the access of automobiles to downtown areas. The urban system in these cities partially rejects the new technology of the automobile and anticipates the future technology of advanced rapid transit and a pedestrian urban environment.

Time lags in urban systems have both cultural and physical sources.[12] Sometimes the cultural framework changes less rapidly than other factors; it is only too common to find technological changes outstripping ethical and aesthetic changes. The first cars were designed as horseless carriages; Greek temples were stone versions of wooden constructions. In addition, buildings often survive for many years, becoming elements of stability that resist change. The many old buildings still used in our urban areas are witnesses to this physical lag; they were designed during the time of the horse and buggy and are being used during the time of interplanetary travels.

The dynamic of urban systems is not one of relentless change, however, but rather one in which fast pace is mixed with stability, change with constancy, and growth with decay. The evolution of urban systems includes internal incoherencies and contradictions and the accident of fate as well as the inheritance of history, the ephemerality of fashion, and the laws of economics.

AGING AND OBSOLESCENCE

One of the most ubiquitous urban images today is that of abandoned buildings and neighborhoods: Deteriorating slums, vacant mills, and closed theaters are all part of our daily urban experience. The optimistic expectation of growth must be tempered by the certainty of decay. Clearly, there is a cultural bias in our society against acknowledging the end of things, but there is no escape from the fact that we are governed by a dualist principle of growth and decay. One of the prices of life is death. "What is everlasting cannot evolve; evolution is a specific trait of that which is born and dies."[13] The processes of urban aging and obsolescence are the result of complex factors within a historical framework; they are the "cumulative effect of causes acting in time."[14] The designer must recognize these factors if he or she is to work constructively with aging and obsolescence.

In obsolescence, elements do not just become old; they also become outdated. Urban obsolescence can be grouped into three categories: physical, functional-economical, and cultural. Physical obsolescence is the one that comes immediately to designers' minds, yet rarely is a building demolished because it is a ruin. Physical degeneration of buildings is a gradual process in which some parts decay faster than others. Mechanical and electrical equipment deteriorates much more rapidly than the structure in which it is housed – air-conditioning and elevators may have only twenty years of useful life.

On an urban scale, the differential decay of built systems is even more critical, leading to "time cycles" in the useful life of urban elements. The longest time cycle in cities corresponds to the circulation network such as streets and roads, as well as some open spaces. In most European cities it is possible to recognize Neolithic hunters' paths, evolving into the Roman cardus and decumanus, and then into medieval market roads and baroque thoroughfares (Figure 5.7). In New York, the anomalous Broadway was originally an Indian hunting path, used later by the European settlers, that managed to survive the nineteenth-century gridiron.

High-technology facilities tend to be more vulnerable to physical obsolescence than are other facilities; this is true of high-speed highways, rapid transit, and other transportation systems. The long-term importance of the urban transportation network lies in its location, its relation to the rest of the pattern, and not on its technology. The most critical design considerations for the urban circulation network are its rights of way and influence on the surrounding urban pattern, as well as its capacity to accommodate future technologies.

Economic-functional obsolescence is caused by the intro-

Figure 5.7. The longest time-cycle elements: streets. (S. E. Rasmussen, *Towns and Buildings,* MIT Press, 1969) (Left) Chester, England: the Roman City. (Right) Chester, England: the city today.

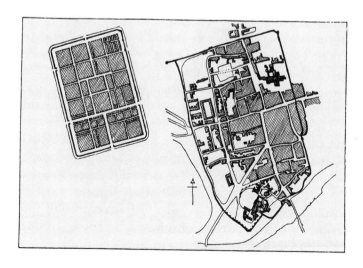

duction of new techniques that may reduce the effectiveness of a facility. Thus, this process is not one of absolute but rather one of comparative obsolescence, since it depends on the relative performance of older facilities vis-à-vis newer facilities designed for the latest technologies. This type of obsolescence is becoming more important, because "the increasing rate of technological change is causing buildings to become obsolete more quickly."[5] In some cases, purely financial factors, such as the tax advantages of depreciation, contribute to the process of obsolescence and influence the feasibility of renewal. The effects of this type of obsolescence cannot be overemphasized, since the accelerated pace of functional change makes many facilities obsolete before they decay.

A design strategy for dealing with economic-functional obsolescence is to identify and isolate the facilities (or areas within facilities) most susceptible to this type of obsolescence and to ease their upgrading or replacement with minimum disturbance to the rest. This, however, is easier said than done, since a technical or managerial change may end up affecting the whole complex.

Finally, cultural obsolescence originates in changes of taste and fashion, which determine not only what looks "old" or "new," but also the economic benefits of a commercial facility in a consumerist market. There are many examples: the old middle-class town houses that were abandoned to low-income groups – and that decades later are being reclaimed in a gentrification process by the same middle class; vacant Richardsonian railroad stations; elegant old movie theaters and hotels – replaced by eight-screen cinemas with parking lots and lavish atriums with rooms around them. Consumerism and profitability spell the end for some of the finest urban facilities, initiating an early, rapid obsolescence involving enormous social waste (Figure 5.8).

The process of obsolescence and, in its most generic form, aging must be seen in relation to the complementary processes of maintenance, rehabilitation, renovation, and reuse – the human response to decay. Typically, as soon as a facility is built, it begins to decay. The downward curve of decay is a natural trend that can be reversed only by human intervention – which may range from the minor and continuous process of maintenance to major rehabilitation and renovation. In the absence of intervention, facilities arrive at a position of full decay. The built environment is never completed, never balanced, and the threat of decline is always present.

Attempts by individuals to arrest the deterioration of private property present basic dilemmas that are at the root of some of the most acute urban problems. For example, in a neighborhood with a number of individual homeowners, the decisions on maintenance and rehabilitation are individual and disjointed, in most cases based on the notion of the house as an investment. Although decisions are individual, external-

Figure 5.8. Cultural obsolescence. (Wayne Andrews) (Top) Chestnut Hill Railroad Station, 1883–4. Henry Hobson Richardson. Demolished. (Bottom) Hotel Ponce de Leon, St. Augustine, 1885–8. Carrère and Hastings. Occupied by Flager College in 1977.

ities are very important: If a homeowner improves his or her house, he or she will thereby increase the value of the surrounding houses as well. But if the neighbors do not improve their houses, the value of the house will not increase as much as it could, because its value is limited by a deteriorating neighborhood. However, if the house of one of the neighbors is improved, the homeowner will profit by an increase in the value of his or her own house, without having to make any expenditure. Under those circumstances, the path of minimum risk is to do nothing, to delay improvements, and to profit from a neighbor's improvements. Clearly, in many well-kept neighborhoods this is not the case, because the stability of the situation reduces the uncertainty for each homeowner. But in many neighborhoods where decay has started, this dilemma is constantly present and helps to explain, to a large degree, the wasteful urban ecology found in U.S. cities. This example indicates that upgrading depends heavily on community-scale actions.

Differences among neighborhoods demand radically different levels of public intervention. Wealthy neighborhoods are very stable and well maintained because of a correspondence between individual and community objectives and an ability to implement these objectives. Each homeowner is faced with minimum uncertainty; each knows that the neighbors are willing and able to pay for the best upkeep of their properties. In poor neighborhoods, economic pressures cause individual objectives to diverge considerably from community objectives. Each homeowner faces a difficult decision when spending scarce funds. Thus, there is a much higher level of uncertainty coupled with a much lower capacity to implement community objectives. Public planning must intervene in such cases to provide assurance to the community, to reduce individual uncertainty, and to help organize resources and actions.

Designs must be able to absorb the pressure toward deterioration and to encourage upgrading within the urban system. Urban complexes, like good wine, must age gracefully and be better when older than when just built. We should learn that technology can backfire because of its built-in potential for obsolescence. We should learn that the tight fit of machine-like designs leads to shorter life, since "senescence is involved in systems which are so tightly constructed, with such sturdy members, and so much complexity of parts and pathways that replacement anew is cheaper than repairs in bits and pieces without interruption of function."[16] We should learn that overspecialization by fitting a design perfectly to the present function or objective, disregarding others with lower priority or simply with future potential, can be disastrous, because "the more closely a design is tailored to a particular function, the more quickly it becomes out of date and obsolete."[17] We should learn how to avoid the evolutionary disaster of pursuing one functional idea to the exclusion of all others. We should learn how to forecast the cycles of change in different facilities, to provide a structure that will encourage rehabilitation, alteration, and other actions stemming decay. We should rescue community design from the grip of consumerism, fashion, and greed and learn again how to build for centuries.

CHAPTER 6

URBAN SCALE

*Or how urban form, size, and function are
interrelated through growth*

LAWS RELATING GROWTH, SIZE, AND FORM

One of the most important lessons to be gained from the
growth process is that it is not an independent phenomenon,
but is closely interconnected with the form of the community.
Form, growth, and size are mutually determined characteristics. Urban growth alters the relationship among the parts,
causing a rearrangement of the urban structure and, consequently, changes in the urban form. Indeed, "growth of any
complex structure is associated with changes in form,"[1] a
phenomenon that is defined as structural growth. Growth
forecasts should be key parameters in the design process, to
ensure that urban form will evolve in a suitable manner as
size increases.

The concept of structural growth is defined as one "in
which the aggregate which 'grows' consists of a complex
structure of interrelated parts and in which the growth process
involves change in the relationship of the parts," even in cases
in which "what grows is not the over-all size of the structure
but the complexity or systematic nature of its parts."[2]
Whether the urban system actually experiences an increase in
physical size, an intensification of uses, accelerated economic
development, or functional changes, new parts develop, existing parts age, and relationships among parts are altered.
These internal rearrangements result in changes in form. Size
and form limit and determine one another. The earliest and
one of the clearest statements on this relationship was made
by Galileo: "You cannot increase the size of structures in-
definitely, in Nature or in Art . . . for increase can be affected
only by using a stronger material, or by changing the shape
to a monstrosity."[3] This relationship is based on laws that
link form and size.

The principle of similitude. Physical form cannot be postulated independently of size: We cannot use the same educational organization for one hundred students and for ten thousand students, or an urban model for a population of ten thousand and for a metropolis of several million people.

This constraint is based on the geometric laws of three-dimensional forms and is formalized in the principle of similitude: With an increase in size, area grows as the square of the linear dimensions, whereas volume grows as the cube of the linear dimensions. This principle is based on the roles that the various "dimensions" of a form fulfill in a structure. A uniform increase in a given form, that is, in its linear dimensions, will result in a square increase in surface area and a cubic increase in volume; this means that the volume will rapidly outgrow that mass which can be "served" by the area. As a result of this increasing disfunction of the geometric relationships, growth must stop, or form must change.

The implications of this principle are universal, affecting systems from biological organisms to urban areas. For example, the upper size limit of a form is bounded by the fact that the volume of a body grows as the cube of its linear dimensions while the surface grows as the square. An elephant's legs are thicker than a horse's legs because they have a proportionally much greater load to support,[4] and beyond this size range, "it would be possible to extrapolate an infinite series of elephants, but it would not be possible to see between their legs."[5]

This suggests an analogy with architecture. The elephant legs of our example can be compared to the stone columns of the temple of Karnak. The thick and closely spaced columns of that temple constitute the upper size limit of this building type (hypostyle hall) and technology (column and beam stone structure), since an extrapolation of the temple would not permit one to see between the columns (Figure 6.1, top). Larger spans and higher ceilings would have demanded proportionally much larger stone beams (due to their poor tension capacity) and taller stone columns supporting much larger loads, which would have resulted in proportionally much thicker stone columns. One way to escape this constraint was to reach for a new technology, which is what the Greeks did with wooden roof structures for their temples; the higher tension capacity of wood allowed larger spans with lighter beams, resulting in less load and, thus, slender stone columns (Figure 6.1, bottom).

The lower size limit of a form is also bounded by the

Figure 6.1. Form, size, and technology. (Top) Temple of Amon, hypostyle hall, Karnak, 1530–1323 B.C. Stone columns, lintels, and roof beams. (Dr. Jonathan Drachman) (Bottom) Parthenon, Athens Acropolis, 447–430 B.C. Stone columns and lintels, wood roof beams.

square/cube law. When the surface area becomes relatively large in proportion to the smaller body mass, there is an increase in heat loss through radiation, and a large amount of energy must be used to replace the loss.[6] However, bodies suitable for small sizes face structural and functional constraints if they grow beyond their size limit. An example of this limitation is found in the insect of science fiction films that grows to the size of a dinosaur. If this could happen, the legs of the poor insect would be crushed under the proportionally much larger weight of its body. In addition, respiration in insects depends on body surface; a giant insect would also be asphyxiated since its body surface would be far too small to serve the needs of the body volume.

This suggests another analogy with architecture. The insect surface can be compared to the exterior surfaces of a building; smaller buildings have a proportionally larger façade surface which, in turn, makes it possible to light and ventilate them through windows, but with a proportionally larger energy consumption to compensate for heat loss and gain. One way to escape this constraint in larger buildings is to reach for a new technology, such as artificial ventilation. But there is another way: through formal complexity.

In order for growth to continue, some proportional changes must take place in the built system to compensate for the disproportionate dimensional effects. For example, in buildings where a relatively constant area-to-volume ratio may be necessary, the surface (façades) would have to increase as rapidly as the volume; because surfaces grow as the square while volumes grow as the cube of linear dimensions, the solution in larger structures is to change the shape to a more convoluted form that would accelerate the increase in linear and areal dimensions relative to volume, as will be discussed in more detail later, with reference to the law of differential growth. This is one of the bases for the assertion that growth brings greater complexity and that larger organizations require, by their nature, more complex structures.

As buildings and precincts evolve, they become more complex, and their form may change radically. Throughout the various stages of a built organization, size and form evolve through mutual adjustments; current design decisions are truly part of a continuum – including both information on past stages and forecasts of future ones – that must be known and understood by the designer. The history of the organization's formal evolution is a critical parameter for future design.

Finally, this suggests that the dictum "Design is all the same, whether it deals with a chair or a city" is fundamentally wrong; on different scales, the levels of complexity present qualitatively different design problems.

Law of differential growth. The interrelationships among growth, size, form, and complexity, and the various modes of escape from the principle of similitude are expressed in the law of differential growth, also called the law of nonproportional change. It has long been apparent in biology that "the organism changes geometrically so as to remain the same physiologically,"[7] that is, functionally. The need to preserve functional similarity results in the systematic modification of the geometric relationships of the organism, leading to the assertion that "the only constancy of form is the constancy of its mode of change."[8]

The constraints imposed by size on built form and the need to preserve functional similarities can be solved by technological means. For instance, building façades constitute the surface of a built form, in which windows perform an environmental function – admitting air and light – somewhat analogous to breathing through the skin in insects. When buildings exceed a certain size that prevents natural ventilation, air-conditioning can be provided; this process is similar to the development of lungs in larger animals. The lower surface-to-volume ratio in larger organizations is resolved by transferring certain environmental functions – such as ventilation – to specialized components. Also, the lower surface-to-volume ratio of larger organizations means that they spend less energy in balancing heat loss and gain.

There is, however, another mode of escape from the constraints of size, which is formal complexity. An example can be found in the morphological history of, and resulting differences in, educational complexes between a one-room schoolhouse at one extreme and a large academic campus at the other.[9] The one-room schoolhouse is a compact building. As a result of its extensive contact surface with the outside environment, it can have windows in its four façades. Compactness means high efficiency owing to the lack of corridors, but the high surface-to-volume ratio means a high heat loss (or gain). As the school grows to a dozen classrooms, the form elongates, although it may remain fairly compact, allowing windows in at least one façade wall in each classroom; the corridors that are now necessary reduce space efficiency, but the lower surface-to-volume ratio suggests a proportionally lower heat loss.

If the school grows to the size of an institution with, say, forty to fifty classrooms, the typical elongated section of double-loaded corridors begins to convolute on the site, creating wings, courtyards, and possibly two-story pavilions. This increase in complexity is caused by the need to provide at least one windowed façade for each classroom – a surface function – subject to the limits of the site and the need to maintain manageable walking distances within the school. If the school becomes a campus, it consists of a number of buildings, each reverting to a simpler structure; multiple forms appear because the upper limit of the single form has been reached. Complexity is apparent in the circulation pattern as well as in the integration of open space and built form in the institutional pattern.

Communications. Another size constraint must be mentioned, one related to the roles of dimension in form as well as to the limits of communication within a system, and hence closely related to the functional organization itself. The communication problems caused by the size of large built organizations are evident everywhere: in the long commuting required by large metropolises, in the proliferation of control systems, and in the monotony of endless institutional corridors. These problems can be ameliorated by the introduction of new technologies, such as instant communications, that eliminate the need to overcome spatial distance. (The implications as well as the limitations of such surrogates for proximity will be discussed in Chapter 9.) Communication problems are not unique to urban areas but are common to many systems. Blenheim Palace, a gift of England to the Duke of Marlborough after the French campaign, was so huge that it became necessary to establish reheating stations to keep food warm when it was carried from the kitchens to the dining rooms.

The universality of the laws guiding growth, size, and form led to the development of allometry, "the study of size and its consequences."[10] Allometry deals with the changes in proportions of growing entities, which result in changes in form, as well as with the structural adaptations that occur beyond certain limits.[11] The study of allometry originated with Julian Huxley, whose research on differential growth within organisms identified the process of positive allometry, whereby the parts grow faster than the body.

The commensurate increase in complexity with size cannot be avoided and is the result of geometric laws constraining size and form. Since the surface grows at two-thirds the power of the volume, growth can take place only as we mentioned earlier, under two conditions: One is a change in shape through elaboration of the surface, toward a more complex form; the other is technological complexity, such as the introduction of internal systems (air-conditioning replacing some environmental surface functions, elevators reducing circulation linear functions). Technological complexity is the result of the introduction of sophisticated mechanical, circulation, communication, and structural systems that reduce the role of the dimensionally "retarded" variable, that is, the variable that grows at the smaller power. Formal complexity is the result of the "geometric solution" to the problem, in which the dimensionally retarded variable must exhibit a faster rate of growth to achieve nonproportional change. The two modes of escape are complementary and are subject to mutual trade-offs.

The technological mode of escape is not without risks. For many, it would appear that technology allows the extrapolation of forms – and institutions – without penalty, or even without limit. It has been estimated that the entire population of the United States could be sheltered in a cube 1 mile × 1 mile × 1 mile, but we know intuitively that this is not a solution – it is a nightmare. If, in reference to our previous example of the school, the surface environmental dependence (the need for windows) is eliminated by the introduction of sophisticated air-conditioning and illumination systems, it is conceivable that a huge compact school could be reconstituted, with interior classrooms devoid of windows. However, this apparent gain in efficiency must be balanced against the appalling human and educational cost of enclosing students and teachers in a beehive without outdoor views. To add to the problem, in the few actual attempts to implement such a solution, the air-conditioning has consistently failed to meet performance standards – a failure that should be seen as a blessing in disguise.

The formal complexity mode of escape is the basic explanation for the fact that "geometric similarity is rarely maintained during the growth of an individual architectural spatial system or among functionally similar architectural spatial systems."[12] In other words, as size changes, the form of built typologies changes: A large mansion is different from a small cottage, a large hospital from a small clinic, a large shopping area from a small retail corner. Also, as size changes, the actual typologies serving the same function change: A town house could be used for small offices, but the form of a large office building is very different from that of a reused town house.

The phenomenon of nonproportional change has three main effects: First, it results in increasing differentiation – a wider range in the size and function of facilities, ancillary spaces, and specialized areas; second, it results in increasing movement patterns; and third, it results in morphological elaboration, elongation, and circumvolution. Thus, forms become more complex, more articulated, with relatively more perimeter and façade and with a wider range of spatial choices and sequences. They may be more expensive in terms of construction and operating costs, but may benefit from the economies of scale of a larger organization (Figure 6.2).

If, however, the process of dimensional compensation is constrained, the size of the structure is limited by its inability to achieve nonproportional change, unless there is an increasing reliance on technological complexity. This is the case in many gigantic built complexes designed in the past decades with deceivingly simple forms. I distrust this approach because of its undue reliance on technology and its disregard for the dimensional roles in form; it is the imposition of an antiformal will that separates itself from the urban system. Its unresponsiveness to the laws of built organizations has made them foreign to urban forms and to human beings; the ruthlessness with which they are imposed evokes a fascistic attitude, alien to true community (Figure 6.3).

The effects of the differential growth laws on urban areas are widespread. We are aware of numerous regularities in human settlements (see Chapters 7 through 9), which are governed by universal systematic laws. Those regularities underlie urban form and establish mutual constraint between the size and the form of a settlement.

If urban land area is considered a two-dimensional realm and if the population distributed over the land area is considered a three-dimensional realm, we have another case of allometry between the surface and the volume of a system.[13] For example, we know that larger cities are denser than smaller ones: As cities grow, populations increase faster than area; specifically, developed land area grows as population size raised to an exponent that ranges between two-thirds and

one, hence increasing density. We know that the rate of increase in density is a positive exponential function of distance
from the center of the city, and that density and rate of growth
are inversely related functions of distance from the center.[14]
We know that land use proportions change with city size:
Residential land use increases in regular progression with city
size, while commercial land use grows less rapidly than total
developed area, indicating the effect of multistory development as a compensatory change in urban form.[15] But our
understanding of the laws of growth has remained largely
confined to the recognition of statistical regularities in urban
systems, with limited normative value for designers.

Urban alternatives to increasing size. Community designers
must be able to manipulate the relationships between size and
urban form. Let us consider a simple example. Assume a
prototypical concentric urban area with a downtown fed by

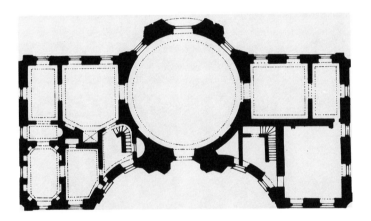

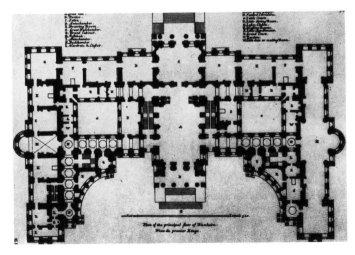

Figure 6.2. Size and
morphological elaboration.
(Top) Amalienburg Palace,
Munich. Small and
compact. (Bottom)
Blenheim Palace,
Oxfordshire. Large and
elongated, circumvoluted,
and differentiated. (Colen
Campbell, *Vitruvius
Britannicus,* London, 1715)

radial highways, and consider the effects of growth on the urban structure, specifically on the capacity of the radial roads to carry daily vehicular traffic to the downtown area. The access capacity is given by the number of lanes available (the sum of the road widths), which is a linear dimension. The number of trips generated is determined by the urban land area and the population densities, which as mentioned grow faster than the area. The combined effect of area and population is three-dimensional and, as is clear, grows faster than the linear dimension of road widths, that is, capacity.

Growth of the urban area, maintaining all proportions constant, would result in the road capacity (number of lanes) growing linearly, while the number of commuting trips

Figure 6.3. Antiurban intruders: Prudential Center, Boston. (Prudential Life Insurance Company of America)

would grow exponentially (area times density). In a short
while, the downtown would be inaccessible. The conventional solution in situations such as this is to accelerate the increase in road capacity, which is reflected in the many highway construction projects in U.S. cities – a shortsighted solution doomed from the start, because it ignores the law of differential growth. For the city in this example to maintain traffic accessibility to the downtown while the urban area is experiencing growth, the number of roads (lanes) must increase at a much faster rate than the urban area itself. Since the roads converge at the center, the growing downtown will soon face the competition of roads for increasingly scarce land, until the roads that were supposed to feed it will end up by destroying the center. The ancillary need for parking will exacerbate the problem. Essentially, a growing urban area fed by radial roads becomes an oversized elephant, whose legs soon fill all the space, until the downtown becomes a collection of highways and parking lots. Thus, what was considered an ad hoc problem is the outcome of growth in an urban form whose size limitation is clearly defined. What are the options for community designers, options that would be consistent with the self-regulation and self-organization processes acting within the urban system?

One option is the technological mode of escape from the area-to-volume problem involving the introduction of a new technology with greater capacity than the road. Mass-transit systems would permit a much larger urban area to thrive, but would also limit the options of populations long used to automobile transportation. Since the introduction of mass-transit technology demands densely populated urban areas, this solution in the United States hinges more on cultural and political issues than on strictly technological ones, as will be discussed in Chapter 8.

The formal-complexity mode of escape involves, at least, three potential paths: branching and convolution of the existing form, expansion of the existing form, and replication of the existing form. Branching of the downtown, for instance, might include creating a composite form made up of several centers and subcenters, which would help decentralize the road system at the core of the metropolitan area – the critical zone where the limits of the form are first evident. These centers and subcenters could develop relatively specialized functions, such as financial-banking, retail, government, theater, and others, and could be linked to form a "constellation" of centers at the core of the metropolitan area.

The radial orientation would still be prevalent on the regional scale, but there would be a dispersion of the points of destination and an increase in land available for roads and parking. This option would follow the tendencies apparent in many large urban areas; for example, Manhattan has several centers, such as Wall Street, the midtown office and hotel area, and the theater district. Formalization of such tendencies through conscious design makes it possible to reap the considerable advantages of branching.

Expansion of the downtown into urban forms radically different from the existing one is another means of altering (and even invalidating) the original radial orientation. A number of the downtown functions and activities could abandon their traditional central nucleus and locate along linear structures in the metropolitan area. Indeed, many offices and retail stores in U.S. cities do locate in automobile-oriented ribbons along radial or circumferential highways in order to avoid traffic congestion and parking scarcity. These outlying ribbons constitute today's major employment areas, providing between 70 and 80 percent of all jobs in metropolitan areas.

Although this solution eliminates the radial convergence on the center, it creates an even more difficult problem: By dispersing employment along low-density belts served only by highways, it precludes the possibility of providing them with higher-capacity and more efficient mass-transit systems. Urban growth is still reflected in linear increases in road capacity; these are more than offset by much larger increases in the number of commuting trips to and from these linear employment belts, which forces the construction of feeder roads and congestion on the highways serving them. The allometric constraints of urban form come back to haunt those that choose to abandon rather than to rebuild, to forget rather than to understand.

An alternative to linear expansion, clustering, consists of concentrating core activities at strategic points and at high-density linear cores, which are served by mass transit so that they are accessible to most residents of the metropolitan area. This alternative brings us to the third path of formal complexity: the replication of the existing form. Here, replication of the original urban center throughout the metropolitan area decentralizes the road system by reducing the former radial orientation. Each of the new centers can be specialized in some activity or serve as a multifunctional regional center. In some of the largest U.S. metropolises, secondary centers have sprung up at key rail and road intersections, often on

the substrata of an old town. The advantages of the reduction
in traffic at the major center, however, must be balanced
against the disadvantages of increasing traffic in the region.
It is not sufficient to assume that each secondary center will
draw from its immediate region only, since the metropolitan
population should have a reasonable choice of centers.

The replication of centers in metropolitan areas has accelerated during the 1980s, leading to an increasing dispersion
of urban nuclei. Some suburbs, such as Glendale near Los
Angeles and Bethesda near Washington, D.C., have developed mixed-use centers of regional importance. One example
is the headquarters of the National Institutes of Health, a
major medical institution and provider of a substantial number of jobs, located in Bethesda. In other cases, strategic
crossroads in outlying metropolitan areas have been transformed by developers into major employment areas, characterized by dispersed low-density patterns served by
regional highways. An example is Tyson's Corner, outside
Washington, D.C., which is soon expected to have more
office space than downtown Milwaukee, Cleveland, or Cin-
cinnati, but lacks mass transit and any measure of environmental quality or urbanity. Other exurban centers have
sprung up, from Century City in California to Schaumburg
outside Chicago, to Perimeter Center outside Atlanta.

Formal replication is a design strategy with historical precedents in traditional preindustrial societies. The Greek and
medieval city-states founded colonies as a way to channel
population growth into underdeveloped regions, ensuring in
this way access to new resources as well. One of the most
interesting cases is that of the Matmata towns in North Af-
rica, which, owing to the strict size limits imposed by their
urban form, replicate the original settlement after a certain
size has been reached, as will be discussed in detail in Chapter
11. In the Third World, since many metropolitan areas are
an aggregation of quasi-rural villages around a modern center, many old towns in the metropolitan periphery that are
engulfed by the mushrooming urban form maintain their
central functions, resulting in a regional "constellation" of
urban centers around the dominant one.

Thus, size and urban form are closely interrelated and mutually constrained, and complexity of the urban system is one
unavoidable result of overcoming the limits of growth. But
complexity does not have only formal or technological roots.
The process of growth also causes functional changes in the
urban system through increasing differentiation; this, in turn,

is the source of much of the functional complexity of large human settlements.

Urban areas of different size exhibit qualitative differences beyond those that are explained by nonproportional growth. These are related to differences in the facilities offered by settlements of various sizes.

Activities that take place in undifferentiated spaces in smaller towns gradually become specialized in larger settlements and institutionalized in differentiated facilities. For example, a large city may have a variety of highly specialized facilities for performing arts and music: large and small theaters, concert and chamber music halls, ballet and opera halls. By contrast, a small town may have a drama society meeting in a church basement, a high school play in the school cafeteria, and a band concert in the bandstand in the park. A large city may have a variety of hospitals and specialized medical facilities, whereas a small town may have only one clinic. This process of functional differentiation adds richness to larger settlements; it also ameliorates the disadvantages of size. The Main Street curb parking of small towns becomes the garages of large cities; many ad hoc informal solutions of small towns simply do not work in large cities.

Determining which activities should be specialized is critical in design, especially in the grouping of urban elements. The aggregation of dwellings in multifamily apartment buildings led to the specialization of many facilities outside the dwelling itself – from circulation, mechanical, and parking spaces in conventional buildings to nurseries, community rooms, and even community kitchens and dining rooms in some of the earliest apartments in the USSR. Larger schools led to the specialization of facilities – auditoriums, gymnasiums, laboratories, workshops – that are absent in smaller schools. In larger complexes these differentiated spaces are justified by the fact that their larger populations can make efficient use of them. Smaller complexes lack the size to justify the creation of specialized facilities; instead, they rely on flexibility to accommodate a variety of activities in multiuse spaces.

Beyond certain thresholds, the size of the population and its economic capacity allow for differentiation; as the size of a settlement expands, more differentiated elements appear, implying more linkages and more functional complexity.

Qualitative innovation lies in the process of differentiation. According to Needham, patterns appear as qualitatively new, because of latent or potential properties, activated by the complexity of the organization.[16] That is, when urban size reaches a certain threshold, new elements, often highly specialized, appear in the pattern. Thus, change, variety, and uniqueness in urban patterns can be traced in part to the phenomenon of differentiation.

Differentiated facilities can add to the richness of a settlement or ameliorate the negative effects of size. But there is always a risk of overspecialization, as discussed in Chapter 4. According to the principle of equal advantage, urban systems experiencing growth exhibit a capacity for functional substitution and regeneration, by which some urban elements tend to take over the function of missing ones, as discussed in Chapter 5. This phenomenon implies flexibility, social imagination, and an ability to improvise, all valued characteristics in an urban system because they reduce the risks of determinism, while generating variety, richness, and spontaneity. In order to preserve the capacity for functional substitution, it is necessary to maintain a careful balance between differentiation and ad hoc informal solutions.

Clearly, some differentiated facilities – concert halls, hospital centers, airports, among others – must be carefully programmed and designed, in order to allow for the full expression of their specialized activity. But sometimes grave errors of overdifferentiation are committed. For example, every residential area is planned with a playground. Playground structures are specifically designed for one play routine each – and thus are antithetical to the creative nature of play, which thrives on imagining extraordinary situations in ordinary environments. Moreover, playgrounds are fenced in to prevent play activities from spilling outside of them. Instead, the whole urban environment should be a playground for children: It is only the increasing poverty of urban environments and the widespread sense of insecurity that could have led to the concept of an official playground. This is just one example of the need to avoid excessive differentiation in many of our urban facilities and, instead, to encourage substitution and improvisation (Figure 6.4).

THE DISADVANTAGES OF SIZE AND DESIGN STRATEGIES

Urban growth has always been considered synonymous with success; only in the past decade has there been increasing discussion of the limits of growth. A frequently cited example of the inevitability of urban growth is the fact that, even in the USSR, cities of more than a million residents are growing despite controls, empirical proof that the trend in urban systems continues to be urbanization and concentration. Moreover, it is well known that the residents of larger cities enjoy greater affluence than those of smaller towns: "Of all the differences among communities of different size ... perhaps the most striking is the pronounced direct relationship between size of place and income."[17] There is no doubt that industrial and postindustrial societies require settlements of considerable size, but this does not mean that the disadvantages of size should not be confronted. It is interesting that while the achievement of external economies from growth (economies of scale, clustering, specialization) is more important in small centers, the amelioration of external diseconomies from growth (maintenance, environmental and social costs) is a priority for large centers,[18] including advanced metropolises such as New York as well as underdeveloped metropolises such as Mexico City.

During the earliest stages of growth, complexity makes

Figure 6.4. The many uses of streets. (Left) Playground: Locorotondo, Apulia, Italy. (Bernard Rudofsky) (Right) Pedestrian promenade: Zafra, Spain. (Opposite top) Market, Fez, Morocco. (Opposite bottom) Pedestrian promenade: Buenos Aires, Argentina.

possible larger and richer urban systems. Beyond some threshold, however, cumbersome complications begin to outstrip the advantages of size: efficiency and richness. Complicated routines, centralized bureaucracies, and expensive physical infrastructures appear to be necessary to keep the largest systems going. And in many cases these systems are unable to eliminate the social costs of size – long commuting and travel time, lack of security, environmental degradation – but only manage to mitigate them.

Recalling the earlier example of the schoolhouse, the development of huge schools has led in many cases to anonym-

ity, a higher incidence of vandalism, and confusion, leaving school administrations struggling merely to stay afloat. Large built organizations and urban complexes should be reassessed when their support and control facilities become so important as to detract from their main functions.

A trend involving large development complexes is to reinternalize functions previously delegated to the urban community, enacting a curious reversal of the specialization process. It is common to find huge built complexes with their own police force, engineering staff to keep air-conditioning, elevators, power, lighting, and other services operational, mail service, janitorial service, parking and traffic facilities, and emergency systems. They constitute enclaves divorced from, and mimicking, the surrounding urban community in their duplication of urban infrastructure and services.

What strategies exist to deal with the threat of excessively large built organizations? There are at least three.[19] The first is simply to allocate more resources to the maintenance of internal order and support; this leads to increasing inefficiency since a proportionally lower share of the total resources is allocated to productive activities and facilities.

The second strategy is to ritualize the behavior of the organization by establishing fixed standards that minimize direct instruction, control, and maintenance or support requirements. This works well under stable conditions but is ineffective when the ritual loses validity.

The third strategy is to decentralize and suboptimize by breaking up the organization into smaller, relatively autonomous units, kept together by general guidelines and selected links. This strategy stresses flexibility and adaptation, though it may not always be optimal.

The first strategy – increasing maintenance – has been the favorite of corporations, governments, and institutions and has formed the mainstream of design practice. Buildings have grown larger and larger; urban lots have been assembled into huge projects within cities. Pedestrian bridges, moving sidewalks, heliports, huge sterile atriums, fully enclosed shopping arcades, and endless office corridors are now a feature of many U.S. urban areas. The costs of the new support infrastructure, including the overhead costs of mushrooming management, security, maintenance, and operation, have risen dramatically.

The second strategy – ritualized behavior – typically found in popular design, is foreign to contemporary U.S. experience owing to the breakdown of cultural patterns and lack of community heritage. Ritual in community design is based on strong cultural values and traditions, and an accepted knowledge of how to put built complexes together and maintain them with minimum control. Clearly, this approach has a limited capacity to respond to increasing size and to meet requirements that are unprecedented in the popular design tradition.

The third strategy – decentralization, suboptimization, and flexibility – may hold considerable potential. It may allow us to maintain the advantages of specialized facilities while reducing the burden of centralized control. The creation of complexes made up by more or less autonomous units may also reduce the number of internal relationships, simplifying the system and thus lowering complexity to manageable levels. There are many examples. Rather than build huge office structures with all their disadvantages – monotonous work spaces, endless corridors, lack of orientation, dependence on artificial environments – for the sake of maximizing real estate profits and corporate power image, we must aim at designing smaller interconnected structures, more highly integrated with the urban pattern and on a more human scale, with a greater variety of spaces allowing proximity to light, air, and view. In the few cases where a high-rise building is warranted, the design must explore vertical decentralization, with major areas of arrival at intervals.

Our obsession with larger complexes must come to an end. Any built precinct is far better if properly integrated within the urban surrounding. A decentralized design approach is closely related to the achievement of human scale in the environment, pluralistic participation, design by combination rather than by aiming at a final form, emphasis on indirect controls rather than on prohibitions, and the delegation of responsibility down the hierarchy. This is a design approach for human communities and not for corporate gigantism or real estate profits.

PART THREE

Which deals with the planning components of urban form: land use and the threat of segregation and homogeneity, density and its importance for urbanity, distribution as a means of restoring an urban culture

CHAPTER 7

LAND USE IN CITIES

Or how segregation and homogeneity have threatened the social ecology of urban areas

LAND USE AS A THREAT TO URBANITY: HOMOGENEITY AND SEGREGATION

Land use is the most basic variable determining the form of a community. Defining an area as one of residences and small commercial establishments, or as a financial center, or as an academic campus immediately establishes some rough parameters. Determining land use can be considered the initial programmatic decision in shaping the future of a human settlement. It is precisely at this critical level of decision making that communities and the essence of communities, their urbanity, are being threatened today by segregation and homogeneity – a threat that in the United States can be traced back to the years after the Second World War.

The process of urban development, as discussed in Chapter 4, is characterized by the complementary phenomena of specialization and interdependence, which lead to increasingly well-defined single-use areas. A certain degree of functional segregation and homogeneity is inherent in the process of development. But in many industrialized cities, most noticeably in the United States, these processes have advanced far beyond the functional requirements of various activities, to define segregated homogeneous areas based on social criteria. In most downtowns, life stops at the end of the working day because there are no downtown residential areas; most residential areas are socially homogeneous zones, where people of the same social class and race live segregated from the rest of the population. Hence, there are the new middle-class suburbs, the working–class dormitory areas, the upper-class enclaves, as well as the slums of the poor and the ghettoes of minorities.

Cities of the past exhibited other kinds of segregation.

Whenever various ethnic groups coexisted in a city, they usually occupied their own quarters. In historical Jerusalem, for example, there arose Jewish, Christian, Armenian, and Arab quarters that exist to this day (Figure 7.1). In other cities, the existence of foreign merchants led to the creation of Genovese, Venetian, and other trader quarters near the docks. Almost all of these segregated quarters reflected the desire of each group to live among its people in a world that was divided between "us and them" along narrow ethnic lines. Nonetheless, the various groups interacted vigorously to create vital communities.

Probably the only exception to this self-ordering of the traditional preindustrial city was the confinement of Jews to ghettoes in European medieval cities – a deplorable cause for shame in the history of Western civilization. It is cause for equal shame that the concept of ghetto has been revived in the U.S. city as a place to "dump" new "undesirables."

In contrast to the traditional case, present-day segregation and homogeneity in land use are forced upon most members of a population regardless of their individual wishes and choices, defining a narrow range of lifestyles for most groups,

Figure 7.1. Quarters in preindustrial cities: Jerusalem (Encyclopaedia Britannica, Inc.)

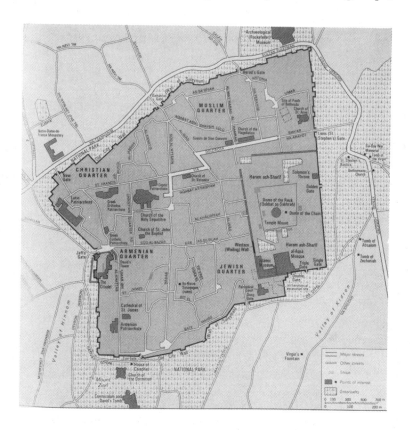

except the upper classes, which retain a wide range of choices. This situation is a contradiction of the stated goals of a post-industrial dynamic society that theoretically aims at freedom and defines itself as a free society. Furthermore, segregated areas are much larger today than they were in preindustrial cities, and homogeneity is extended to practically every activity, leading to a reduction in social (though not functional) exchange. Thus, the most precious characteristics of urbanity, that is, choice and interaction, are being lost in a society with the highest potential to achieve them.

This internal cleavage occurs between two levels: what has been referred to as the formal and the community organization levels.[1] The stated concept of a free society is generated at the national level, where specific goals are expressed in legal documents; segregation takes place at informal local levels, where a community's behavior is shaped by widely held beliefs, unofficially supported by local government and real estate practices.

As mentioned in Chapter 5, land use segregation is related to the typical processes of urban ecology and, specifically, to the process of succession. Urban succession defines the cyclical replacement of social groups in urban areas, sometimes involving the abandonment of a zone by a group and its occupancy by another group, sometimes involving the expulsion of one group by another. The formation of suburbs, the decay of old dormitory areas, the spread of slums and ghettoes, the deterioration and renewal of downtowns can all be traced to the process of succession.

In the succession process, higher-income groups tend to move to the periphery, being replaced by progressively lower income groups with a parallel deterioration of buildings, until in some cases the process reverses, giving way to gentrification. Each neighborhood becomes a temporary living space for increasingly poor populations, living in increasingly substandard dwellings, until, in some cases, renewal arrives and the poor are expelled by a new affluent group. Succession usually takes place through a combination of fear and hope; the need felt by poor and minority groups to move out of their slum neighborhoods and the opportunity they perceive to obtain houses with more space in other neighborhoods are combined with the fear of more affluent groups living in these neighborhoods, accustomed to segregated lifestyles.

The typical urban pattern in the United States is one in which homogeneous areas of constantly increasing size cause segregation in space for activities and people. Curiously, this spatial allocation is a reversion to the most elemental notions of territoriality found in animal societies and very primitive human societies, where boundaries clearly define segregated areas with the main purpose of avoiding open conflict.[2] Today, this primitive notion is expanded to include segregation by class, income, race, ethnic origin, and even age. The negative effects are pervasive, since "apart from the ethnic enclaves, virtually everything about [U.S.] cities today is sociofugal and drives men apart, alienating them from each other."[3] Thus, urban patterns are being increasingly "simplified" owing to the narrower range of activities and population within each segregated enclave, where less variety demands less complexity.

This segregation process is a case of overspecialization, which, as mentioned in Chapter 4, leads to a rapid reduction in the capacity of the system to adapt, an especially dangerous constraint since "adaptability is essential for social as well as for biological success. Therein lies one danger of the standardization and regimentation so prevalent in modern life: we must shun uniformity of environment as much as absolute conformity in behavior."[4] Visual monotony is a counterpart of the aggregation of similar groups in homogeneous areas tied by simple social relations, with the ironic result that "the emergence of a new city life in an era of abundance and prosperity has eclipsed something of the essence of urban life – its diversity and possibilities for complex experience."[5] What are the effects of such patterns?

The most obvious effects of segregation are found in the slums and ghettoes of every U.S. city, from Watts in Los Angeles to Harlem in New York. However, the roots of the problems of "ghettoization" should not be sought in the slums, where the crisis is visible, but rather in the places from which segregation has spread to the whole urban system, places that have imposed a rule of simplification – and in some cases elimination – of urban life, with negative consequences even for themselves.

Suburbia, criticized by some and defended by others, is where segregation and homogeneity originate. Explained as a haven from urban problems for people living in an urban economy, suburbs offer a low-key lifestyle that combines informality with affluence. My criticism of these segregated and homogeneous residential areas for the middle and upper classes is based not on personal preference, but rather on the negative effects of suburbia on the community, which be-

comes simplified to the point of being socially primitive. In
the words of Richard Sennett

It is the simplification of the social environment in the suburbs that
accounts for the belief that close family life will be more possible
there than in the confusion of the city. The simplification of the
social environment in suburbs is the logical end in the decline of
diverse communities, . . . [for] in the suburb, physical space becomes rigidly divided into functional areas. . . . The desire of people
beyond the line of economic scarcity is to live in a functionally
separated, internally homogeneous environment.[6]

The cultural implications of this lifestyle are profound, since
"suburbanites are people who are afraid to live in a world
they cannot control," resulting in "this society of fear, this
society willing to be dull and sterile in order that it not be
confused and overwhelmed."[7] The homogeneous environment of the suburbs presents no incentive for exploration and
discovery; "why venture beyond home, since it is a mirror
of all that lies beyond?"[8] The total is no longer more than
the sum of the parts.

The simplified routines of suburban life lock the population
into an adolescent lifestyle dominated by fear of conflict and
interaction and a desire to be surrounded by peers and peer
groups.[9] Adolescent social characteristics are based on "a fear
of experiences that might create complexity or disorder,"
with the result that "social life becomes more primitive, in
the quest of a mythical solidarity, even as the technological
resources for more complex social structures increase."[10]

In order to perform on the scale required by a society of
consumption, this culture has created a number of new facilities made possible by technological capabilities. The ubiquitous shopping center, the "mall," with its oversimplified
routine based on available parking space adjacent to a group
of buildings that are devoted exclusively to shopping, is devoid of any urban richness, complexity, surprise, or choice.
It allows a minimum of social contact while increasing the
number of highways, traffic lights, and parking lots.

Homogeneity affects everyone adversely, but young people suffer the most damage. As René Dubos wrote:

One can take for granted that the latent potentialities of human
beings have a better chance to become actualized when the social
environment is sufficiently diversified to provide a variety of stim-
ulating experiences, especially for the young. As more persons find
the opportunity to express their biological endowment under diversified conditions, society becomes richer in experiences and civ-

ilizations continue to unfold. In contrast, if the surroundings and ways of life are highly stereotyped, the only components of man's nature that flourish are those adapted to the narrow range of prevailing conditions.[11]

It is said that a lion's share of the knowledge that a person acquires in a lifetime is learned before the person is five years old, that is, before formal education begins; a child's environment is the critical "schoolhouse" during those early years.

In a diversified urban environment a child has an amazing array of educational experiences: Many adults, often not family members, have contact with neighborhood children; the children themselves belong to different social groups; streets and alleys, plazas and markets, shops and workplaces, churches and political headquarters, love and conflict are all there to be explored. Children know that food does not "grow" in plastic bags in supermarkets, for they see butchers and fishmongers, farmers and vendors at work. Life is not a picture book of neatness: They see chauffered limousines and beggars, mansions and shacks, power and exploitation, as well as the struggle for justice.

The social question for young people is still where to find an enlarged forum for experience and exploration. This . . . is the true task of planning modern cities. The ills of the city are not mechanical ones of better transport, better financing, and the like; they are human ones of providing a place where men can grow into adults, and where adults can continue to engage in truly social existence.[12]

Social life for young adults in true cities has a richness impossible for suburban teenagers to imagine – teenagers whose weekend is highlighted by a trip to the local shopping center.

Though there are still central cities – ranging from world metropolises to regional towns – with an urban core, new threats to urbanity can be found even there. The trend toward homogeneity and segregation is reflected in a comparatively recent intruder within cities, the "project." Except in the case of some institutions, buildings in cities are traditionally products of pluralistic decisions reflected in a relatively small scale of development; even the largest buildings in central areas represent a parcel-at-a-time venture that fills an urban block with several individual buildings. There are exceptions that confirm the rule: Rockefeller Center in Manhattan represents a major venture, but each tower maintains the scale of an individual development, and the plaza with the skating rink on Fifth Avenue is a significant gesture of integration into the surrounding pattern (see Figure 3.14, p. 59, top).

In every age there have been major urban enterprises, but they have all respected and exalted the surrounding pattern; for example, the earliest real estate venture in Paris, Place des Vosges, was a magnificent addition to the urban pattern (Figure 7.2). Even when major public works were required, such as the filling of swamps and wetlands, some new developments continued to create true urban patterns – witness Le Marais in Paris with its community of "hotels," or Back Bay in Boston with its community of town houses.

In the past few decades, the "project" approach has been the conventional solution to housing the poor. Public housing, for example, takes the form of project housing, a large number of low-rise and midrise apartment buildings assembled in huge tracts, without any reference to the surrounding urban pattern, street network, or scale of development. Although the inadequacy of apartment buildings for poor families is slowly coming to be understood, the inadequacy of segregated institutional enclaves for the poor, and the stigma attached to them, have yet to be grasped (see Figure 12.10).

Today there are also projects for the affluent. With monotonous regularity, new commercial ventures characterized as "projects" assemble large parcels for the construction of

Figure 7.2. Preindustrial real estate ventures: Place des Vosges, Paris, the earliest real estate venture in Paris, laid out under Henri IV in 1607–12. (French Government Tourist Office)

segregated multibuilding enclaves in urban centers. More often than not these projects turn their backs on the street and the pedestrian sidewalk to create internal air-conditioned malls surrounded by shops, allowing people to move from stores to offices, to hotels, and to other functional elements without coming into contact with the city. This problem is compounded by the scale of the projects. Though by assembling a number of parcels they are able to create a superficial image of autonomy, the large size of the projects has an enormous negative impact on the urban pattern (see Figure 6.3).

Suburban shopping centers were built for the middle classes living on the periphery of metropolitan areas; we are now experiencing the selective suburbanization of central areas. The idea of controlled, antiseptic, functional commercial centers is transferred from suburbia to downtown, with its parking garages and antiurban attitudes. It is possible to drive downtown on an expressway, reach a garage, walk into a mall, eat at a hotel restaurant, shop in stores, meet in an office, and not once be in the city. Those projects are the urban analogue of a cancer in biology: One component grows beyond its size, threatening the normal behavior of the surrounding system and, eventually, destroying the organism. The city is being threatened by large real estate corporations who are displacing urban decision makers: individuals, groups, and the community at large. In this process, the city itself is being pressured to transform into an aggregate of homogeneous segregated enclaves, owned by huge corporate interests that will undermine and eventually destroy its urban pattern.

One of the most disturbing situations is the lack of balance between the forces of change and opposition to change in metropolitan areas. Change is predominant in some central cities, whereas opposition to change controls suburbia. Growing central cities are under the unchallenged pressure of many types of change: Huge projects are destroying urban patterns while neighborhoods are experiencing deterioration and, sometimes, gentrification. In contrast, established suburbs have created a series of defenses against change aimed at preventing the introduction of low- and moderate-income housing and the influx of minorities. The effects are negative: environmental degradation and social strife in central cities; restrictions on the less affluent groups in suburbia.

Some ills of homogeneity have not gone completely unnoticed. In some new exurban centers, there is an emphasis on providing employment as well as certain urban services and amenities – from medical offices to restaurants – in order to enrich the surrounding suburban areas. Social segregation, however, remains as strong as ever, assured by real estate prices and lack of mass transit facilities.

Slums, ghettoes, and deteriorating areas are not accidents, mistakes, imperfections, or exceptions; they are the result of the land-use-segregated patterns on which the U.S. city has been developed. And there is nothing unavoidable or "natural" about segregation; it is the result of cultural conditions that prevail in the United States – and increasingly the Western World – in the latter half of the twentieth century.

CAUSES OF SEGREGATION AND HOMOGENEITY

Land use segregation is not only the result of planning practices; it also appears to be responsive to some cultural requirements found in urban areas of industrialized countries, especially the United States. The basic characteristic of these cities, that of being formed by the aggregation of large zones of homogeneous use, can be traced to the effects of socio-cultural preferences, formalized and reinforced by the planning profession. The most common planning tool, zoning, is, of course, ideally suited to the enforcement of land use segregation.

The demand for segregation lies at the core of a society's cultural norms. Culture is one of the four social systems that Lang identifies according to the functional theory expounded by Talcott Parsons (the others being social, personality, and physiological).[13] Culture is composed of beliefs, values, and symbols that control much of human behavior. Most people, however, are not consciously aware of these superstructures; cultural influences are transmitted through mediating norms that are patterns of commonly held expectations,[14] in other words, people accommodate their behavior to what they believe is proper.

One possible explanation for land use homogeneity is based on the role of spatial segregation as a reinforcer of the social class system. In an affluent society based on a class structure, the personal symbols of class differences such as clothing are to some degree eroded, concealing class differences. Consider the striking difference between a peasant and a bourgeois in a Third World country; they are recognizable from far away, as they were in Classical times or in the Middle Ages. With affluence, the superficial difference between the

139

janitor and the chairman of the board is far narrower – inexpensive suits look remarkably similar to tailored suits in a crowd. A good address, however, can clearly establish one's class status.

This explanation is corroborated by a comparison of British society – which retains considerable class symbolism – and U.S. society. Whereas in the former, "it is the social system that determines who you are," in the latter, space is used "as a way of classifying people and activities."[15] It appears that "a society compensates for blurred social distinctions by clear spatial ones," since "space allocation not only indicates status but also reinforces it."[16] Thus, spatial segregation restores class differences camouflaged by material prosperity.

In preindustrial cities, as well as in most of the Third World today, where the personal symbols of class are clearly visible, spatial segregation is much less common and there is a much greater mix of land use in space, reflected in the heterogeneity of these cities. The Third World integration of upper and lower classes in space results in a symbiotic relationship that includes domestic work, clientele, and maintenance jobs. Economic growth without social equality results in a greater degree of material comfort, but it does not eradicate society's internal privileges and may even break up what is left of a community because of the emergence of spatial segregation and homogeneity.

Segregation can also be explained by the fact that it is based on an idealization of the lifestyle of small towns and a concomitant contempt for urban life. There is widespread nostalgia for what is assumed to have been the simpler life of small towns. The single-family home on a lot, the small community, and social homogeneity define this paradigm of independence and self-reliance.

Segregation is reinforced by economic barriers erected by both the private and the public sectors to protect the affluent. Clearly, better houses clustered together in good locations command higher prices; the homogeneity of higher-income areas is, in itself, a powerful barrier to the entrance of lower-income groups to these areas. Furthermore, the high property taxes in most affluent areas enable residents to enjoy high-quality services without subsidizing other groups, since less affluent groups are discouraged by high total housing costs from moving to privileged areas. The so-called market forces of real estate are reinforced by the municipal fiscal structure in establishing land use and social segregation from the top down.

Among the most damaging effects of segregation are widening educational difference among income groups. Since public primary and secondary education in the United States is administrated and financed by local political subdivisions, the wealthiest ones are able to devote more funds to their school systems; as it happens, the residents of these areas tend to have a greater familiarity with and interest in education and actively lobby for it. As a result, the children of the wealthiest and most highly educated families tend to receive a far better education than children of lower-income groups, in a fashion reminiscent of Huxley's *Brave New World*, in which alphas bred alphas, betas bred betas, and gammas bred gammas. Invisible, yet very real internal walls divide the U.S. metropolis, maintaining and increasing the social distance among the segments of its population.

Finally, segregation is also strengthened – or at least not challenged – by the fact that many professional planners and designers tend not to be politically conscious and easily become instruments of power groups; thus, professionals often support the status quo by reinforcing segregated patterns. As Herbert Gans said:

From about 1920 on, the new planners planned and zoned. They developed master plans which segregated land uses by a variety of criteria, most of them class-based, so that the upper and middle class residences were separated from working and lower class residences, affluent shopping districts from poor ones, and industry, which employed mainly working and lower class people from everything else. . . . Although city planning has been concerned principally with improving the physical environment, it has also been planning for certain people, although only indirectly and implicitly. These people were the planner himself, his political supporters and the upper middle class citizen in general. . . . The planners' ideal city was good for business and for property ownership.[17]

Planning efforts have often resulted in a mechanistic, antiurban, and violent metropolis:

This century of city building has, in Lewis Mumford's phrase, confused a machine-using society with a vision of a society as a machine itself. Until the peculiar calculus of efficiency guiding much of city planning is united with a new conception of the humane use of cities, . . . planners will create urban conditions that intensify purity drives and so promote voluntary withdrawal from social participation and the willingness to use violence as a final solution.[18]

Even the Modern movement in architecture contributed to this effort, through the Congrès Internationale d'Architecture Moderne (CIAM) with its "four functions of cities," which fostered the notion of segregated land use as the optimal organization for cities, based on an aseptic image of clear differentiation and low-level order. Since then, a relentless passion for tidiness has become one of the greatest enemies of city planning and community design. This has been accompanied by a strong reluctance to probe the goals and objectives of dominant groups. Planners should question the reasons for fostering the lifestyle of the elite, which is widely imitated by the middle classes, as well as the effects of behavior aimed at pursuing such a lifestyle.

THE NEED FOR DIVERSITY

The major causes of succession in urban areas are found in the demands of the affluent for areal homogeneity and segregation. I believe that this behavior is equivalent to seeking to establish dominance in the community. In ecological terms, dominance occurs when a certain group (species in the ecosystem) so pervades the community that it exerts a powerful control on the existence of other groups.[19] In urban space dominance is the appropriation of potential habitats (niches in the ecosystem) of subordinate groups by the dominant one.[20] Thus, the segregated pattern of homogeneous habitats is based on the preemption of the most desirable urban niches by the dominant group.

In the process of allocating space and land uses, the dominant group not only takes the most desirable urban niches, but also manages to preserve a greater flexibility; subordinate groups are forced to specialize. In ecological terms, members of dominant species have greater "niche width," becoming generalists adapted to a greater variety of habitats.[21] Clearly, in urban space this has been true of the most affluent groups, which have chosen to settle in a variety of desirable habitats, from exclusive suburbs in the "horse country" to gentrified, elegant central areas; elites have a wide range of choices, and they change habitats and lifestyles at will. In contrast, less affluent groups occupy areas undesired by the dominant group. The poor and minorities scavenge habitats in slums and deteriorating housing projects, working-class families in neighborhoods of small bungalows or triple deckers, and lower middle-class groups in remote tract developments or in a few blocks carved out by a highway in suburbia. They have very limited choices and must be highly adaptable in order to survive. This restriction of choice implies a curtailment of urbanity and is particularly damaging in a heterogeneous society, since a diversity of people requires a diversity of built environments.[22]

The social-physical phenomena of land use segregation and the related ecological processes of succession and dominance lead to an increasingly homogeneous and specialized community, the effects of which have far-reaching consequences in terms of survival probabilities. At the root of these effects lies the ultimate trade-off between efficiency and adaptability. The scenario for the trade-off is clear: The territorial division of labor is a mainspring of economic growth;[23] it is the link between technology and the spatial conditions of economic progress. Indeed, advanced urban societies offer a wider range of opportunities and have a greater need to specialize locationally than simpler societies, increasing the probability of survival through higher efficiency,[24] but they must be able to change their areas of specialization with little warning.[25] Surprise is intrinsic to evolutionary social systems; "one thing we can say about man's future with a great deal of confidence is that it will be more or less surprising."[26] Diversity is essential for coping with uncertainty.

Diversity, which implies generalization, is the opposite of dominance, which implies specialization. Diversity is the key factor in maintaining flexibility and adaptability in a system. Ecologically, diversity depends on a variety of groups and the degree of equality among those groups,[27] which can be translated as socioeconomic equality in urban systems. The greater the variety of groups and the greater the equality among the groups, the lower will be the chance of any one group dominating the others. But under some conditions, the process of development tends to threaten diversity; increases in the size and complexity of groups, as well as in the competition among groups, may reduce the number of groups and allow dominance to occur.

The economic process closely follows the ecological process: Early stages with small, simple elements and rapid rates of reproduction – the capitalist world of Adam Smith – are followed by stages with larger, more complex elements and slower rates of reproduction – the corporate world. In the urbanization process as well, early stages with high rates of growth are followed by mature phases with lower growth potential but better capabilities for achieving a dynamic equilibrium. Thus, although stability increases as development proceeds from the early stages, it is also threatened if overspecialization and undue dominance occur. Diversity and stability seem to be linked.

How important is diversity? Is it worth attempting to modify the segregated and homogeneous patterns of urban development in order to obtain diversity? "Is variety only the spice of life, or is it a necessity for the long life of the total ecosystem comprising man and nature?"[28] I strongly believe that there are many reasons to reduce dominance and increase diversity and thus to maximize the richness of urban communities: "The community best organized to cope with site contingencies may be objectively defined as the community on the landscape with minimum dominance."[29]

Diversity is the best assurance a community has that it will be able to minimize crises and deal with uncertainty, since most crises originate in the dominant structure of urban communities.

Diversity is a strategy for increasing control of the social and physical environment and achieving greater protection from perturbations and surprising events. A diversified urban community with economic and political balance is not only resilient but enjoyable and fair. In contrast, overspecialized cities controlled by dominant groups are subject to periodic crises owing to their unbalanced concentration of power, homogeneity, and segregation.

THE GRAIN OF LAND USES: KEY TO DESIGN

We should work toward integration, because it is fair and essential to the long-term viability of urban communities. But urban patterns in the United States are becoming more and more segregated, and at the same time, areas of homogeneity are growing larger. In other words, the grain of land uses – for example, the texture, the size of the constituent elements – is becoming coarser. Increasing scale of land use patterns ensures spatial segregation. The large size of homogeneous areas makes land uses in other homogeneous areas progressively "invisible," unless one specifically wants to see and reach them. It is possible to travel antiseptically, via highways or commuter rail, between an origin and a destination without seeing unwanted areas with "different" people. Someone can live in a homogeneous and relatively autonomous affluent suburb without ever visiting other areas or even without going downtown.

How can we begin to reverse segregated patterns? In terms of residential land use, there is some evidence that a forced mixing of different people within a zone may have unintended results. Michaelson found out that the completely random location of working-class families within middle-class neighborhoods results in the isolation of the former, rather than in any positive integration.[30] In another case study, low- and middle-income groups were included in an urban renewal development planned originally for upper-income groups exclusively. The mix was restricted to the apartment building scale, each income group being assigned a different building. The study showed that "an indiscriminate mix of social classes seems to be too simplistic a solution, ignoring many of the abrasive differences in social behavior among classes."[31] In other words, the higher-class groups strongly resented living close to the lower-class groups. Contributing to this sort of conflict is the fact that segregated classes are ignorant of the behavior and lifestyles of other classes, breeding differences, distrust, and even contempt among groups.

Nevertheless, it must be stressed again that there is nothing "natural" in this situation and that the classist mentality is purely another cultural burden; this is proved by the fact that "the most extensive mixing between classes occurs among the children"[32] since they are naturally unencumbered by such prejudices until they learn it from their families.

Planners and designers are faced, in the U.S. metropolis, with the conflicting objectives of a class-based society. One is homogeneity, an objective sought by those who want to live with members of the same social group; this includes people whose concept of lifestyle is shaped by notions of race and class segregation, as well as people who enjoy the company of others with the same cultural background (e.g., the residents of ethnic neighborhoods). The other objective is heterogeneity, or a desire for integration as a matter of "public good." Established communities have different reactions to integration; affluent communities generally oppose it, and their local governments reflect their position. It is up to planners and designers to seek advocates of integration within each community.

Professionals who plan land uses and design communities in such environments, implementing objectives that are not fully shared by some groups, face a problem. The achievement of integration can be subsumed under what Gottschalk calls the major goal of redistributing resources and power, based on the fact that there is no freedom without equality.[33] In such cases, planners and designers must become advocates of disadvantaged constituencies to assure them a share of power; we have an overriding responsibility to redistribute power. In Gottschalk's words, planning as an "attempt rationally to control future events, in the light of that which cannot be controlled, . . . rarely challenges the fundamental assumptions of economic and technological growth – usually identified with progress – upon which it is based." Our task includes "the need to invent, and if possible to experiment with alternative social institutions and physical arrangements which are expressive of the actual or anticipated changed circumstances of life," as part of an unavoidable "obligation of planners to join, and often to take sides in the arbitration of moral issues."[34]

Our approach should be based on both idealism and realism; we want to effect change toward a better society and a better community, and we want to be sure that our proposed changes will be implemented. The key may be found in the manipulation of the scale of areas under homogeneous uses. Although we must assume that variable degrees of homogeneity will be maintained in the near future in order to satisfy individual objectives, there is some flexibility in the size of homogeneous areas, which would allow a reversal of the trend toward larger segregated zones. A progressive reduction in the size of homogeneous areas would increase community-wide heterogeneity. If people were unable to avoid other groups, social contact would be increased, cooperation and a healthy degree of competition would take place, and the ignorance that breeds distrust would slowly be eliminated. The approach is not to expect fully heterogeneous communities to develop immediately, but to erase myths born of ignorance, to increase groups' awareness of one another, and to enable them to recognize one another's real positive and negative features.

Progressive integration should be introduced in a series of incremental steps, leading to a reduction in class and racial prejudices through increasing understanding and, eventually, cooperation. At the same time, we should expect a heavy dose of minor conflict to occur, as different people meet personally for the first time; but if this takes place on a continuous and low level basis, explosions of pent-up social violence will be averted. This design approach is viable because it does not threaten the segregated pattern all at once, but erodes it like a guerrilla operation – if you cannot beat it frontally, work around it. Slowly, the segregated mosaic of homogeneous areas will have a finer grain, and while each zone will still be internally homogeneous, it will be less and less autonomous, depending more and more on – and hence unable to ignore – the rest of the community.

Throughout this process, planners and designers must work at two different levels, corresponding to what Hillery called formal and community organizations. Planning would be implemented through local governments, formal organizations with the necessary powers, legal and functional structures, and stated goals. However, local governments are influenced by community organizations, which are based on cooperation, independent actions with immediate, practical low goals, and what has been described as structured freewheeling.[35] Planners and designers must reach out to community organizations in order to establish dialogue, develop possible consensus and early awareness of conflicts, and search for advocates of common objectives.

An important question is: What is the minimum size range within which people can still feel they live in a homogeneous neighborhood? The interest of sociologists in neighborhood size was originally sparked by Louis Wirth's hypothesis that neighborhoods can re-create primary relations, the traditional kinship and family basis for social solidarity, which urban areas are assumed to have weakened.[36] Since that time, and acknowledging the probabilistic nature of social research, the findings on neighborhood size have tended to cluster around specific ranges: A neighborhood with which people identify could have a population as low as 2,000,[37] or cover an area as small as 75 acres, which represents 2,500 people at 10 families per acre.[38] Other studies indicate the existence of smaller local units with only a few dozen families,[39] but they are really areas of close geographic interaction that are one level lower than the neighborhood in the urban hierarchy. It is important to remember that people tend to have varying interpretations of their neighborhoods;[40] their definitions of size are not exact but rather are gross approximations.

Considering the obstacles encountered in residential areas, it is clearly easiest to break land use segregation in nonresidential areas, where symbiosis can be used to advantage. "Symbiosis" is a term borrowed from ecology defining a situation in which activities benefit by propinquity, either linearly along a consumption or production chain (as with theaters and restaurants), by sharing an activity (as with theaters and offices, both related to restaurants), or by having a common need (as with college students and elderly, both of whom need laundries, restaurants, and similar establishments). Symbiosis may take place in time as well as in space; activities may "time-share" facilities, as in the community use of schools. The maximization of symbiosis should be another priority of land use planning.

Land uses must be designed to increase their linkages: One activity produces what another needs; the grouping of some activities generates still others. Only rarely does a zoning bylaw allow residential units above a commercial space, yet a prototype of this is found in most urban neighborhoods built in the United States before World War II as well as in Europe, Latin America, and other areas of the world, creating unique vitality, richness, and diversity.

Also, we have been slow in creating new prototypes that stress symbiotic relationships, such as commercial areas adjacent to school complexes, which would offer children a place to eat other than the cafeteria, while allowing them occasionally to combine their trips to school with shopping. This has a precedent in some regions of the country, where school children "convene" at nearby fast-food establishments, sometimes to the chagrin of the establishments' managers. Such prototypes would form small neighborhood centers for isolated schools in dispersed suburban areas, where children could meet on their own turf, while shop owners could provide informal control.

INTEGRATING LAND USES

No planning variable has been misused as much as land use; metropolitan areas have been officially divided by city halls into mosaics of homogeneous use. In reality, major objectives of land use planning have been to preserve the status quo and to create new opportunities for real estate profit. Their implementation has been limited to the establishment of zones that are easy to administrate by planning boards and building inspectors. Much of the essence of urbanity has been lost in this process.

Land use planning has been based on the recognition of major "functional areas." The definition of these areas can be deceptively simple: Work areas include industrial and business zones; living areas are residential zones with their ancillary community facilities; recreation areas encompass cultural facilities as well as open space. The simplicity so highly valued by those who deal in classification becomes a dangerous oversimplification for design purposes; "much of the sterile formalism of our plans arises from the habit patterns of our activity language."[41] The pitfalls are innumerable.

The artificial separation of areas through zoning results in sterile designs, not in communities. Residential areas and workplaces are typically zoned apart with almost fanatical fervor. One result is that children grow up without seeing people at work, while in isolated office and industrial parks workers see only mirrors of themselves. Residential areas are classified by means of zoning parameters such as minimum lot size or density in order to admit or reject specific income groups and household types. Urban areas become a parody of themselves, a kind of human zoo with every "species" segregated in its own zone.

Urban patterns suggest many ways to integrate land uses. For example, in university towns, regardless of conflicts, there is a certain integration of town and gown since most facilities are used by both communities. Many urban precincts are often composed of overlapping functional areas, as with medical schools and training hospitals or technical-vocational schools and industry. At the same time, some single-use areas are unnecessary. Large cultural complexes, such as Lincoln Center in New York, consist of an assembly of facilities with the same general classification in the same site, although there is no overwhelming need for the symphony to be near the opera. Each of these facilities could have created a unique node of influence in the city while dispersing the traffic flow that now converges on the same place at curtain time.

Is the separation of land uses valid? Separation is based on one of two criteria: The first is environmental incompatibility; the second, sociocultural prejudices and attitudes. The environmental criterion is far easier to deal with than social prejudices because it requires scientific proof; a case for the separation of some activities such as those creating dangerous levels of pollution, heavy traffic, noise, and so on, can easily be made. Otherwise, urban activities should be planned to interact, overlap, share – in short, to be symbiotic.

Among the few uses that require strict limits is open space. Land can be zoned as open space for agricultural production, natural resource protection, aesthetics, or recreation, in any combination,[42] important functions that provide privacy, a sense of space and scale. Open space works in less visible ways to protect water supplies, prevent floods, and play other ecological roles[43] and may be used to shape urban development through land banks and buffer areas. However, some activities usually assigned to open space, like children's play, may take place in other areas not designated for them.

Zoning and land use integration. Land use planning, implemented mainly through the drawing up of master plans and legislation of zoning bylaws and ordinances, has tended to create single-use areas of considerable size. While it accepts ancillary activities, it generally consolidates homogeneous uses and avoids small-area definitions, which are pejoratively called spot zoning. In most cases, spot zoning is used to benefit a property owner or to legitimize an illegal situation, as is well known to many planning boards.

The strategy of making the grain of land use patterns less coarse, however, indicates that conventional master plans and zoning must be changed in several ways. One possible way to achieve a finer grain is to reduce progressively the size of the areas under single-use classification, which would eventually result in more complex patterns replacing the simpler ones of extensive homogeneous areas under the same land use. This course of action would revive spot zoning, this time as a deliberate, long-term strategy, responding to the complexity of urban systems, wherein land uses could be carefully legislated according to the nature of the urban pattern.

An alternative would be to assemble "packages" of mixed land uses that were symbiotic, complementary, or at least not manifestly incompatible, supplemented with design guidelines, allowing individuals and groups to make their own decisions within these frameworks. These design guidelines would establish the rules of land use combinations, determining relationships, ratios, and buffers, as well as physical elements, from fences to signs.

The downsizing of homogeneous areas in land use patterns through zoning should take advantage of the ecological changes in population and activities that take place in metropolitan areas, to steer these processes toward integration. Even the most homogeneous areas have places with at least the potential for transition; this potential represents the "cracks" of segregated areas, where change can be introduced. As mentioned, planners and designers must establish alliances with progressive members of local government boards and present recommendations for zoning changes supported exclusively by rational land use arguments. Let us discuss a few examples. Proposals to zone residential areas above retail spaces should be related to downtown revitalization; those to zone residential areas with smaller minimum lots should be related to more efficient use of municipal infrastructure; and those to cluster residential units should be related to open-space preservation. In these three cases, residential areas have the potential to include affordable housing; this potential should be reinforced through other channels independent of zoning, from state subsidy programs to local incentives for developers.

The ultimate difficulty with zoning and land use master plans is that, ideally, they are aimed at legislating environmental quality; this is a major problem when a cultural consensus on quality is lacking. (One can also argue that in times of cultural consensus, legislation on quality is not needed.) Thus, master plans and zoning fluctuate from soft positions that allow multiple infringements, to hard positions that stifle spontaneity and creativity. As a result, settlements shaped by these tools are distorted images of true communities, not unlike the absurdly fat and thin reflections of people in carnival mirrors.

By changing the two basic dimensions of zoning – the areal definition of land use maps and the classification of regulations and bylaws – we can expect to transform them into far more responsive and valid planning tools, which would help to shape communities in agreement on the nature of urban systems and long-term stability to be gained from integration, flexibility, and variety.

Air rights and vertically mixed uses. Imaginative approaches to integration and the creation of symbiosis are essential; urban areas are places of unrealized potential that offer opportunities to develop creative solutions. A common shortcoming of land use planning is its identification of "land" with soil: In planning, land must be synonymous with location. A focus on physical land may be limited in many cases; it is preferable to plan for space use, because it shifts the mental framework from soil zoning to space design, including concepts such as vertically mixed uses.

One of the most interesting concepts, tested in only a few areas, is that of air rights, which transforms the practice of land use planning into space use planning:

The friction of space (transportation costs) not only produces the clustering of people and activities – that is, relatively high density – but in fact suggests that multi-purpose use of space is at its essence a cost-saving device. Seen in this light, city building today tends to be highly inefficient. The present basically two-dimensional rather than three-dimensional city planning simultaneously promotes an outmoded single purpose view of urban space (regulated by a simple set of zoning principles). . . . Efficient and compatible multiple uses in a city require expert multiple dimension planning.[44]

It would be a mistake, however, simply to credit technology for the possibilities of space use; an excellent example of the application of space use to community design is the monastic town of St. Michel in France, built over and around a hill during the eighth to the eighteenth centuries. A cross section of this town reveals layers of use from bottom to top that include storage places, offices, residences, transient lodgings, religious structures, meeting and dining rooms, cemeteries, infirmaries, recreation areas, and gardens (Figure 7.3). The technology of the time, which did not change radically throughout the centuries spanning its construction, was based on stone and wood structures, staircases, and natural ventilation.

In major urban centers, some multifunctional complexes have created very successful prototypes, and as early as the beginning of the century, air rights complexes were built in New York City. One of the factors behind such complexes, of course, is the high price of central urban land in major cities; the capitalized value of the use of three-dimensional space minus the additional cost of space use – complexity of construction and amelioration of externalities such as noise,

Figure 7.3. Low-technology air rights: Mont Saint Michel, built 996–1776.

vibration, and fumes – can result in a competitive option to conventional development.[45] High land prices being the result of active demand, multiuse and air rights structures are an answer to high prices in urban areas where their success as business centers leads to increasing competition of land uses in downtown areas.

There are many other possibilities for innovation in the reduction of segregation and homogeneity. Most of the single-use precincts built in the past few decades have deteriorated; their rehabilitation and reuse should be geared to the creation of islands of heterogeneity in metropolitan areas. For example, many shopping centers built in the 1950s along highways on the outskirts of metropolitan areas are now economically obsolete, being scheduled for redevelopment. Most developers are simply planning larger and more up to date shopping centers, with the same homogeneity and negative environmental effects, such as acres of parking lots and traffic congestion. Instead, these shopping complexes could be redeveloped as multiuse community centers, with benefits for themselves as well as the surrounding suburban areas. In addition to retail, they could integrate other uses, as has been done in some pioneering cases: There might be a market for specific office space, or for hotels if the center were located near business areas or combined with assembly facilities. A more radical addition would be residential uses; these centers could provide dwellings at a higher density than in the surrounding suburbia, combined with generous open space that might take advantage of the wetlands and flood plains often found near old shopping centers. Such residential areas would offer not only affordable housing but also wider choices of market housing, including family units. In addition, a residential community adjacent to and/or over the shopping area would be a valuable asset to retail businesses.

This new type of center would require public support in the provision of transportation and community facilities. Public transit would be emphasized through linkages with metropolitan systems and the development of commuter and express buses, parking garages at entry points, local shuttle buses or trolleys, and pedestrian sidewalks in streets. Community facilities, ranging from post offices to child care centers, would complement the center.

A community center developed jointly with a renovated shopping center would be a place where local opposition to integration and mixed land use would be greatly reduced. Most towns would appreciate the benefits of a reduction in development pressures in their residential area and of better public transportation and environmental conditions. In order to make these centers a reality, however, local governments should develop specific plans, including special zoning districts with incentives and guidelines. From the debris of mid-twentieth-century shopping centers the reconstituted centers of the twenty-first century could rise, creating much needed anchors for suburbia.

BOUNDARIES AND BRIDGES

Separation of land uses leads to the explicit and implicit establishment of urban boundaries. Two types of separation – distance and physical dividers – can be used in any combination to create boundaries, the relative importance of each being a function of the incompatibility of the uses they separate and of their location in the urban area. Land uses that are heavy polluters, for example, require a considerable distance – an open-space buffer, heavily wooded if possible – to protect surrounding areas. Quite often rivers, streams, and gullies constitute boundaries within cities, across which incompatible uses may be located.

In many cases, a boundary may be a man-made feature that is institutionalized as a separation; it can take many forms, many of them based only on symbolism, such as a street dividing two racially different zones. The boundaries between white working-class areas and black ghettoes in U.S. cities are a stage for the tragic violence between these two groups. Boundaries between people are not always negative, however; in some cases, such as in the North End in Boston, working-class areas have been protected from the real estate pressures of nearby higher-value areas because a strong boundary existed between them, discouraging easy movement and even negating their proximity. Such boundaries can be highways cutting through urban areas, creating major barriers, "Chinese walls" that divide neighborhoods and encourage differences to emerge on both sides.

Where boundaries are required, they should in most instances be complemented by bridges – either literal bridges over rivers, railroad tracks, and other obstacles or urban "bridges." The latter constitute any physical space where contact between different groups can take place without the turf of either group being infringed upon; they are agreed-upon places where violence is not allowed so as to permit a certain level of interchange. The ugly reality of segregation

demands the constant building of bridges between different
groups. Bridges often facilitate intergroup contact with the
aim of increasing mutual understanding and acceptance of
growing interaction, as does a marketplace, for example, in
a working-class area that is patronized by middle-class people. In other cases, bridges establish the first link between
two hostile groups, by providing a meeting ground where
conflict can be changed to competition – for example, through
athletic facilities – and where the personal contact between
people from both groups can begin to erode prejudices. Planners of community facilities in urban areas must place the
highest priority on bridges.

Normally, community facilities have been programmed,
planned, and designed simply to satisfy the functional needs
of a neighborhood or a sector of the city. However, if seen
as urban bridges, these facilities have another important role
to play: reducing conflict in cities and offering an opportunity
for peaceful exchange. Clearly, not all community facilities
qualify for this role. But many do, and should be used to
provide the meeting grounds so urgently needed in U.S.
cities: Athletic centers could provide neutral ground for
healthy competition, as already mentioned; a transit station
would allow different groups to meet without pressure; childcare centers would eliminate conflict in the earliest years;
churches would provide another powerful link by bringing
people together for worship. This strategy would in no way
minimize the difficulties; there have been too many cases in
which a community facility, say a beach, located on a boundary has been appropriated by one group, which violently
expelled the other. The management of a public facility and
participation of public officials and local and community leaders must be an integral part of a public policy for the creation
of urban bridges.

Planners and designers can, and must, work toward the
erosion of segregation by taking action at the edges. They
should design or recognize boundaries only where appro-
priate, making the best use of natural and man-made features.
And they must prevent spurious boundaries from being established, or remove them, and create bridges over them.

The ultimate argument for land use integration is not an
economic one. There is an urgent need for social integration
to restore the sense of community and interaction and a true
choice of urban lifestyles. There is an urgent need for land
use integration to avoid damaging and wasteful urban ecological processes and to restore diversity and variety while

ensuring stability. There is no optimum even in the best homogenous zone; life in a homogeneous and segregated environment can, at best, be too much of a good thing and too little of the real thing. The true long-term optimum for human communities is found in environments where variety, diversity, and heterogeneity exist.

The strategy of planning urban systems and designing urban communities with the aim of achieving diversity and stability could be carried out only at the expense of a reduction in the short-range economic yield (profits) of the system. Design for diversity and stability would also demand basic changes, either in the social goals of dominant groups or in dominance itself. The wasteful and painful process of succession in U.S. cities is a highly destructive one that keeps degrading and pulling the city apart. Its negative effects originate in the behavior of powerful elite groups with antiurban images of "the good life," whose main objective is to prolong their own dominance, taking advantage of urban resources to feed corporate power as well as to satisfy consumerist needs. If highly efficient zones of industrial production are required, they must be compartmentalized so that their negative effects are isolated, allowing the rest of the community to develop in diversity. If competition must arise among groups or activities, let it happen during frequent contact, rather than delaying it through segregation, only to find that the cumulative effect of normal conflict – which contact naturally works to diffuse – has mushroomed into violence. Community design must aim at diverse and complex urban organizations offering a range of lifestyles, where competition as well as cooperation, and development as well as stability, occur together.

CHAPTER 8

DENSITY IN COMMUNITIES

Or the most important factor in building urbanity

DENSITY IN URBAN SETTLEMENTS

Urban settlements are characterized primarily by a high concentration of people and activities in space relative to the surrounding regions; that is, they are characterized by high density. Density is basic to settlements because it generates urbanity, that elusive yet essential quality that is both cause and effect of dense clusters of human habitats. Urbanity can be defined as the potential capacity of the inhabitants of a town or city to interact with a sizable number of people and institutions concentrated in that town or city. This large potential for interaction is created by density and, in turn, encourages higher density.

Urbanity has also been defined in terms of sophisticated behavior – courtesy, refinement, politeness, and civility. Civility is related to a Latin word for city, *civitas,* to which other major concepts, such as civilization and citizenship, are related. The realm of the city, that is, the realm of dense human settlements, has always been identified with high levels of culture and linked with the most civilized expressions of social behavior. Clearly, because historical cities were not homogeneous, fairly uncivilized behavior coexisted with the most refined lifestyles; one need simply recall London in the writings of Dickens or the engravings of Hogarth. Today, especially in the United States, the identification of cities with civilization is rapidly losing validity, as shown by the association of social problems such as crime, vandalism, illiteracy, addiction, and morbidity with "urban problems," as if it were the nature of cities and not social factors that caused them.

Consistent with contemporary cultural values, no design variable has been so maligned as density. Most people associate density with crowded slums; and the complementary relationship between urbanity and density is ignored in favor of dispersed suburban environments. Myriad factors contribute to the reduction of density in U.S. metropolises. One factor is the private automobile, which enables people to live in scattered patterns. Another factor is a nostalgic desire to re-create the lifestyle of rural areas and small towns. A third, and seldom acknowledged, factor is the aim of excluding people of lower social strata from upper-class areas, where larger lots ensure higher land costs. Such government policies as federal housing and highway programs have provided critical support for low-density suburbanization – which has become, by default, practically the only choice for middle-class families.

The densities of U.S. cities today are the result, for the most part, of disjointed decisions by investors and developers pursuing financial objectives within the limitations of zoning regulations. Perceived market demand and the potential for profits are the guiding principles, quite often supported by incentives built into zoning regulations or the granting of special variances. The result is over-urban densities in downtown office centers and sub-urban densities in residential areas. In European cities, the influence of the public sector is far stronger than it is in the United States; decisions are, in general, affected by notions of public interest and acceptance of higher residential densities. But the differences between urban areas in the world are rooted in more than political systems; they are rooted in the cultural values of each society, as is to be discussed later in this chapter.

Let us first make some comparisons of density within the so-called industrialized Western countries. To take well-known European examples, the gross residential density of Paris is 84 people per acre, and that of London, 60 people per acre. In the United States, the gross residential density of New York is 47 people per acre, that of San Francisco is 24 people per acre, that of Chicago and Philadelphia, 23 per acre, and that of Boston, 21 people per acre.[1] Thus, the most dense U.S. metropolis, New York, has only between one-half and three-quarters the residential density of its European counterparts; the remaining major U.S. cities are in a completely different range, with residential densities that are barely one-fourth to one-third of the European values. And if we consider the almost three hundred urbanized areas in the United States, which include the gammut of smaller cities and towns, gross residential density decreases to a mere 6 people per acre, a value that raises serious doubts about the urbanity of U.S. cities and towns.

Localized density values also reveal differences between U.S. and European cities. In Paris, the central city residential density is 380 people per acre;[2] in Manhattan, residential density is around 100 people per acre. The lowest residential densities in Paris, in single-family-home neighborhoods, are around 12 to 15 people per acre, which correspond to fairly dense single-family-home areas in U.S. cities – less than one-quarter-acre lots. But most Paris residential areas are composed of midrise apartment buildings, with values of around 60 to 75 people per acre (Figure 8.1).

New planned settlements show similar differences. To restrict the comparison to British new towns,[3] the net residential densities are 45 people per acre in Harlow, 48 in Peterborough, 62 in Runcorn, and 90 in Cumbernauld. In contrast, Reston, Virginia – heralded as the most urbane of the U.S. new towns – has a net residential density of 22 people per acre, while Columbia, Maryland – probably the most successful new town from a financial point of view – has only 15 people per acre. Indeed, the average net density of U.S. new towns is between 12 and 18 people per acre, which represents a gross density of 8 to 12 people per acre – that is, suburbs with single-family homes in quarter- and half-acre lots.

Clearly, the wide disparity between planning standards can

Figure 8.1. Urban density: midrise apartment buildings in Paris.

be traced to radically different cultural expectations that translate into market acceptance. At the core of these cultural differences we will find the trade-off between the assumed negative sociopsychological effects of density – most of which have to do with crowding – and the positive effects of density – which have to do with urbanity, as will be discussed below.

A critical difference in the density structure of cities is found in the social allocation of density zones to population groups. In urban areas, there is a systematic organization of density values, with the highest values at the center and exponentially decreasing values toward the periphery. Within this general principle, as mentioned in Chapters 5 and 6, there are complex relationships between density gradients, size of the settlement, level of economic development and technology, history and growth rate of the urban area, and other factors. Typically, in historical cities, the elite occupied central areas of high density and perhaps some outlying sectors of summer residences in low-density patterns. Typically, the land use heterogeneity of historical cities meant that there were congested poor areas near the center as well as poor suburbs at the periphery.

This has all changed in U.S. cities – and in other regions under their cultural influence – with the suburbanization of the upper and middle classes, as discussed in the preceding chapter. As a result, most poor people live on expensive high-density, centrally located land, and most of affluent groups live on cheaper low-density, suburban land. Some urban economists explain this apparent paradox as an efficient allocation of resources by allowing factor substitution of land and building inputs in the production function. Wealthy suburbia uses more land, the cheaper input, in relation to buildings, because its affluent population can afford long trips to work; central city housing uses less land, the expensive input, in relation to buildings, because its poor population cannot afford long trips to work and must be near the largest concentration of employment.[4]

The line of argument stemming from this explanation is that location is the result of social choices in a set of optimizing trade-offs. The wealthy select the cheaper suburban land because they can afford large tracts as well as the cost and time involved in long commuting trips. Correspondingly, the cheaper land is less dense than the expensive land closer to the center.[5] This choice, which the middle class follows closely, can be explained by a cultural "hunger for land" typical of most of U.S. society, which willingly trades off propinquity for space. The resulting decline in density prevents the extension of mass-transit systems to most outlying residential areas, thus forcing residents to commute by private car at costs that are beyond the capacity of low-income groups to pay.

These cultural preferences are supported by local governments when, for example, they enact zoning limitations that block the development of greater density in suburbia, a major factor in the maintenance of suburban land values per acre at relatively low rates but land values per parcel at higher levels owing to the extensive area requirements for minimum lots.

In central areas, the need to enlarge the supply of higher-density housing owing to the relatively limited capacity of these areas to expand, and the opposition of the inner suburbs – the old residential areas developed based on trolley car accessibility during the early decades of the twentieth century – results in higher land values for landlords[6] and higher rents in the slums and ghettoes. In effect, the only option for expanding housing for the poor has been to accelerate deterioration, which results in social conflict with surrounding neighborhoods and increasing degradation of the urban environment.

A trend that has become apparent in the past decade or two, employment suburbanization, has increased social inequality and further eroded urbanity. Rather than having a major employment center in the downtown area, cities have begun to sprout suburban low-density employment belts dispersed along highways and, lately, major exurban employment centers (Figure 8.2). Only a fraction of urban employment today is located in central cities. The result is that the overwhelming majority of employees in suburban workplaces drive to work because public transportation is simply not economically feasible. The poor and minorities, locked in slums and ghettoes in central cities, have been particularly hard hit by this trend, since the only advantage of their location – easy access to downtown employment and urban transit systems – is becoming increasingly irrelevant as they, too, seek employment in the newer highway-oriented areas. The trend has been reinforced by the willingness of local governments to zone huge parcels of land for low-density business (e.g., the so-called office and industrial parks), guided by their own goal of expanding the local property tax base.

Indeed, local governments, which are responsible for the regulation of zoning, have been unanimous in adopting the objective of density reduction. Their purpose in establishing density ratios is not to encourage densities high enough to achieve urbanity, but rather to prevent densities from reaching certain maxima, supposedly for health and amenities reasons. Only rarely is a minimum density required for urban services, mass transportation, and social interaction.

Clearly, the emergence of segregated, low-density patterns in U.S. cities is, to a large degree, a self-fulfilling prophecy. By using zoning controls to limit densities, as well as by downgrading mass-transit systems to a "second rate option," cities have ensured a segregated pattern whereby the poor are crowded into expensive land near the center, the wealthy expand to cheaper land far away from the slums, and the image of success is a low-density estate. None of the social costs of this urban system are accounted for.

LOCATIONAL EFFECTS OF DENSITY, URBANITY, AND THRESHOLDS

Density is the critical variable in determining urbanity because of its locational effects. Density determines the accessibility of people to people, of people to work, of people to

Figure 8.2. Employment suburbanization: Route 128, Boston Metropolitan Area. (Robert Perron)

services and recreation; in short, it allows urban relationships to flourish.

As discussed in Chapter 4, interaction among the elements of an urban system is a precondition for the system's existence. Interaction with a large number and variety of people and groups is at the core of the concept of communities, that is, organizations with sustained interpersonal relationships, because it not only fulfills the need for affiliation and belonging but offers an opportunity for a wide range of human behavior. Indeed, "interactions are the basis for the formation and continued existence of social organizations."[7] The presence of dense settlements maximizes the potential for such interactions.

The relationship between density and urbanity is based on the concept of viable thresholds: At certain densities (thresholds), the number of people within a given area is sufficient to generate the interactions needed to make certain urban functions or activities viable. Clearly, the greater the number and variety of urban activities, the richer the life of a community; thus, urbanity is based on density.

Urban interaction is ultimately equated with communication. Traditionally, the interactions of a population within an area were based on spatial propinquity, that is, on personal communication. Today instant communications have reduced our reliance on physical propinquity – and thus density – to generate interaction. This topic will be discussed at length in the next chapter, which deals with urban distributions; here I shall concentrate on the types of personal interactions required to make urban activities viable.

Public transportation and density are closely intertwined. High density makes feasible various transportation modes, as well as pedestrian access to trains, subways, and buses, and thus is a crucial determinant of accessibility in an urban system. Capacity, technology, and the cost of transportation systems are intimately related to density; subways can move large amounts of people, for example, but because of their high cost they must run through high-density corridors to be efficient. Each mode of urban mass-transportation technology – with its respective cost and capacity – is associated with a density threshold.

The effect of density on transportation is visible in the process of daily commuting. The separation of workplaces from residential areas, forced by large-scale land use homogeneity and segregation, means that very few people can walk to work. In addition, because of the low density prevalent in many residential suburban areas, people have no way of getting to work except by automobile, since even buses are uneconomical to operate below certain thresholds. And to make the situation worse, the dispersion of employment in low-density outlying zones means that urban mass-transit service cannot be provided to those areas – forcing full reliance on the private automobile.

Many programs have been implemented in U.S. cities to remedy the shortcomings of a low-density urban pattern. Commuter rail and outlying subway stations have parking facilities to permit suburban residents to drive to the stations. This solution is limited by the capacity of parking lots – or the patience of driving spouses – except when costly parking garages are provided, and is tailored mainly to commuting and other scheduled trips. Highway lanes are reserved for express buses and cars with more than two people. Given their constraints, some of these programs have succeeded in fulfilling their modest objectives. It is apparent that the largest of the U.S. metropolises could not function without mass-transportation systems, but the fact remains that those systems at best provide a second-rate service and at worst are poorly maintained and vandalized systems where crime is an everyday experience.

A comparison between the urban transportation systems of Boston and Paris illustrates the effects of density.[8] The city of Boston proper, with a population of more than 600,000 in 46 square miles, has a density of 21 people per acre, whereas Paris, with a population of more than 2,200,000 over 40 square miles has 84 people per acre – a density four times higher than that of Boston. As a result, every Parisian is within four to five blocks of one of the 279 Metro stations, where silent and clean trains run every 60 to 90 seconds. For a Bostonian, this is a dream that could never be matched, simply because four very expensive miles of subway would be needed in Boston to serve the same population that can be served with only one mile in Paris.

The relationship between density and urbanity extends beyond transportation, reaching to the viability of, and accessibility to, most urban services. In the retail sector, for example, there is an increase in the number of shops and stores as residential density increases. Population density and the available income of the population living within an accessible distance determine a series of thresholds. Below a certain density, no retail stores can exist; as density increases, feasibility thresholds are reached, allowing an increasing number and variety of stores. From the point of view of the merchant, commercial feasibility is an economic consideration; for residents, easy accessibility of commercial services is not only a convenience but a social amenity.

Recognizing density thresholds is thus critical to understanding the effects of density on urbanity. In the retail sector, for example, the effects of density on the number and variety of retail stores in a commercial center can be studied through the effects of distance on shopping trips, the size of the center as an attraction to shoppers, and balance with competing commercial centers. It is also possible to sketch a series of residential density ranges and suggest an initial set of thresholds; the relationships presented below, expressed in dwelling units per acre (du/acre), correspond to the ranges commonly found in the United States; other countries have different density thresholds.

A detached single-family house normally ranges from a net density of 1 to 5 du/acre. Tighter clustering would allow a density increase of up to 8 du/acre. A semidetached two-family house ranges from 5 to 12 du/acre. A town house with party walls could range from 10 to 16 du/acre. The net density of 12 du/acre is the first urbanity threshold, since below that level it is difficult to provide community facilities in close proximity to the dwellings.[9] The tight pattern of single- and two-family houses is commonly found in many inner metropolitan areas and in most small towns of Middle America. It is a small-scale, true urban environment, catalyst of many vital communities, immortalized by Frank Capra in his films of the 1930s and 1940s. The town house (or row house) has been the basic raw material for many cities, its density allowing the generation of an urban environment with community facilities nearby; the brownstones of New York and the town houses of Boston are among the many examples found on the eastern seaboard.

Tighter clustering with perhaps some mix of two-story flats would allow density to increase to 20 du/acre. The net density of 20 du/acre is another threshold, since above it direct access to the ground cannot be provided from each unit, leading to a radical change in the nature of the outdoor open space, a reduction of unit identity, and a need for common parking areas.[10] Thus, the threshold of 20 du/acre is the watershed that divides the types of dwellings that can maintain a unit identity from those that are merged into larger combinations.

Low-rise apartment buildings, such as three-story walk-ups, have a net density that ranges from 35 to 50 du/acre. At the upper level of this range, 45 to 50 du/acre, visual intimacy can begin to be lost,[11] and a concentrated urban scale emerges. Midrise apartment buildings, six stories high, range from 65 to 75 du/acre. The upper range, 75 to 80 du/acre, is another threshold, since above this level there can be a wide variety of facilities and activities easily accessible to each dwelling, indicating that from two points of view – space and accessibility – we are already in the realm of the higher hierarchical levels of the urban environment. At the same time, the provision of parking and open space becomes an important design issue.[12]

At the top of the urban hierarchy, high-rise apartments can range from 50 to 100 du/acre. Above that range we enter the level of high-density central city buildings, with all the limitations and advantages that the core of urbanity can provide – maximum accessibility, but also limited open space, congested streets, and, in general, pressure for space. Clearly, cities that provide substitutes for the automobile in the form of good mass transit and some major open space – Central Park in New York, Luxembourg or Les Tuilleries in Paris, Hyde Park in London, Palermo in Buenos Aires – certainly offer attractive central locations.

SOCIAL AND PSYCHOLOGICAL EFFECTS
OF DENSITY AND CROWDING

The pervasive aversion to urban density and the implementation of density control measures have been justified on the basis of the assumed negative effects of density on people. But how real are these effects?

It is important, first, to distinguish density from crowding. Although often confused, density and crowding are measures of different phenomena. Density is the ratio of people or dwelling units to land area. Differences in density have economic and physical implications but no clear social or psychological effects. Crowding is the ratio of people to dwelling units or rooms. Different degrees of crowding have clear social and psychological effects. Studies of urban patterns have shown that, at the neighborhood level, there is no correlation between density and crowding and that different densities have no systematic relationship to people's perception of crowding.[13] The difference between the two ratios can be shown by example: High density and low crowding can exist in a high-rise, upper-class apartment building, where there are many dwelling units per acre but few persons per dwelling. In contrast, low density and high crowding can be found in isolated rural shacks in a depressed region, where there are few dwellings per acre but many people per room.

The most important difference between the two concepts is that density reflects mainly physical and economic conditions, whereas crowding reflects social and psychological conditions. Thus, density is a measure of the physical (univariate) condition, involving limited use of space. In contrast, crowding is a perceived condition of limited space; it is a multivariate phenomenon due to the interaction of spatial, social, and personal factors and is characterized by stress.[14] As a result, density is a quantifiable index that is easy to apply universally and to measure physically and economically, whereas crowding is a subjective and highly personal experience translated into psychological stress, involving numerous factors, and impossible to apply universally. Clearly, many of the objections to density can be legitimately directed toward crowding.

The most general way to study the relationship among social variables is statistical correlation. This method will not prove that the relationship is one of cause and effect, but it will associate phenomena, highlighting areas for more conclusive research. In this respect, we must reiterate warnings about conceptualizing the relationship between the built environment and human behavior in a deterministic way, by mistakenly assuming that behavior is a direct response to environmental stimulus.[15] The effects of density have been statistically studied, and although on first impression density appears to be related to pathological behavior, more detailed analysis indicates otherwise. The small apparent effects of density on pathological behavior are reduced to insignificance when controls for social class and ethnicity are introduced.[16]

For example, a statistical analysis of census data involving a number of public housing projects around the world[17] correlates measures of population density with indices of social and medical pathology, as well as with the effects of intermediate variables such as income and education controlled through partial correlation. The results indicate that, although high population density is commonly associated with social disorganization, the positive correlation between density and pathology disappears when measures of social status are utilized as control variables.[18] In other words, such factors as poverty and low educational levels are at the root of social disorganization and pathological behavior. I should add that even this statistical interpretation must be qualified. There are many societies in which people with extremely low incomes and poor education lead a structured social life without such pathological behavior. The difference seems to lie in the existence of a traditional social order within the community pattern. This phenomenon is observed in the Third World, where rural migrants who lived a structured life in villages are traumatized by the breakup of traditional ties in cities, leading to social disorganization and environmental degradation, on top of economic poverty.

High density in U.S. slums is the result of the poor being forced to concentrate on expensive land around the city center in order to be near jobs and transportation, and being unable to move to other areas because of segregation barriers. Crowding is the result of the poor being forced to fit large families into small apartments because of high rents. Such concentration of poverty, with people living in crowded, deteriorating quarters, with limited access to jobs and education, is the cause of high incidences of disease, socially pathologic behavior, and the creation of a "lumpen" subculture.

Crowding, measured as the number of people per room, has been found to be highly correlated with such indices of social pathology as high mortality and juvenile delinquency since the earliest studies conducted in this field.[19] This conclusion has been supported by later studies, which strongly suggest that interpersonal pressure or crowding may be linked with pathological behavior.[20] It is important to note that studies conducted on different neighborhoods found no correlation between crowding and density and an inverse relationship between the level of crowding analysis and the importance of physical density measures at the city level.[21] But residential crowding has consistently been found to have negative consequences.[22]

Recall that crowding is a perceived condition. The perception of crowding is inversely related to one's ability to exercise behavioral freedom and to exert control over one's social and physical environment.[23] That is, crowding is experienced when the number of people in one's environment is large enough to reduce one's behavioral freedom and choice.[24] This gives rise to overmanned situations;[25] it imposes behavioral restrictions and creates social interference, leading to competition for scarce resources.[26]

Crowding is perceived when a person's demand for space exceeds the supply of space.[27] But this situation could originate in physical factors – restricted space, arrangement of space, light conditions – as much as it could originate in social factors, such as the presence of other persons felt to be competitors, since "an individual may feel crowded in the midst of strangers, but quite comfortable and secure in the presence of an equal number of friends."[28] In addition, laboratory research has shown that conditions that potentially cause crowding have no negative effects on the performance of human tasks if the physical consequences of spatial restrictions (high temperature, stuffiness, limited movement) and other environmental stresses (noise) are controlled.[29] Spatial restriction is a necessary precondition of, but is not sufficient by itself to cause, crowding stress. Thus, crowding is not objective and abstract, but subjective and personalized. The demand for space, however, originates in fairly universal needs for privacy and personal turf. Privacy does not mean withdrawal, but the ability to control visual and auditory interaction,[30] and can be defined at various levels: solitude, intimacy, anonymity in a crowd, and control of intrusion through psychological barriers.[31] But even privacy is not an absolute concept; it depends on the cultural milieu.

One of the most critical factors affecting the perception of crowding, as well as of density, is culture, which, as we mentioned in Chapter 7, controls much of human behavior. In addition, expectations and past experiences affect one's perception of crowding. Correlation studies show that spatial restriction is not always associated with social pathology and that cultural traditions define different parameters for density and crowding. The fact that Hong Kong, with a residential density ten times higher than that of Manhattan, is a thriving city not particularly burdened with behavioral pathologies is one indication of the importance of cultural framework. Indeed, the relationship between high neighborhood densities and social pathology is mediated by personal and cultural factors.[32]

The mediating effects of culture in spatial perception in general, and in the perception of crowding and density in particular, are probably the most important obstacle to the generalization of research findings outside of a specific environment. Different social groups have different perceptions of what constitutes trespassing in space and what constitutes permissible involvement in public and private areas, leading Hall to assert that "culture is possibly the most significant single variable in determining what constitutes stressful density," because "people brought up in different cultures live in different perceptual worlds. . . . People perceive space quite differently."[33] Cultural norms mediate the perception and adjustment of interpersonal space and, thus, the sensory thresholds for residential crowding and urban density.

It has been suggested that crowding may be the result of perceived urban congestion and excessive social stimulation;[34] the inability to avoid or reduce social or visual contact[35] may cause a cognitive overload leading to stress and withdrawal.[36] Cultural norms radically change the thresholds of such perception.

However, cultural differences in the perception of crowding and density cannot be adjusted through an anthropological classification of cultures. It has been said, for example, that urban scale must be consistent with ethnic scale, since each ethnic group seems to have developed its own scale.[37] Does this means that an Irish neighborhood must be planned in a different way than a Polish one? To what extent should subcultures be disaggregated in environments as rich as urban areas? A clue to understanding this issue, at least for planners and designers, is given by one of the oldest neighborhoods in Boston, the North End, which today is largely Italian; its tightly packed, midrise, relatively high density pattern, its narrow streets and alleys seem to be ideally suited for an Italian neighborhood. However, the North End was built and settled by groups migrating from England in the eighteenth century (some of whose descendants now live in exclusive suburbs with quite different lifestyles). The explanation for this is that the original English settlers belonged to the same European urban culture from which the more recent Italians originated. Thus, a straightforward ethnic label may not account for the truly differential factors within urban subcultures, or the common elements they share.

The complexity of the relationships between built environment and human behavior has led to the formulation of various theories that go beyond the effects of crowding and density. Barker has proposed the concept of behavioral settings, in which the built environment is interpreted as affording (but not determining) behavioral opportunities;[38] in order to survive, an urban environment must be adaptable to different behaviors and to changing behaviors, as discussed in Chapter 4. One of the criticisms raised by Frampton to Modern and Postmodern architecture is that they offer limited alternatives for patterns of behavior.[39] In addition, because of cultural variations in activity, family and gender, privacy and social intercourse,[40] the same environment would be perceived and used differently by different people, according to their values, experience, and motivation.[41] In the context of the postindustrial metropolis, where cosmopolitans share urban space with locals of various cultural extractions, these concepts are critical to community designers, as we shall discuss in Chapter 12. Sommers developed the concept of personal space, in which territoriality is a way to attain privacy through physical or symbolic barriers, and space is personalized to satisfy one's needs for identity, security, self-fulfillment, and a frame of reference.[42] The personalization of the suburb of Levittown or Le Corbusier's project at Pessac is an indication of people's preference for diversity, which will also be discussed at length in Chapter 12. Territoriality, like many other urban concepts, is culture specific; the hierarchy of private to public turfs varies with different cultural parameters.

In summary, crowding stress cannot be predicted on the basis of spatial considerations alone; it is determined by a combination of environmental and personal factors acting over time. The psychological stress of crowding involves not only the realization that demands for space cannot be met by the supply, but also an emotional imbalance in which a person feels infringed upon, alienated, and deprived of privacy. The size of physical space – and thus the number of people per area – is only one of the variables of crowding. The noise and light levels in a space, the number of objects and their arrangement, the social situation, the activities taking place, and the personal psychology are all factors that, together, determine the perception of crowding and the level of stress. The close, personal proximity of urban life, when seen from the vantage point of suburban life, may seem threatening since the attraction (or focus) of urban activities may not be sufficiently perceived by suburban observers. A dense urban situation may be unappealing to a person not familiar with the activities taking place in that environment and unaccustomed to the urban rituals and routines that structure – and give meaning to – dense urban life.

Crowding has an opposite: undercrowding. Undercrowding is defined as an excessive abundance of space in which an individual suffers social isolation and needs enclosure and contact with others – sometimes manifesting as agoraphobia, or fear of large spaces. Too much space can be as undesirable as too little.

Thus, the limitation of density in a community does not address the problems caused by crowding. In the design of a community, crowding must be prevented through a sensitive handling of the various relationships between people and inhabited space. In contrast, density must be based on community-related considerations in order to reach desired thresholds of urban services.

TOWARD URBAN DENSITIES

As already mentioned, density planning has been used almost exclusively to establish maximum density limits, with a clear preference for low levels. Zoning is the typical mechanism for establishing density limits, using such criteria as ensuring adequate daylight, sunlight, air, usable open space, room for community facilities, a feeling of openness and privacy, and adequate relationship of building cost to land and improvement costs.[43] Except for the last one, an economic objective legitimately influenced by density, there are very few objective justifications for these requirements. Consequently, controls on density are frequently unwarranted, their real use being to prevent undesirable development.

Daylight and sunlight are, in fact, only very loosely related to density, since they begin to be restricted only at the highest values; they are influenced to a much greater degree by the type of building, landscaping, and fenestration. Usable open space has a tenuous connection with density; it is possible to obtain a large amount of open space in high-density areas (with high-rise buildings) and, vice versa, a small amount of open space in relatively low density areas (with single-family-unit subdivisions). Nor does privacy bear a consistent relation to density: Some low-density areas have little privacy because windows open to surrounding yards facing neighboring windows without fences, and there is no transition between houses and the community.

There are better ways to fulfill these requirements than through the stringent application of density indices. If ensuring daylight and sunlight is the objective, then the establishment of a sky exposure plane would be more adequate. This control approach, tailored for central areas, limits the vertical height of buildings along the street line, but could allow setbacks determined by a sloping plane. If ensuring usable open space is the objective, then the use of an open-space ratio is recommended. This ratio states the percentage of a lot that must be kept undeveloped. If an adequate relationship to land in terms of future demands on municipal utilities and street capacity is the objective, then the establishment of a floor area ratio would be suitable. This ratio, equally valid in central or peripheral areas, limits the building gross floor area (i.e., the sum of all its floors) for given uses per lot area—which would ensure a balance between development and infrastructure capacity.

A more flexible use of various control approaches to suit the needs of a particular problem would be desirable: Incentives could be introduced in order to foster additional community objectives. For example, if a setback at the sidewalk level were desired at a specific intersection, the sky exposure plane could be allowed at a steeper angle; or if more open space were desired, the incentive could be higher allowable density.

There are two distinct areas of concern. One is crowding on a residential scale; the other is density on an urban scale. Residential crowding, a cause of pathological behavior, is the result of the segregation of poor people in high-rent areas. Attempts to solve this complex problem must be an integral part of our efforts to eliminate discrimination in all its dimensions and to give everyone a share of the community wealth. Land use and housing integration, access to education and good employment, and provision of housing for all income groups must be high-priority public policies. Clearly, this amounts to a radical program, and in no way can one understate the seriousness of the obstacles likely to be encountered in trying to implement it; these will be discussed in more detail in the Epilogue. However, it is essential to recognize that the orthodox application of density limits in order to solve the problem of crowding has absolutely no effect on this problem.

On an urban scale, density can, and should, be handled through density regulation, among other planning and design tools. Yet regardless of the flexibility with which various control approaches can be used, the fact remains that the application of all of them is biased by cultural values. As already mentioned, the concern for overdense areas has led to an almost complete disgregard for the opposite problem – that of underdense areas. Metropolitan densities are affected by two extremes, which we shall call areas of over-urban density and areas of sub-urban density. Over-urban density can create a perception of crowding. It reduces choice, privacy, and opportunities for personalization. The environment loses adaptability, flexibility, and opportunities for alternative human behavior. In short, people lose control of the environment. Sub-urban density can lead to isolation. It reduces the capacity for interaction and, thus, choice. The environment provides few options for human behavior. In another way, people also lose control of the environment.

The basic question is, How can we reestablish density as a building block of urban life and urban communities?

The pattern of density: balance and variety. The major obstacle to reestablishing a range of urban densities is that there has been a polarization of densities at both extremes of the spectrum. In addition, these density extremes are experienced daily by the metropolitan population, giving rise to a polarization that feeds on itself. The crowding of daily commuters in packed trains and buses or on congested highways, and the regimented anonymity of huge corporate workplaces, lead people to seek respite in quiet suburbia, with identifiable houses and patches of green. Millions of people experience daily the rather traumatic shift from a suburban environment to an over-urban one, and vice versa, in the belief that the first extreme is a cure for the ills of the other.

One design strategy is to ameliorate the crowding experienced during the trip to and from work and in the workplace itself, thereby reducing stress and thus the need for compensation in the form of low-density suburbs. This strategy assumes that, in order to restore a range of community densities, it is necessary to erode the two pathological extremes of over-urban and sub-urban densities. We could call this a strategy of balance.

This strategy faces serious obstacles. The improvement of the trip to and from work – making it shorter and more comfortable – is clearly linked to the existence of density corridors that make high-quality mass transit feasible. To paraphrase the chicken and the egg question, What comes first, urban densities or good mass transit? We will return to this issue later in this chapter.

Speculation in land values and gigantism in organizations and projects constitute another vicious circle that feeds on itself. As mentioned before, land values rise to astronomical levels in the expectation of huge profits reaped by giant developments; giant developments exist because land values are astronomically high and corporations demand ever larger built complexes. The reduction of over-urban densities; the elimination of huge anonymous lobbies, elevator banks, corridors, and office pools; the introduction of human scale in the workplace and of civilized urban scale in the community

– these appear nothing short of impossible. For community designers to lead the charge against these corporate trends would seem folly . . . until one remembers David and Goliath. We shall return to this issue later as well.

A large proportion of the population in metropolitan areas is caught in the daily stressful swing either between over-urban and sub-urban areas or between suburban residential life and suburban employment. The balance strategy aims at restoring a wide range of urban densities. It must not be misunderstood, however, as leading toward a homogeneous environment. Far from it. Another design strategy is to open this wide range of urban density options to all population groups.

Optimal density is not one constant value but many different values. In the continuum between personal privacy and community-wide interaction, density is one of the key factors in increasing choice. The challenge for planners, designers, and civic leaders is to create neighborhoods of varying densities, with small semiprivate community areas as well as large public spaces, so that both interaction and seclusion can be enjoyed. These are necessary conditions for a true community design. The optimal situation is to be able to choose, at different times, the thrill of urban life as well as the soothing quality of small-scale environments.

By "urban thrill" I do not mean Times Square, and by "small-scale environment" I do not mean an isolated suburb – not necessarily, at least. These two types of spaces, which could be near one another, need not evoke the stereotypical images of skyscrapers and single-family estates. London offers many urban-scale dense areas that do not oppress with crowding, anomie, or exhaustion, and yet constitute the highest level in the urban hierarchy – Regent Street is one of many examples – as well as intimate areas in close relation to the former – the famous Mews are delightful examples – plus many in between – Grosvenor Square, to mention one.

It is very important that the range of density options be kept open to all population groups. Today there is a wide range of options for only a very few – elite groups who could choose any space from a luxurious penthouse in the city center to a rural estate. As income decreases, choice narrows; the poor must accept subhuman conditions in marginal environments. The importance of the strategy proposed here lies in the opening of density choices – and thus lifestyles to some degree – to all.

The regulation of density. The implementation of the design strategy of balance demands a certain control of densities across the metropolitan area. A reduction of over-urban density and crowding in some central areas, a reconcentration of suburban workplaces in denser centers, and an increase in suburban densities require planning efforts on a metropolitan scale, with participation and consensus of the various municipalities forming the metro area. The most critical argument for metropolitan integration of efforts is the need to coordinate density and public transportation. One of the most ironic planning contradictions in the United States is that decisions on density and mass transportation not only are made independently but often are at odds with one another.

Although every transportation authority has responsibility over a metropolitan area, most planning of transit networks and services is undertaken without minimum coordination with the local municipal agencies responsible for density (and land use) zoning. Furthermore, every municipality has the right to veto improvements or extensions of mass transit to its residents, thus hampering the effective planning of urban transportation. In the past few years, for example, several Boston suburbs have rejected a plan to extend the subway system to their communities: The probable reason was a fear of "undesirable people" gaining access to the community, as well as an aversion to converting low-density residential areas in the vicinity of the proposed transit corridor into higher-density multifamily residential and commercial uses.

Clearly, the selective coordination of zoning of key areas on the metropolitan scale would be a breakthrough of major proportions, because every municipality jealously guards its right to zone the land within its boundaries. There is a growing number of reasons to change this archaic political mosaic into a more responsive and integrated metropolitan organization. Among them are the need to develop a first-rate public transportation system, to protect water resources (including reserves and aquifers) and open space, to treat sewage properly, to isolate and clean contaminated waste dumps, as well as to open up location and housing choices to people of all races and social classes.

Meanwhile, planners and designers must explore a number of fronts in order to implement the design strategies of balance and variety in density. The reduction of overcrowding and anomie in corporate and bureaucratic workplaces demands a number of complementary controls and incentives, only the most important of which I will mention here. The

scale and bulk of office buildings should be reduced through
a combination of maximum floor area ratio (building floor area over land area), height, gross floor area served by one elevator core, and distance to windows. These controls aim at disaggregating the building bulk and providing less crowded, less anonymous, and more humane workplaces. This approach is part of the general decentralization and sub-optimization strategy for dealing with large organizations, as discussed in Chapter 6.

The introduction of giant office complexes, completely out of scale and character with the prevailing urban pattern, has resulted in over-urban densities and led to major environmental conflicts, as mentioned in Chapter 3. Designing buildings in scale with the existing pattern is a first step toward regaining an urban community without overcrowding. Limiting the floor area that can be served by one elevator core and designating the maximum distance from a work station to the nearest window are controls that aim at providing a better environment while eliminating the disorientation, anonymity, and crowding of oversized buildings. The purpose of establishing realistic floor area ratios is to bring development in scale with, among other parameters, the traffic capacity of streets.

Central city zoning must support public transportation, offering incentives to developers and agencies that cooperate in improving it. Among other possibilities, buildings should provide access to underground subway stations, should give first priority to the upgrading of station entries with visibility and light from sidewalks, and should contribute additional amenities at the sidewalk level for pedestrians – for example, arcades to protect people from bad weather, waiting areas for bus and taxi stops, and restrooms. This type of public-oriented facility designed in coordination with the city and transit authorities – rather than the currently fashionable consumerist "atriums" – must be encouraged. A historical precedent are the gallerias that flourished in the preceding century (Figure 8.3).

At the same time, incentives for the provision of small plazas in the front of every office building could well be eliminated. Most of these plazas are wind-swept barren spaces that break the continuity of streets and avenues. They are a clear example of an urban pattern being undermined by building types without community sense. Open space in central areas must be the result of a conscious planning decision within the urban pattern; Central Park in New York, the plazas of Savannah, the squares of London, and the tree-lined boulevards of Paris are examples of properly planned open spaces (Figure 8.4).

A strategy of reconcentration should be used to redirect the trend toward suburbanization of employment, as discussed in Chapter 6. Strategic nodes with actual or potential access to extensions of public transportation systems should be zoned for secondary or tertiary employment centers, with mixed uses and urban densities. Large dispersed employment areas along highways should ideally be phased out if serving

Figure 8.3. Urban amenities. (Top) Galleria Vittorio Emanuele, Milan. Interior. (Bottom) Entry to the Galleria.

them with public transportation proves to be unfeasible. Unfortunately, this is easier said than done because of a specific fiscal characteristic of many U.S. municipalities: the local property tax.

Most suburban towns, except the most affluent ones, compete strenuously to induce businesses to locate within their boundaries; they offer tax incentives, sometimes very generous ones, to tilt the balance in their favor. The major reason for this competition is that businesses pay more to towns in property taxes than what they consume in municiple services, thus providing substantial fiscal benefits. However, in the heat of the competition, towns offer incentives such as tax breaks to such a degree that they often end up losing the benefits.

Any strategy for reconcentrating suburban employment must face the fact that some municipalities would lose their property tax base. A solution to this problem is the already mentioned establishment of a metropolitan authority, which would be responsible for pooling the collection of property tax revenues and their distribution to each municipality based on some agreed-upon criteria. Currently, property taxes are used within the municipality that collects them, and tax revenues are raised on the basis of valuation and rate. A criterion for redistribution could be revenue allocation by population in general, and low-income groups in particular. This not only would assure each municipality of tax revenues regardless of the business uses within its boundaries, but also would improve the equality of distribution. If this approach were taken, land could be devoted to the best use – free of fiscal considerations – and densities could be more easily reconcentrated.

Finally, strategies for increasing suburban residential densities should combine a number of alternative approaches. Minimum lot sizes should be reduced; for areas with single-family units, quarter-acre lots satisfy the need for private open space while permitting some form of surface public transportation. Zero line lots should be encouraged in more urban situations. Several communities have begun to experiment with cluster zoning, whereby the same number of dwelling units that can exist in a given area under normal zoning are concentrated in a much smaller area and the area remaining is devoted to open space. This approach, which is very valuable in low-density suburbs, could be improved by requiring that the remaining open space be planned as an integral part of the open-space system in the community and that the cluster of dwellings also be planned in relation to the existing built pattern.

Cluster zoning could be expanded into a full policy of channeling peripheral developments into "villages." In many suburban and exurban areas, new construction could replicate traditional settlement forms, such as villages and hamlets. If those villages were zoned at crossroads, certain thresholds would be reached: Services and facilities within walking distance of the village inhabitants, as well as bus service, could be provided and rural areas and farmland preserved. The village approach is related to our previous proposal to redevelop obsolete shopping centers as mixed-use integrated local centers. Both approaches involve reconcentration and achievement of higher densities and urban thresholds.

Density and dwelling types. One of the problems of defining density in operational terms is the relatively weak relationship between density and building types. The same density can

be obtained with radically different building types, and the
same type can be used to obtain different densities. For example, the myth that high density is equivalent to high-rise
construction has been dispelled by the "rediscovery" of
tightly packed, high-density, low-rise types. Since density is
nothing more than a quantitative index with perhaps some
clues to possible design solutions, it has few deterministic
implications in terms of visual images and behavioral settings.
Even environments with the same density and building type
can be very different in character, depending on the design
nuances – as the differences between old town house neighborhoods and newer versions in countless developments
clearly show. Yet dwelling types offer some key opportunities for achieving certain density levels.

The Mediterranean cultures – Greek and Roman, Egyp-
tian, Italian and Spanish, Moroccan, Portuguese, and French
– all used a recurrent dwelling type in endless variations: the
patio house or court house (which is also found across most
of the American continent; see Figure 3.16, bottom). The
first known example is the so-called House of Abraham in
Ur. Using this dwelling type, these cultures built urban communities that became the cradle of civilization. Their cultural

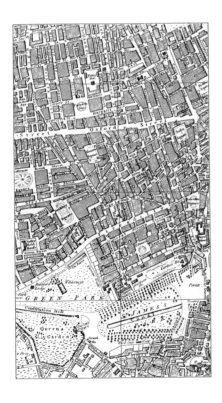

Figure 8.4. Urban open
spaces. (Opposite) Central
Park, New York City,
1857. Frederick Law
Olmstead. (New York
Convention and Visitors
Bureau) (Left) London
with seventeenth- and
eighteenth-century squares:
Bedford, Cavendish, Soho,
Hanover, Grosvenor,
Leicester, Berkeley, and
St. James. (MIT Press)

values are reflected in the Arab proverb "Paradise without people should not be entered because it is hell." Middle Eastern culture treasures privacy, as shown in its architecture of walls and private gardens. And yet it allows itself the luxury

Figure 8.5. Rediscovering apartment buildings. (Top) Apartments with retail shops on an arcaded ground floor, Evora, Portugal. (Bottom) Apartments with ground floor arcade around a square, Plaza Mayor, Madrid. (Opposite top) Apartments with enclosed balconies, La Valetta, Malta. (Bernard Rudofsky) (Opposite bottom) Bullring, half arena, and half apartment building, 1770; boxes converted to additional apartments in 1870; Tarazona, Zaragoza, Spain. (Bernard Rudofsky)

– indeed, the basic requirement for human life – of a rich community life.

Another widespread dwelling type, originating in northern Europe and later transferred to North America, is the party-wall row house or town house, which has formed, with multiple variations, the majority of urban patterns in those countries. This type, like the preceding one, while preserving individual privacy within the house, combines into dense

urban patterns that encourage community interaction (see Figure 3.16, top).

At the level in which dwellings combine to form apartment buildings, there is a rich variety of types offering a trade-off between the advantages of higher densities and a lack of direct access to the ground (Figure 8.5). At the opposite end of the spectrum is the single-family dwelling on a lot with a range of options in terms of frontage, side yard requirements, and fences.

In all cases, a successful pattern should offer a proper gradation between the privacy of the house and the various levels of community. A proper sequence of intermediate levels must account for elements both on private turf – front yards, fences, entrances to buildings, balconies – and on public turf – residential and metropolitan streets, neighborhood and urban centers, quiet plazas and bustling squares. A successful density control system must consider those intermediate levels.

Ultimately, the repossessing of community densities, with all that this implies in terms of urbanity, will depend on the establishment of urban patterns in which suitable building types can be developed, a variety of conditions and environments can be achieved, a hierarchy of urban thresholds can be reached, and human beings can choose the level of community interaction at which they wish to participate.

CHAPTER 9

DISTRIBUTION IN CITIES

Or a key to reconstituting the culture of cities

DISTRIBUTION IN SPACE

Distribution reflects the location of sets of finite elements in geographic space, that is, the allocation of activities, population, and facilities to specific sites and the resulting spatial organization of urban systems, whether metropolises or neighborhoods. One cannot understand an urban system simply through knowledge of each of the component elements separately, or even through knowledge of the sectorial relationships among elements. By far the most important characteristic of urban systems, as discussed in Chapter 4, is their structure in space, or their geographic relationship.

The interaction among urban elements, translated in spatial and sectorial linkages, shapes relationships of mutual interdependency among individuals, groups, and institutions, forming urban communities. This is well understood by the "laissez faire" counterpart of planners, the private real estate market, whose land values depend on location – that is, location of each parcel with reference to the rest of the community. Location determines the specific effects and interrelationships of the urban system acting upon a particular site. Urban distribution is the result of the interaction of people and activities in concentrated urban space, all of them aiming at reducing the cost and time of overcoming distance – for example, travel cost and time – and increasing the advantages of their roles in the urban system.

Distribution is the key planning variable in community design. Distribution characterizes spatial organizations, and as such constitutes a unique area of expertise. Community design's first concern is the relative location and distribution of elements in space. Some of the most negative tendencies of cities, particularly in the United States, are related to the increasing unraveling of urban distribution. Loosely distributed locations, reflected in the dispersion of population and employment and the creation of dispersed centers – together with segregation – foster socioeconomic inequalities by preventing access of lower-income groups in central cities to suburban jobs. This also results in wasted resources and erosion of the notion of community in nonurban isolated settlements. Communication technology has led many to postulate that spatial relationships are less important than they in fact are. Finally, the regimentation with which planners conceptualize settlements has been another threat to urban distribution.

Let us begin by identifying some problems. First, dispersed distribution has very serious implications for energy and environmental conservation: Because mass transit cannot be extended to dispersed residential or employment areas, transportation is provided largely by private automobiles, which consume huge amounts of energy and are the main contributors to air pollution. During the oil crises of the 1970s there was a heightened concern with this problem, but it was immediately forgotten when energy prices stabilized. Yet finite nonrenewable oil resources and the huge consumption of energy in metropolises with a dispersed, low-density distribution constitute a very dangerous situation; this distribution is mortgaging the resources of the whole planet just to maintain the U.S. suburban lifestyle. Second, dispersed distribution has important social effects. Urban agglomerations are constantly expanding outward and abandoning the city center; at the same time, the upper and middle classes are pushing for new dispersed developments on the fringes of the city. In contrast, the poor are forced to concentrate in deteriorating central slums, increasingly removed from the dispersed places of suburban employment.

Accessibility plays a critical role in the distribution of urban elements. On the metropolitan scale, a key factor is the location of basic employment, which influences the location of other elements. The relationship between employment and residential areas is established through the urban transportation system. The location of industrial employment is in some cases rather flexible,[1] while in others it is determined by the accessibility needs of a given technology. Railroad-dependent technologies led to central, or at least concentrated, industrial areas, while truck-dependent technologies allowed the suburbanization of employment along highways.[2] For the tertiary sector (services), dependence on mass transit led to a concentrated distribution at the city center, while dependence on the automobile allowed decentralization of employment in suburban and exurban areas. In the United States, the impact of employment suburbanization cannot be overestimated; even in centralized, concentrated metropolitan areas such as Boston, downtown employment represents no more than one-third of all metropolitan employment. On average, not more than 20 percent of metropolitan employment is located at the center, the majority being distributed along highway ribbons and exurban centers (see Figure 8.2).

Employees and workers want to live near their jobs – whether industrial or office-oriented. Residential areas, in turn, generate secondary places of employment – from laundries to restaurants – to serve the needs of the population; this secondary employment generates a second wave of residential location consisting of the people working in these establishments, which in turn creates even more secondary employment, and so on.[3] Within this broad scenario, the actual location of residences and employment is the result of a complex set of factors.

Faced with the problems and opportunities offered by urban areas, people and activities distribute themselves with the aim of reaping locational advantages. From a residential viewpoint, housing costs and transportation costs are optimized according to the particular objectives and limitations of various social (income) groups.[4] In metropolises with vital downtowns, there is competition for the most accessible land at the center of the city. In this competitive game, the land uses that stand to gain most from accessibility to employees and customers – retail and office uses – acquire the prime land, using it intensively to reduce the unit impact of high land cost. As a result, only those activities with large value added per unit of land can locate in prime locations.

A key point is that residential location follows employment, with lower-income groups settling near the concentration of employment in the center and upper-income groups settling on the periphery of the metropolitan area. The choice of location by income groups can be explained, as mentioned before, in terms of how close to the employment center each group needs to be. The poor, who cannot afford expensive trips and frequently change jobs, locate near the employment center; since this is very expensive land – owing to its accessibility – the poor can live there only at the cost of crowding into tenements in order to reduce the total rent paid per family. At the other extreme, the wealthy, who have a cultural hunger for land, can afford longer commuting trips and enjoy employment stability; thus, most exchange commuting trips for space, which they can get in abundance because the land is cheaper. The social and geographic spaces between the two extremes are filled with the middle classes in the inner suburbs and other intermediate areas. It should be added that those of the wealthy who still value an urban lifestyle have the option of living in the luxury town houses and apartments of gentrified neighborhoods near the city center. Thus, as we mentioned in the preceding two chapters, the upper classes have a wide choice of location, which they base mainly on considerations of lifestyle; the poor, in contrast, have very few choices, all of them involving substandard and subhuman conditions. For those in the middle, the options range from working-class neighborhoods threatened by racial strife to middle-class suburbs offering a quiet retreat.

This pattern of urban location is not universal, but is the result of the cultural assumptions behind the economic behavior of the participants. Mainstream U.S. culture, as already mentioned, values dispersed, segregated, homogeneous, low-density settlements, preferences that are based on a "hunger for land" – which is probably the key to explaining the U.S. locational structure. In history, many centralized cities have been populated by both poor and rich, but nowhere did the same distribution observed in U.S. cities exist in other cities, since their elites valued proximity to the center of power, urbanity, and social interaction above other considerations, and they thus settled in central locations.

In the past several decades, there has been a trend toward substantial dispersion of employment, leading to an array of metropolitan distributions – suburban centers, linear industrial and office parks, major exurban centers. The dispersion of employment has occurred selectively; the old industries may still be close to the railroad yards, but the fast-growing high-technology industries, as well as the equally important tertiary places of employment, constitute the core of the dispersed employment. In other words, much of the dynamic and higher-paying employment is moving out of city centers and settling on the periphery of metropolitan areas, more often than not accessible only by private automobile (see Figure 8.2). As a result, low-income groups living in crowded central city slums are farther and farther away from the most promising sources of employment; in contrast, the more affluent groups and middle classes in suburban locations are finding their commuting distances shortened.

Municipalities are assisting this process, partly through zoning bylaws and regulations that encourage the location of employment in dispersed distributions. In addition, local zoning has strengthened the barriers that prevent the poor from moving to small low-cost dwellings in suburbs, near the new employment centers. Even the old industrial towns absorbed into metropolitan areas have resorted to zoning to protect their middle-class residents from encroachment by low-income families. Increasing inequality and decreasing opportunities are some of the results of the urban trends of the past several decades.

PROPINQUITY AND COMMUNICATIONS TECHNOLOGY: MYTH AND REALITY

Since the emergence of the automobile as the mode of private transportation in the United States, cities have begun to disperse; the telephone has complemented the automobile in allowing people to leave the close physical contact of traditional communities. In the past few decades, new communication technologies have appeared to decrease even further the need for physical propinquity. The widespread use of television as the main form of family entertainment, and of personal computers with their capacity to link individuals to national information networks, have also reduced the need for propinquity. For some families, the idea of living in an isolated rural area, linked to the rest of the world by car, telephone, radio, television, fax, and computer, is very desirable. Children would be educated via television and computer, adults would work via computer and fax, and recreation would be provided by television, video, and cable. The surrounding environment would be an idyllic setting, and by driving to the nearest shopping center one could buy whatever one needed.

This "island" ideal has in some cases been extended to the workplace. Some corporations are considering the possibility of employees working from their homes or on the road, using personal computers to send and receive information. (Although this concept is being tested by many firms, sales of computers aimed at decentralizing the workplace to the home appear to be disappointingly low.) This arrangement is reminiscent of one that prevailed in the early years of the Industrial Revolution when entrepreneurs traveled over the countryside distributing yarn to peasants and collecting the textiles they wove in their huts. An electronic peasant world is being born out of an antiurban culture that does not know how to use cities and does not value the community of human beings.

Something critical to humankind is being forgotten. Civilization, the culture of cities, was always central to human development. The Agricultural Revolution and the "invention" of cities from the third millennium in Sumer and Egypt to the first millennium in Mesoamerica and Peru, and the later Industrial Revolution with the emergence of the modern industrial metropolis in Europe and America, are landmarks of human history. The role of cities as catalysts for interaction covers the whole range of economic, social, and cultural changes in world history: Urban universities fostered human thought and science; urban patrons financed art, literature, and music; and the nomadic Jews established the first monotheistic faith in the city of Jerusalem, the holy city where also Jesus preached during the end of his messianic years. Cities are indeed the environment in which humankind has evolved.

The need and potential for increasing contact within an urban area, coupled with the generated economies of urbanization, act as powerful forces that pull people and activities together. The size and the concentration of an urban cluster determine the degree of interaction, the capacity to create wealth, and the costs inherent in the system, as well as the level of external economies and accessibility.[5] The exchange of goods, services, and ideas within a diverse concentration is the essence of urban life. Ultimately, urban centers can be seen as giant communication devices generating and distributing information. The resulting intercultural exchange has been equated with civilization, and civilization is based on propinquity.

But this belief has been challenged in recent decades by the introduction of technologies that are touted as replacements for the communication role of cities and, thus, for physical propinquity. The dawn of electronic instant communications promises (or threatens) a new civilization. Urbanity can be defined by the amount and variety of one's participation in the cultural life of the world of creative specialists. However, urbanity is seen by the proponents of the electronic peasant world as no longer the exclusive experience of urban dwellers, but also of suburbanites and exurbanites.[6]

According to this interpretation, interaction transcends the place where people live, and the "urban" community becomes a vastly dispersed, non-nodal one. The focus of attention has shifted to human interaction without reference to space, since "the physical boundaries of settlements are disappearing; and the networks of interdependence among various groups are becoming functionally intricate and spatially widespread."[7] The interdependence that ties individuals and groups to one another is seen as increasingly aspatial – an invisible connection among groups and businesses indifferent to location, environment, and physical distance.

The debate about whether physical proximity is a factor in a world flooded with instant communications misses a critical point: Those technologies can enrich communication but cannot fully substitute for physical propinquity in space. Historically, new technologies have not always replaced the old ones, but they have often provided a specialized option that increases choice and have made available unique tools for specific needs. Witness the coexistence of theater, film, and television, all of which have carved a niche in a pluralistic performing arts field.

Instant communications are best suited to the provision of highly specific information, the retrieval and manipulation of data, the transmission of news. Though functionally very important and a real contribution to our capabilities, they neglect a huge portion of human communication. How can we articulate our hints and suggestions, conduct intuitive searches, enjoy unexpected events, explore the meaning of expression, communicate our anger and enthusiasm, savor the richness of the world? Many people find it difficult to express some subtleties by telephone and prefer personal contact. It is often said that the best ideas are generated at a water fountain or over a cup of coffee, when scientists, artists, or politicians meet by chance, talk openly, and from time to time enjoy the spark of a new idea. Communication technologies enhance one another, each becoming increasingly specialized.

There are so many activities enjoyed by people living in a community that cannot be replaced by electronic communications. Remember the rituals around which urbanites organized their recreation in the past: A trip to the theater, the opera, the ballet, or the movies usually included a visit to a restaurant or café, a meeting with friends, and perhaps conversations about art, politics, or business, or just plain gossip. In contrast, watching television is a drastically simplified and impoverished experience, and though it may be relaxing on occasions, it cannot replace the rich and thoroughly urban experience of attending a public performance and enjoying its ancillary activities. Some of the most attractive features of small-town life include trips to the stores on Main Street, where informal conversations constitute a ritual that reinforces the community structure and satisfies people's social interaction needs.

An excessive reliance on instant communications has eroded our humanity by eliminating a wealth of interaction and replacing it with canned images and information. We have lost visual contact with faces, with art, with the environment; we have lost emotional contact with people, places, and nature. Television from three or four sources transmits information and editorial opinions to millions of people who have no way of questioning the sources, opposing them, or even discussing the issues. Computer users "interface" with networks of information as isolated subscribers, and a common form of entertainment is to play electronic preprogrammed games. It is almost as if a fascistic nightmare of dehumanization is being fulfilled, and it has certainly created a vulnerability to fascism on a scale never imagined before. An electronic culture by itself would constitute a noncivilization, and life limited to an electronic environment would be a reductionist nightmare.

A seldom-noticed fact is that dispersion based on instant communications is practiced mostly by the "consumers," not by the "suppliers," of information, as is obvious from studies of the locational patterns of the very people who, presumably, could profit most from dispersion. Research, scientific, artistic, and professional elites are distributed in highly clustered patterns, and not dispersed all over the countryside – not even all over the country. Their concentration generates a further concentration of similar people and related activities, and it is fair to say that today U.S. intellectual and scientific elites are far more clustered than they were a century ago. The bulk of the "intelligentsia" in the country are located in Boston–Cambridge, San Francisco–Berkeley, New York, Ann Arbor, and a few other places; and within each area, these people concentrate in tight clusters such as Harvard Square. Here research firms, individual consultants, scientists, artists, and academicians all share the positive externalities and amenities generated by their critical mass and the wealth of information available in those centers.

By contrast, the distribution patterns of development and

production activities in the same metropolitan centers show that the more narrowly defined high-technology industries are dispersed on cheaper land that allows one-story production and assembly buildings – as, for example, along Route 128 in Boston, in Silicon Valley south of San Francisco, and in New Jersey. There, office parks, research labs, and industrial plants, removed from urban centers, have been forced to provide retail stores, restaurants, and athletic clubs in office buildings in order to attract prime tenants. They are becoming caricatures of the central area whose congestion (and high rents) they wanted to escape in the first place.

Urban distributions are being undermined in many areas of the world, in some countries, like the United States, because of a technology that fulfills antiurban values, in other countries because of huge population migrations caused by unviable social structures. In the United States, the technological mirage is attracting many to a search for electronically linked rural lifestyles. In the Third World, many countries are experiencing the ruralization of cities and the creation of whole villages around the old centers. The scarcity of urban values in the United States and the pressure for radical change felt by many Third World countries suggest that the shift toward an urban society has not been completed at all.

THE DETERMINISTIC DISTRIBUTIONS OF THE STATE OF THE ART

Architects and planners well understand that distribution in space is the core of community design. But the fact that distribution in space tends toward complex, systematic, rich hierarchies is not as well understood. The state of the art seems to be based on a deterministic approach that conceptualizes towns as being organized in exact echelons of residential subunits – what we may refer to as "nested" distributions. For example, many proposals and plans have been based on the concept of neighborhood units or related ones and have established population modules as building blocks for urban design.

The concept of neighborhood units, first heralded in 1929, recommended a rank of units with increasing numbers of families, all neatly related to one another in the nested fashion of Russian dolls, such that, let us say, ten parish units of six hundred families would form a neighborhood unit of six thousand families, which in turn would form part of the larger whole. This neighborhood unit would be self-

193

contained, bounded by main roads, providing housing, schools, shopping, and recreation facilities for its population.[8] This module was described as a "social unit comprising a certain number of people from a variety of classes, occupying a definite area of land, served with the amenities and facilities necessary for a healthy social life, sited at convenient distances, with a service center where the social institutions of day-to-day life are grouped."[9] This theory was first implemented in Radburn, New Jersey, where each neighborhood unit was defined as the area within a half-mile radius around an elementary school, and three neighborhood units joined to form a larger unit within a one-mile radius around a high school and commercial center. A notion emerged of a community curiously resembling a prefabricated village set at the edge of a modern metropolis, with the main service area being determined by the elementary school, and a strong sense that, in order "to retain its unity, a neighborhood should be physically self-contained in respect to most of the daily necessities of life."[10] This planning concept, simplistic and regimented at the same time, soon spread, and has been part of the USSR planning approach since the 1930s, of the London Plan in 1943, of Chandigarh, India, in 1957, and of most new towns built in England and the United States, as well as of the less ambitious planned unit developments and other real estate ventures started in the past few decades.

The limitations imposed by the use of such planning modules became increasingly clear to some social scientists. It is important to recognize the difference between a neighborhood – a geographic area – and a community – a system of interpersonal relations.[11] There are several types of communities, as well as neighborhoods. Some communities are related physically to the land through their settlements in space.[12] Other communities establish nongeographic social relations,[13] such as networks of scientists active over the whole country and even the world. Lee has recognized several types of neighborhoods: social acquaintance neighborhoods based on social interaction, homogeneous neighborhoods based on homogeneity, and unit neighborhoods based on sharing service areas.[14] Keller has further refined our understanding of neighborhoods by identifying some specific characteristics: They have ecological positions in urban areas, embodying social symbols and fulfilling functional roles, while often creating a special atmosphere.[15] Clearly, there are obvious advantages in maintaining the concept of neighborhoods, if this concept is kept flexible enough, limited to loose territorial groups "whose members meet on a common ground within their own area for primary social activities and for organized and spontaneous social contacts,"[16] since it aids social integration of the community within a large metropolis. However, social research has found that neighborhood units of five to ten thousand population are not large enough for a whole range of social relations.[17] Increasingly, the orthodox applications of neighborhood units have been discarded, such as in Cumbernauld, Scotland, and other late new towns.

What is left of the planning module is a stripped-down version of the theory, that is, neighborhood units providing a narrower range of services because of economic factors that tend to favor major urban centers: the ability to provide specialized services, the economic advantages of large catchment areas, and the realization that self-contained neighborhood centers may detract from the main town center. There has been a growing awareness of the variation of demand among local areas – caused by differences in social class, family status, age, car ownership – and the influence of demographics and parochial and private schools on the catchment area of public elementary schools.[18] The rationale for using planning modules has become increasingly thin, but the deterministic attitude has remained unchanged.

The original, and often forgotten, goal of the theory was to fight what Lewis Mumford called "depersonalized societies" and "desocialized organisms" that he saw threatening urban life. But the result of the application of the theory was the opposite of the one intended. The idea of self-contained and self-sufficient neighborhoods in twentieth-century U.S. cities is paradoxical at a time when specialization fosters increasing interdependence. In reality, the social system is structured around nodal centers – schools, stores, churches, transit stations, clubs – which in turn give rise to a whole range of catchment areas, many of which are ill-defined and often overlapping.[19] Clearly, a plan specifying that three elementary school districts be equal to one high school district or to one commercial center market area ignores the complexity of urban hierarchies.

Social life develops in "fields" that are not always coincident with established boundaries of territorial groups; geographic demarcation is only one definitional element of community; there are many other demarcations – environmental, social, institutional, and special interest.[20] A planning approach that is based on the assumed (and highly questionable) needs of children and women, giving them no excuse to go outside their small community, is more than inadequate: It is undesirable. Condemning children to monotonous routines between home, school, and playground, and women to an impoverished world of home, shopping center, and childcare – both within the small neighborhood unit – is plainly wrong.

It has been asserted that extreme compartmentalization and dissociation of internal elements are the first signs of the imminent destruction of an organization or a human being; anarchy in societies and schizophrenia in people are extreme cases.[21] The planning approach of deterministic nested distributions leads to extreme compartmentalization and dissociation of artificial "neighborhoods" – really planning modules. It fractures what should be a community of communities and transforms it into a forced aggregation of strangers.

Parochialism, charming as it may be in remote villages, becomes ugly in urban areas, antithetical to the interaction that cities should provide. Indeed, nested organizations are a model for secret organizations: Their reliance on nested cells is aimed at reducing information to the minimum amount necessary to carry out orders as well as to minimize interaction within the organization. And, as we know, minimum information is entropy, that is, minimum order.

Paradigms of clarity and simplicity, when applied to urban systems, are only parodies, unlikely to reflect the nature of urbanity and the complexity and intricacy of the hierarchy of urban centers and their areas of influence. In modern society there are no closed groups; groups overlap, as do centers and areas of influence. But state-of-the-art urban designs are closely related to such nested organizations as armies and corporations: they have clearly defined ranks, with distinct levels of subordination in a rigid order that allows no improvisation or creativity. Cities are not military camps; cities are not company towns either. Their organization does (and should) resemble that of freer institutions – where any definition is qualified by exceptions, where currents meet and diverge, and where the accident of history is always present.

NONNESTED DISTRIBUTIONS: HIERARCHIES OF COMPLEMENTARY AND COMPETITIVE CENTERS

In urban distributions, as is the case with many systems, the form is the activity, and the activity is the form. Urban distributions are the result of the interaction of process and form. It is possible, on the one hand, to identify functional inter-dependencies of urban activities on various levels. It is possible, on the other hand, to recognize the form of the spatial arrangements of networks, patterns, and buildings.[22] It would be a mistake to assert that one determines the other; process and form evolve by mutual adjustment.

Urban distributions are defined by sets of centers – from small corner stores to downtown business cores – character-ized by related urban forms and activities and with corre-sponding areas of influence. These centers are organized into hierarchies, where certain specialized activities tend to be found in higher-order centers whereas more standard activ-ities tend to be found in lower-order centers. For example, stock exchanges can be found only in the largest and most specialized centers, whereas grocery stores are ubiquitous.[23] An area of influence is correlated with a type of center, since the quality of the activities in the center affects people's will-ingness to travel, and quality is often associated with a center's size. Shopping for clothing, for example, involves longer trips than more routine weekly trips to buy food, because clothes buying involves a wider choice of merchandise and prices and constitutes a less frequent event that may incur considerable expense. It is also clear that a university draws its area of influence from a much larger region than does an elementary school.

Urban centers are of two systematically different types. The two types, complementary and competitive centers, de-fine bounded and overlapping market areas, leading to rad-ically different distribution patterns. Complementary centers are based on cooperation and the rationing principle, whereas competitive ones are based on competition and the pricing principle.

Complementary centers provide public services, such as elementary education, and goods allocated on the basis of community needs. Students are assigned to neighborhood schools in a fashion that establishes bounded areas of influ-ence, leaving them no choice. The aim is to provide schools of approximately equal quality and approximately equal dis-tance from home to school to all children in the community. By contrast, private schools provide education based on pric-ing and individual choice, their distribution resembling that of commercial centers more than community facilities, since they are located at strategic sites accessible to high-income population groups.

Competitive centers provide private goods and services allocated on the basis of market considerations, as in the case of retail stores. People shop in a way that defines overlapping market areas without clear boundaries, choosing different centers for different shopping cycles: day-to-day convenience shopping, weekly shopping, nonroutine comparative shopping of goods ranging from clothes to furniture to jewelry. Even within this classification, people try different centers at different times in order to optimize the combination of price and quality with the effort needed to reach each center. Thus, urban distribution comprises an array of competitive and complementary centers, with their corresponding bounded and fuzzy areas of influence.

These centers – and the ancillary transportation networks feeding them – are the points of reference for distribution patterns and the establishment of urban hierarchies. The distribution of land uses and densities in the urban realm is based, generically, on accessibility to centers and on the hierarchy (size, type) of the centers. Several factors shape the differences in the appeal of different centers. In commercial centers, for example, the costs of comparable services and goods vary with the economies (and diseconomies) of scale and agglomeration of centers of different sizes.[24] The quality of services and goods varies with the level of specialization and, thus, with the size of a center.[25] And the size of a center may itself be an element of its attraction. The hierarchy of a commercial center (i.e., size and specialization) is a function of the market (i.e., population and income within the area of influence), but the market area is also a function of the hierarchy of the center. Similar considerations would apply to other centers. As a result, the influence of urban centers, defined as the spatial distance of their catchment or market areas, has a definite relation to their level in the hierarchy, a fact that highlights the relationships that shape distributions. Those relationships define the series of economic and physical thresholds of centers.

Urban centers are distributed in two different types of spatial pattern. Complementary centers, providing public services according to a planned allocation, have a homogeneous distribution at each level – at least to the extent that the population distribution allows such homogeneity. Elementary schools are distributed homogeneously and their areas of influence are determined by their distances from homes. Similar distribution occurs for high schools, kindergartens, public clinics, police and fire stations, libraries, post offices, and other public service centers. Their public nature and controlled allocation explain why their areas of influence have clear boundaries.

Competitive centers offer private goods and services on a competitive basis; each tries to maximize its locational advantages to capture a larger market. Consider the locational sequence of unplanned commercial centers. The first step would entail a number of small stores locating in accessible spots. Sooner or later, some of them, by fate or accident or perhaps by better management, would grow more than others, and their larger size would attract larger markets, establishing a hierarchical rank. As a result of this positive feedback between population behavior and centers, as well as the inherent complexity of urban systems, the distribution of competitive centers may appear to be a random process.

However, a detailed study would show a distribution in which the larger competitive centers formed patterns with a few large clusters, while at the other end of the hierarchy, the smaller centers were distributed fairly homogeneously – since their quality–price equation is rather uniform. Different intermediate-level centers would fill the gaps in the market landscape between these two extremes. The competition among centers would preclude any clear demarcation of market areas, while the influence of larger centers would overlap that of the smaller ones.

It is important to realize that design solutions to urban distributions may be easy to visualize only when their areas of influence are planned through the rationing mechanism of complementary centers. However, when people's trade-offs and choices and competition among centers play a critical role, there is no immediate solution.

The hierarchy of competitive and complementary centers is fundamental in conceptualizing the total distribution, because the area of influence of a given center will not, in all likelihood, be composed of a finite number of areas of influence lower in the hierarchy, nor will it join with a finite number of centers on the same level to form a center higher in the hierarchy. The various levels of areas of influence are related in a nonnested hierarchy.

The recognition that nonnested hierarchies are inherent in urban areas is essential to community design, for more than one reason. Designing urban areas in such a way as to foster nonnested hierarchies would go a long way not only toward creating communities with vital urban complexity, but also toward reducing the ills of segregation. It would provide opportunities for people to share education with one group, to shop with somewhat different groups, and to enjoy recreation and cultural facilities with yet other groups. These experiences would be radically different from those offered by conventional designs, where one is limited to associating with the same people within clearly bounded neighborhoods.

It is critical during the design programming stage to distinguish the various centers' real typologies, that is, their systematic relationships with their areas of influence. Is it valid simply to assume that community facilities will always follow a complementary distribution pattern and that competitive centers will consist of businesses only? Not in all cases. We have already mentioned that, whereas public education is a typical complementary function, the distribution of private schools resembles that of competitive centers. Even within public education systems, the location and specialization of so-called magnet schools resemble the pattern in competitive centers based on choice, without pricing. In cities with a predominant religion, the distribution of places of worship follows the pattern of complementary centers, with strictly defined parishes; but in cities where there are several major religious groups, the distribution patterns are far more complex.

One obvious difference between the two types of centers in the United States is that complementary centers are the result of government intervention and are subject to the planning of the public sector; in contrast, competitive centers are in the domain of the private sector. This difference raises two questions: Are nonnested hierarchical distributions possible only under conditions in which a private sector fosters competitive centers? Should there be competitive centers, and thus nonnested hierarchies, in cities under noncapitalist conditions? These questions touch on a couple of critical issues: the degree to which planning should intervene in the distribution of competitive (private-sector) centers and the degree to which it is desirable to maintain a nonnested distribution of both complementary and competitive centers in societies with a reduced private sector.

In most U.S. cities, planning has not fulfilled its role of ensuring the community welfare as against the welfare of a few individuals; there have been only a few interventions to enforce public responsibility in the private sector. In many cases, the equilibrium of market situations may be less optimal, from the community point of view, than the equilibrium of a planned distribution, which would more than justify the intervention of the public sector. The example of ice cream vendors at the beach will suffice: Two vendors at a crowded beach, regardless of where each starts selling ice cream, will soon gravitate toward the middle in order to capture at least half of the beach market. This central location, though considered the equilibrium one from the market viewpoint, is not so good for the bathers, who must walk to the middle of the beach to get ice cream. The bathers would be better off, and the vendors no worse off, if each vendor located at the quarter points from the ends of the beach; in this way, the bathers would reduce their walking distance and the vendors would still command half of the market. Equilibrium could be achieved under only one condition: There would have to be a public authority forbidding the vendors to start inching toward the middle. If, however, there were a difference in the quality and price of the two vendors' ice cream, the central location might be better because it would afford the bathers a choice. Planning can (and should) improve the welfare of a community without curtailing its richness and complexity.

The development of cities under socialist conditions has always presented the challenge of restructuring the urban pattern to reflect the new society. Limiting the discussion to distribution, the absence of individual capital owners may be mistakenly construed as leading to the generation of exclusively complementary centers throughout. Remember that the restrictions on private capital ownership are aimed at avoiding an undue concentration of economic power in a few corporations without community control. This need not affect the multiplicity of urban enterprises – from market vendors to stores – where there could be a range of other "entrepreneurs," such as cooperatives, neighborhood shops, and even competing branches of publicly owned stores or services.

I believe that the richness and vital complexity inherent in nonnested hierarchies was, is, and must continue to be part of urban systems. Competitive centers enhance the range of choice open to people, and thus enhances urbanity. Political and social changes aimed at achieving more democratic conditions should not confuse egalitarianism with uniformity.

DEVELOPMENT AND REDISTRIBUTION OF
URBAN CENTERS

The current urban landscape seems to be one of decentralization and dispersion, and it is generally believed that this trend has been the only possible outcome in a motorized society. In other words, the postindustrial city in the West is dispersing because this is assumed to be its destiny, dictated by technology. This is the "city of the future" (as Los Angeles has often been called), a dispersed settlement based on movement so effortless that people can expand over the metropolitan area at will. The only significant artifacts this city has created are the mazes of highways that connect vast urban regions (see Figure 5.6, bottom).

However, lower transportation costs and higher speeds have had a paradoxical effect. Nationally, the U.S. population is reconcentrating in a few urban regions and vast areas are being depopulated. It is only on the metropolitan scale that dispersion is apparent. This double process of national reconcentration and metropolitan dispersion occurs because, once moving becomes easier, people relocate to centers with greater opportunities and greater appeal – which happens to be certain metropolitan areas in selected locations. It is cultural values, facilitated by the transportation technology, that lead a society to chose a dispersed – but localized – distribution around these urban centers.

The effect of transportation on distribution can be illustrated by a fascinating ecological example: the locational pattern of beetles and wasps.[26] Beetles have a high transfer cost because they expend considerable energy and move at slow speeds. They follow an absolute dispersed pattern, with very small concentrations at each location; they spread out fairly evenly. Wasps have lower transfer costs because they can cover large distances at high speeds daily; they certainly appear to have considerably more freedom to choose nest locations. However, wasps have a highly concentrated distribution, with a large number of insects at each location. The capacity of wasps to cover large feeding areas allows them to concentrate in sizable nests, whereas beetles are forced to disperse in order to survive within a much smaller feeding area.

Historically, improved transportation technology and lower transfer costs have led to increasing concentration of human settlements. Thus, we have seen empires and nations emerge, capitals and world cities develop. And until relatively recent times, the urban hierarchy has become richer because of the quantitative and qualitative growth of the total system.

Beyond some threshold, however, the large metropolises have not added to the total wealth of the system, but have begun to drain the resources of moderate-sized cities, towns, and villages. In many areas of the United States, for example, large hinterlands are far poorer, by many standards (except perhaps income), and far more economically and culturally dependent today than they were several decades ago. To take the hinterland of Boston as an example, each town once had a valuable social and cultural life. Lawrence had legitimate theaters with high-quality nightly performances; today, it has only shopping center moviehouses. Concord, the home of Henry David Thoreau, Ralph Waldo Emerson, Nathaniel Hawthorne, and Louisa May Alcott, had a vital and rich literary life; today, it is a suburb with historical houses visited by curious tourists. The cultural life of the region is concentrated in Boston, leaving nothing in these surrounding towns.

It is important to begin taking steps to regain a fuller life, with more personal control and greater access to varied information. Whether a settlement is in the middle of a hinterland or is a suburb of a metropolis, the agenda should be reconcentration, redistribution, and rediscovery of community – which means rediscovery of ourselves.

Reconcentration and nodality. Some of the design strategies discussed in Chapter 6 – those aimed at branching, expansion, and replication – call for the establishment of new nodes and reconcentration beyond old centers. These new hierarchies of centers must be reconstituted on existing public transportation corridors, or in such a way that transportation can be extended to the new centers. But reconcentration should be expanded alongside the key centers of employment, to residential areas.

We mentioned that the location process is based on residential land uses following the distribution of major employment centers. This should not be interpreted too literally, however; in reality, the world is far more complex. The cycles of change in employment and in housing do not overlap neatly; people may change employment but do not necessarily move to another dwelling unless their new job is located in another region of the country. In a spatial framework in which there is a combination of central and peripheral employment locations, the key to good residential location is proximity to transportation systems that make commuting distance and time reasonable. Thus, areas near highways and rapid-transit systems (trains, subways, express buses) are desirable residential locations of potentially high density and can become nodes with mixed land uses and small commercial centers.

Finding opportunities for nodality in residential areas and developing potential centers into actual ones are major tasks of community design. In undeveloped areas, this concentration should be accompanied by experimentation with new residential patterns; for example, "villages" should be revitalized as an environment for those searching for small communities in rural areas, with zero lot line, party-wall two-family houses, and other clustered options. In developed areas, reconcentration could take several paths – for example, the creation of mixed-use centers out of obsolete shopping centers (as mentioned in Chapter 7), with community facilities and housing – some of them on air rights – or out of isolated school buildings. This strategy could be extended to many other clustering opportunities: around churches, libraries, town halls, and post offices, located in isolated road intersections.

Planning new centers. Reconcentration and the achievement of nodality must aim at the distribution of nonnested hierarchies of competitive and complementary centers. To some designers this creates a dilemma: How can one plan what should be eminently spontaneous? The fact that this question is being asked at all is evidence that an understanding of urban systems has been gained. Indeed, many centers in urban areas were not "planned" in the strict sense of the word, which gave them a special vitality that helped disguise some of their rough edges. In its simplest form, planning for distribution is basically finding strategic locations in the urban pattern. For complementary centers, it is easy to define areas of influence and center size. For competitive centers, a thorough design involves fairly complex iterations in which alternative locations and sizes are proposed and assessed in terms of their capacities to justify their size and their eventual growth. Alternatively, it is possible just to identify key locations and allow the urban development processes to operate in space within design guidelines.

Some locational characteristics of centers are important in assessing their capacity to create an area of influence, and transportation is foremost among them. Centers extend their influence to the surrounding area through movement – not merely geographic distance. Centers around mass-transit stations often operate on two scales: the metropolitan scale of the transit network and the pedestrian scale. The areas of influence of these centers may extend over part or most of the metropolitan area – for instance, to employment and major shopping areas – as well as a few blocks around them – to minor shopping areas and community facilities. Thus, we see the importance of a good pedestrian system for making a reality of the many potential hierarchical levels in a single center.

Centers located at road or street intersections or around highway ramps extend their area of influence along these thoroughfares, as a function of the potential travel speed of these thoroughfares: centers with access to highways may affect the metropolitan area, while those that abutt urban streets have more local effects. It is extremely important to provide a good pedestrian system in these cases in order to "civilize" the automobile and establish urban precincts with pedestrian networks.

Another locational characteristic critical to centers – or at least to those that do not draw exclusively from a regional area of influence – is sufficient density. The latter ensures a level of urbanity and pedestrian movement that can easily be grafted to other scales and transportation modes. The reconcentration of densities around centers is a prime strategy for reducing the sterility of typical highway-oriented nodes.

Finally, the location of centers may take into consideration the need (or lack thereof) to create bridges with neighboring communities, as we proposed in Chapter 7. When the functions and levels of a center are clearly local, centers should be located internally, within the community. But in many other cases, either because it is socially important to create bridges or simply financial common sense, boundary locations may be desirable.

A design strategy aimed at reconcentration is ultimately aimed at reconquering civilization as the culture of cities, in communities alive with complex hierarchies of diverse centers.

PART FOUR

*Which deals with the lessons learned
from traditional settlements and
their applications to community design*

CHAPTER 10

MORPHOLOGY

Or the roots of design in traditional settlements

MORPHOLOGY

The urban form of traditional settlements, most of them of the popular tradition, but also a few produced by elite designers in preindustrial times, is rooted in pervasive factors that shape physical organizations and spaces. We can say that the "design" of traditional settlements sprung from the morphology of the problem – morphology being the science of form, or of the various factors that govern and influence form. Traditional settlements have been so consistently shaped by morphological factors that their "designers" appear to have acted as channels for them. As facilitators or interpreters of powerful telluric forces, they repeatedly chose the same solutions throughout the world – for example, high ground or strategic crossroads as key sites for settlements.

The morphology of traditional settlements has its roots in the physical characteristics of a site as they interface with the requirements of the social group. The key morphological factors can be grouped into four sets based on (1) the way in which nature and man-made features satisfy needs for protection and defense; (2) the way in which the physical and economic landscape allows for communication with other regions; (3) the way in which the topography of a site suggests the construction of a human settlement; and (4) the way in which climate leads to building solutions adapted to it. These four sets combine in various ways to explain major settlement typologies, land uses, densities, distributions, systematic organizations, and growth and change characteristics. Their influence on community form is not merely utilitarian; it is both cultural and spiritual. And it has greatly enriched human inheritance, for it has produced design solutions that have persisted for centuries.

There are three realms of interface between morphological factors and community form: physical, social-psychological and supernatural. The physical realm corresponds to the immediate level of utilitarian design solutions, such as locating a city on high ground for reasons of defense.

The genius of traditional societies was to have lifted utilitarian solutions to highly expressive levels and developed ancillary cultural interpretations and beliefs to ensure the validity of these solutions beyond their time and place. They did this by attaching to their design solutions values related to the social and psychological realm of the community. Solutions became symbolic and so much a part of the culture that they became "second nature" to the members of the community. For instance, high ground was valued long after it was no longer crucial for defense, being continuously reserved for the use of the elite (Figure 10.1). Even today in Washington, D.C., people say "up on the Hill" to refer to Congress.

Some design solutions were invested with magical, spiritual, and religious beliefs and values, embodying the highest symbols of the culture. For example, high ground evolved into the traditional site for religious buildings and sacred precincts (Figure 10.2)

Figure 10.1. High ground, sociopolitical use: Velez Blanco, village and sixteenth-century castle, Almeria, Spain. (Bernard Rudofsky)

These three realms constitute an integrated cosmology, and permanently affect one another: Utilitarian solutions affect patterns of behavior, which affect patterns of belief, which affect utilitarian responses and behavior. This integrated cosmology provides manifold rewards in terms of satisfaction, pleasure, gratification, and reassurance, ranging from community pride in the symbolism of the town's gates to divine protection from the temple. Reinforcement from each realm ensures the internal coherence of the cosmology and adjustment to new conditions.

In order to be accepted, a design solution must satisfy the social, psychological, and spiritual needs of the community. During the Agricultural and Urban Revolutions (from the eighth millennium B.C.) utilitarian responses to the physical

Figure 10.2. High ground, supernatural symbolism. (Top) Acropolis, Athens, fifth century B.C. (Bottom) San Miniato al Monte, Florence, 1075.

world took precedence and helped shape cultural values and beliefs. For example, the courtyard, a utilitarian response to hot climates, contributed to the development of lifestyles and social patterns, and acquired sacred connotations as the proper space to locate in front of temples.

After a time period which could take centuries, pragmatic solutions and cultural beliefs increasingly converged to form an integrated cosmology within which traditional societies evolved. Radical changes in design came only as a result of cultural, technological, and/or social changes; the community then made adjustments in its cosmology. For example, the creation of national states with new defense capabilities led to changes in the locations of buildings at the top of the political hierarchy: Royal palaces abandoned walled high grounds in capital cities for expansive sites in rural areas, from El Escorial to Versailles. Yet the new solutions preserved certain cultural elements; while El Escorial preserved the "wall" image of a fortress, the formal gardens of Versailles offered an expansive view of the landscape that recalled the commanding views from high ground and symbolized human power over nature – a belief that flourished in the baroque era (Figure 10.3).

The contrast between traditional and contemporary settlements could not be more striking. Compare Los Angeles with Paris; Houston with London; Detroit with Florence; and El Camino Real in California or Route 1 on the East Coast lined with discount stores, fast-food restaurants, and shopping malls, with the "Chemin Français" or "Camino de Santiago," the medieval pilgrimage route in Europe dotted with chapels, inns, charitable institutions, and elaborate stone crosses as landmarks. Cultural disintegration and loss of community building traditions in wealthy societies with advanced technologies have had appalling results.

The integrated cosmology of traditional societies has been replaced in our age with single-minded utilitarian objectives; utilitarian designs lacking any cultural value brutally simplify the physical environment in order to achieve "efficient" solutions. Morphological differences are eliminated – hills are bulldozed away, the climate is air-conditioned – along with our cultural symbols, behavior, and beliefs.

In the process, communities in some industrialized societies have lost the richness and rewards of a universe alive with symbols that fulfill our many psychological and spiritual needs. Their affluent residents have become unidimensional people desperately using their wealth to drown the anguish

Figure 10.3 (*facing page*). Change and continuity of cultural values. (Top) El Escorial, Madrid, 1572–84. Juan Bautista de Toledo and Juan de Herrera. The "wall." (Bottom) Palace and garden of Versailles, 1661–1708. Jules Hardouin Mansart and André le Notre. The "view." (French Government Tourist Office)

of standing alone, facing an incomprehensible universe without dimension or meaning. Their poor residents have lost the cultural frameworks that give meaning and support to traditional communities.

We shall now examine the four sets of morphological factors that have shaped traditional community design solutions: defense, transportation, topography, and climate.

DEFENSE AND PROTECTION: THE WALL

From the beginning of time, the threat of predatory animals and human enemies has led to the selection of easily defended settlement sites, such as caves or lake dwellings. We call this universal behavior "site plus," that is, taking advantage of the characteristics of a site as well as adding reinforcements to achieve safe ground. Two types of sites offer initial advantages for defense: those with water protecting part or all of the perimeter and those with steep slopes protecting all or part of the perimeter. Water and high ground, alone or in combination, are still highly valued for more than utilitarian reasons.

Among water sites, islands, of course, provide the ultimate protection. Venice was founded by tribes searching for safety from incursions by neighboring tribes. Tenochtitlan (the capital of the Aztec Empire) was also founded by a wandering tribe seeking safety from powerful neighbors (Figure 10.4, top). Other locations offer only partial defense. Sites on peninsulas and rivers are used to advantage when supplemented with the foremost man-made defense feature: the wall. Istanbul (the former Constantinople) is located on the Golden Horn overlooking the Strait of the Dardaneles with walls enclosing the otherwise exposed "flank." When Paris, originally an island on the Seine, expanded to the shores, it required the protection of walls (Figure 10.4, bottom).

The unique advantage of bodies of water is that they not only act as a barrier but are a channel for communication – essentially trade. Venice, Tenochtitlan, Istanbul, and Paris all developed into major commercial centers and, in the process, created a network of physical elements and institutions to facilitate trade: docks and bridges, boats and shipping companies, banks, shipyards, and merchants' quarters.

Among high-ground sites, peaks offer the ultimate protection because of the high cost of approaching them; they were selected for the location of hill towns from Tibet to Italy. Other locations with partial slopes require, in addition,

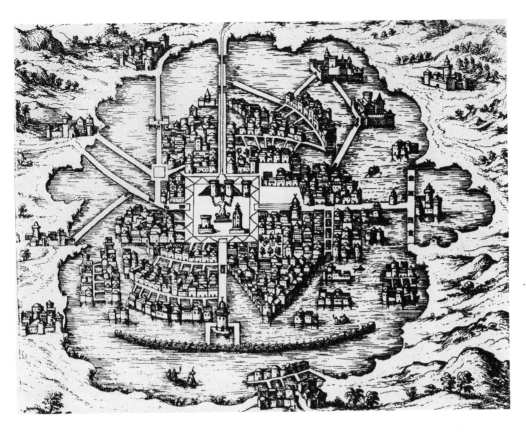

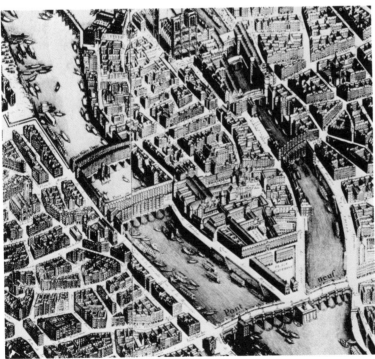

Figure 10.4. Water sites: islands, peninsulas, rivers. (Top) Tenochtitlan, capital of the Aztec Empire, sixteenth century, located on an island in Lake Texcoco. (Georg Braun, *Civitates Orbis Terrarum,* Cologne, 1576) (Bottom) Paris, 1739, the center and origin of the city on Ile de la Cité. (The New York Public Library, Map Division. Astor, Lenox and Tilden Foundations)

man-made protection; the artificial hill – the defense wall – establishes a vertical barrier between the settlement and the outside world. In Mt. Athos, Greece, some walls simply continued the defense provided by mountains. In other cases, as in Carcassonne, France, walls were the only "mountain" (Figure 10.5). As in port cities, devices invented to complement the barrier, most prominently the gate, the tower, and the moat, evolved into cultural symbols.

It is interesting to speculate that traditional builders developed design solutions based on natural examples. A moat translates a river or island into a man-made defense. A wall duplicates high ground. Water and high ground, in natural and artificial versions, were combined in a thousand and one forms to protect settlements.

These solutions, though effective, had a price. Walls were expensive to build and maintain; islands were limited in area. As a result, most traditional settlements were concentrated. Defense costs were not the only factor; there were also transportation costs, for example. Concentration itself provided some additional benefits: A tight pattern was easier to defend if an enemy managed to break through the walls. The "core" of the community, with its centers of power, was tightly set within the walls, whereas peasants and fishermen who lived in the surrounding regions were always ready to seek refuge there during times of conflict.

This type of urban system had limitations: Growth took place only by a conscious, community-wide decision after the space within the walls had been filled. In some cases, old walls were demolished and new ones built farther out, as in Vienna, Paris, and many other cities. In others, new walled precincts were built, as in Nancy or Fez, which were composed of two or more closely situated settlements, each built within its own walls (Figure 10.6).

These morphological factors eventually acquired symbolic value. Water and high ground have found meaning in most cultures as the most desirable characteristics of a site. Views of water and views from high ground have always been considered assets in community design and landscaping, as well as in real estate. How much of their desirability lies in their objective beauty and how much in atavistic remnants of their role as protection elements? When we command a view over the landscape, we experience not only a detached appreciation of its natural features, but also a powerful feeling that we are able to exert some control over that landscape, over who approaches it and over what is going on in it. Long after the

Figure 10.5. High ground and artificial hills. (Top) Monastery of Simon Petra, Athos, Greece, eleventh century. (Bernard Rudofsky) (Bottom) Carcassonne, France, thirteenth century.

217

defense role of high ground became obsolete, elite buildings and habitats continued to be designed with commanding views. In Versailles, nature was domesticated across acres of controlled gardens and placed under the eyes of the Sun King; in the crescents in England, bourgeois town houses, designed as palaces, were given the same visual control over the landscape (Figure 10.7).

Design solutions also became physical symbols that influenced attitudes. One of the most important contributions of settlements founded on water and/or high ground was the

Figure 10.6. Growth within walls. (Top) Paris. Central core: early Middle Ages; walls of c. 1180, 1370, 1676, 1784–91, and 1841–5. (S. E. Rasmussen, *Towns and Buildings,* MIT Press, 1969) (Bottom) Nancy. Old town on right; new town on left. (Edmund N. Bacon)

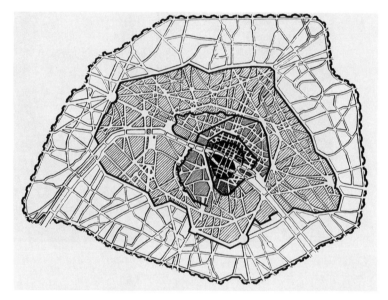

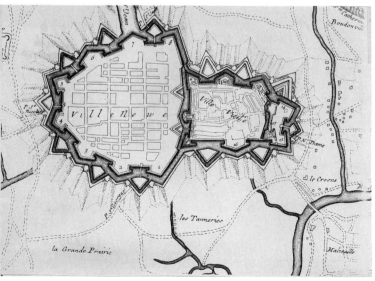

reinforcing of the division of the world into a "we" and a "they," the assignment of "turf," in a word, the establishment of a cosmology understandable in a threatening world.

The sense of enclosure provided by walls satisfies more than the need for physical protection; it provides psychological reassurance. Complementing it is the sense of anticipation and passage provided by entry gates. The combination of walls and gates enclosing, say, a courtyard, where it is possible to anticipate and experience a spatial sequence, to enjoy an outdoor space that is different from the outside space, to feel that one is in a "world" of its own, and from there to contemplate the building that is the final destination, is uniquely rewarding, no matter how often it is experienced (Figure 10.8).

This satisfaction originates, to a large degree, in the fact that these design elements carry powerful symbolic messages that we are able to understand and enjoy, much as we understand and enjoy a well-known and liked piece of music. Walls become more than brick and mortar; they are in effect boundaries between two worlds. Gates and doors become more than utilitarian openings; they are transitional elements allowing us to penetrate another world. Towers and campaniles become more than structures for observation; they are powerful landmarks guiding us to our destination. These design elements have such strong cultural connotations that they are even a part of our everyday expressions – like "a door to success," "a wall around our liberties," or "landmark legislation."

Communities on the water have also developed powerful cultural symbols, as well as memorable images, out of their

Figure 10.7. Visual control over the landscape: the royal crescent, Bath, 1767–75. John Wood II. (Marburg/Art Resource)

Figure 10.8. Anticipation, passage, and enclosure. (Top) Purmamarca, Jujuy, Argentina. Walled precinct and gate. (Middle) Forecourt with church at left and interior gate and upper court at right. (Bottom) Upper court, with church at left.

220

design solutions. Most are apprehended upon arrival at these cities, through the harbors, the city "gates." In Venice, the Piazza San Marco extends to the docks, and the campanile announces to incoming boats the presence of the city. On one's arrival, the city's power is magnificently displayed before one's eyes: first the temporal power of the doges with their palace and then the divine power of God with the basilica (Figure 10.9). Arrival at Lisbon is dramatic, with the Praca do Comercio edging on the Atlantic Ocean, as if the heart of the city were opened to the mystery of the sea beyond. And arriving at Istanbul by boat is a splendid experience, with the profile of the city in the background, every hill crowned by a mosque and minarets, the Golden Horn with its hundreds of ships and boats of all descriptions, and the Galata Bridge linking both sides in a constant stream of humanity.

If we compare any one of these arrivals with landing at the airport of most industrialized cities, we realize how impoverished our present experiences are. Except when the awesome power of a modern metropolis impresses us, as when we arrive in New York by boat, it is only at night, when the lights magically transform a city, or when nature offers an exceptional gate as it does in San Francisco, that "arrival" has any meaning left at all.

Design responses to morphological factors in traditional

Figure 10.9. Arrival by water: Venice, arrival at the *molo* of the Piazza San Marco by boat.

settlements have reached the level of the sacred in each culture. The sacredness of high ground is an almost universal feature of human culture: in the Greek temples on acropolises, the Mayan temples on pyramids, the Christian temples on hills. The idea extended far beyond the expedient use of a convenient site. If there was no high ground, people created some: *Temenos*, platforms, and pyramids were all erected for the deity. Reaching for the divine while leaving humans below, building a cosmological model with heaven above and earth below, was the climax of almost every culture. The symbolism extended to other design elements: Gates became processional thresholds marking the boundary between the human and divine realms, and courts became assembly spaces in front of restricted temples.

Have we succeeded in incorporating these morphological factors in the urban areas of our industrialized world? Not at all. Considering again the basic needs of defense, we are faced today with two very different threats. One is the threat of nuclear war, to which the only answer can be disarmament; the other is a new threat to which the tradition of community design – as well as systems analysis – has no answer: internal conflict. The industrialized metropolis, especially in the United States, is under internal siege as a result of social and racial conflict and the invisible – but very real – internal walls dividing social groups. Today's defenses are land use homogeneity and segregation, low density and dispersion – patterns dictated by elites that create social conflict and at the same time protect the elite and middle classes. The fractionalism typical of multiethnic capitalist cities has not been resolved and may not be as long as the tenets of a class- and race-based society are maintained.

Urban areas in the industrialized world also fail to provide cultural satisfaction beyond the most immediate and utilitarian objectives. It is true that sites near water and on high ground are prized, but their worth is measured monetarily, in terms of their real estate value. On the other hand, land is often violated whenever bulldozing can simplify construction operations and increase profits. Land has lost all but its monetary value, and how it is to be used is decided by individuals – not by communities. An example of the privatization of land, a common resource, is the pattern of development in settlements facing the sea. In fishing villages, the streets are often perpendicular to the seashore, and private dwellings are located on them; usually one can see the water from the streets, for they are veritable corridors to the beach

(Figure 10.10). By contrast, in resorts, a wall of high-rise hotels and apartments facing the sea blocks everyone else's view of the water.

The very important experiences of entry and enclosure are mostly absent today. Urban spaces tend to lack any modulation that establishes spatial measures and denotes turf. There are no walls – apart from mostly inert building façades – and no gates – apart from building doors. Exceptions, such as the small triumphal arch in Washington Square in the Greenwich Village area of New York, stand out in our mind not because they are intrinsically outstanding, but because they are the only ones we have. There is no sense of belonging, of arriving, of protection; there is no sense of spatial qualities. Urban space is homogenized, banal, and without beginning or end.

It is unfortunate that the very design tools that might have mitigated the internal divisiveness of our pluralistic society have been wholly forgotten. As mentioned in Chapter 7, the working-class ethnic neighborhood in Boston known as the North End felt threatened by plans to rebuild the elevated Central Artery underground. Residents believed that the removal of this "wall" would open up an influx of real estate ventures and hasten the process of gentrification, whereby they would lose their neighborhood and homes. They were placing their hopes for protection on a "wall" as people have for time immemorial. Though I neither advocate a romantic revival of historic urban forms nor believe that design can

Figure 10.10. Views as community resource: Cadaques, Catalonia, Spain. View of the harbor.

cure deep social ills, I think that community designs far more responsive to existing conditions and problems would go a long way toward civilizing the industrial city. We have a rich treasury of design solutions with symbolic values that speak of turf definition, of protection, of leaving and entering, of areas for everyday activities, and of areas for special rituals.

TRANSPORTATION AND COMMUNICATIONS: THE CROSSROADS

Whether harbors for settlements on shore or roads for settlements in a hinterland, transportation crossroads are vital for the survival of a community. Harbors enable one to reach far-away lands and to create opportunities for trade, which in turn allow port cities to monopolize trade in their own hinterland. Inland cities sometimes develop a similar privileged position if they are located at the crossroads of several regional roads, especially if one of these is on a continental trade route. Transportation systems are truly the lifelines of a settlement, and their locations at strategic intersections and transfer points greatly increase their economic, and eventually political, capacity. Transfer points, such as bridges, harbors, mountain passes, and route crossings, are natural locations for settlements.

The physical and economic determinants of regional and continental trade have influenced communication channels throughout history, with different technological and political conditions. Old caravan routes and shipping lanes were powerful factors that helped to shape the various cultures that successively occupied the same region; this resulted in layers of historical settlements living at the same basic crossroads, adapting to evolving technology and markets. Only with the advent of a radically new technology – such as steamships, railroads, or airplanes – or with a radically new political situation – such as the closing of the land routes to Asia by the Ottoman Empire – were age-old crossroads truly affected, bringing life or death to settlements.

What had been a road in the countryside became a civilized street in an urban area. Indeed, streets are the foremost urban invention; they combine in one spatial vessel movement and space, through traffic and local activities, and access to dwellings, workplaces, and temples (Figure 10.11). Most spatial urban inventions derive from the concept of street. Main Street is simply the urbanized section of a regional road, where commercial activities concentrate along a linear spine.

224

Processional routes such as the Via Sacra in Rome are streets serving religious areas and are laden with symbolic meaning. Plazas, which developed out of the magnificent idea of creating a centripedal space for people, are the result of widening one block of urban street and changing its linear orientation (Figure 10.12). In the United States crossroads are sometimes emphasized in what are called squares, which are not squares or plazas at all, but intersections where commercial activities are clustered around vehicular and pedestrian flows intermixing in a dynamic way. Indeed, the "crossroads" is the center of town, the marketplace of goods and ideas; this location has taken many different spatial forms, from the common in New England towns to the plaza of southern European towns.

The invention of the street had very important implications. The space of a street is never banal, is never left over or undefined space, but because of the tightness of the urban pattern demanded by defense needs and high transportation costs, buildings and open space – including streets – shaped a mutually defined gestalt. This does not mean that all streets are restricted; quite the contrary. Some, like the boulevards of Paris, the Mall in London, and multiple other versions of avenues, alamedas, and paseos, can be generously wide. These wide streets were very consciously designed as such to offer a striking contrast with other streets, and thus to be perceived as even wider and more magnificent. The traditional settlement is a world of measure, some spaces having a large scale because others have a small scale, but in every case it is possible to define the limits of even the most majestic areas. It is precisely the sense of measure, the recognition that large spaces must be bounded in order to be magnificent, and that even the sense of infinity must be controlled, that characterizes traditional settlements.

The balance between buildings and streets, between center and roads resulted in several urban typologies, the logical conclusion of the interplay of morphological factors. The road that passed through small settlements overwhelmed any possibility of a center, resulting in linear villages; examples include Japanese rural villages and the small towns of the midwestern United States, though they can be found in many other areas of the world. In contrast, the centers of larger settlements clustered around crossroads or of settlements located near a barrier to land routes (water or mountains) were far more important than their roads – which in fact were transformed into streets (Figure 10.13).

Today, transportation remains one of the most important morphological factors in shaping settlements. And yet in our impoverished culture, the function of roads has been reduced to the purely utilitarian one of transporting people and goods. Today, what should be streets have been changed back into roads without spatial measure, or scale, or capacity to encourage urban activities around them, in a reversion of the

Figure 10.11. Streets. (Top) Village in Extremadura, Spain. (Bottom) Gothic quarters, Barcelona. (Opposite top) Cuzco, Peru. (Opposite bottom) Beacon Hill, Boston.

civilization process. Regardless of the technology involved, urban areas are changing back into dispersed clusters developed along roads. A historical search for a case approximating this primitive (nonurban) kind of settlement reveals a similar situation among Mayan peasants who were clustered in no particular order along roads radiating from ceremonial centers. Archaeologists are still debating whether these settle-

ments can legitimately be called urban. Most see them as a grouping of peasants around a rarified elite compound.

The impoverishment of cultural values and the urban community ideal has greatly eroded the concept and viability of urban centers, resulting in a growing imbalance between center and roads, with the roads assuming increasing importance and the centers becoming obsolete. The industrialized U.S. metropolis, in particular, is rapidly adopting this pattern on a large scale. Strip development – commercial or industrial along highways, and suburban tracts – is the industrial-world version of the linear village or Main Street.

One of the major problems here is the incompatibility of

Figure 10.12. Plazas. (Top left) Piazza del Campo, Siena. (Top right) Piazza San Marco, Venice. (Bottom left) Plaza Mayor, Trujillo, Spain. (Bottom right) Main plaza, Cuzco, Peru.

a simple typology (the linear village) with large urban areas. Another problem is the erosion of cultural symbols and their corresponding urban activities; streets are being replaced by utilitarian roads, and the social role of urban spaces for peoples' encounters is being replaced by instant communication. Main Street is nothing more than a memory, and with the loss of the concept of the urban street we have lost the concept of community.

SITE TOPOGRAPHY

The topography of a site is, in addition to the defense considerations mentioned earlier, a major morphological factor. Interestingly, topography in most cases favors the same site characteristics as defense. High ground – important for protection – is also excellent from the point of view of drainage and public health; and it saves agricultural land.

Since their beginnings, towns have relied on the production of agricultural surplus in the immediate area to support the urban activities of craftspeople and traders, as well as soldiers and priests. Historically, agricultural land was the

Figure 10.13. The road and the settlement. (Left) Village in Japan: the linear village. (Bernard Rudofsky) (Right) Piazza del Popolo, Rome: urban streets. Nolli's map, 1748. (MIT Press)

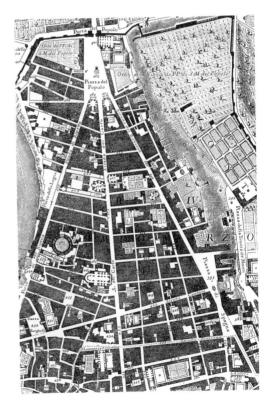

most important resource and settlements were planned to preserve it; if there was an agricultural plain, the settlement was located on rocky hills over the valley. The Incas developed daring agricultural terraces out of mountain slopes and located towns, such as the famed Macchu Picchu, at the very top (Figure 10.14).

The topographical advantages of high ground led to the development of various high-ground settlement typologies. One of them is the well-known hill town, examples of which can be found all over Italy, Spain, and other countries where dwellings are built on the slopes of hills, some streets running parallel to the topographical contours and others ascending via a series of stairs. The display of a hill town's buildings as if there were a gigantic tapestry spread across the hill and the breathtaking views commanded from almost every place in town are assets difficult to match in other settlements (Figure 10.15).

Another high-ground typology is that of cave dwellings. For most people today, caves connote prehistoric settlements, with the probable exception of the legendary Mao Tse-Tung caves in Hunan, which were developed into complex communities. But even now there are a large number of cave villages and towns in southern Europe and other regions of

Figure 10.14. Agricultural land and settlements: Machu Picchu, Peru.

the world. Gypsies in southern Spain prefer cave dwellings, many of which have elaborate façades to make them look like conventional houses (Figure 10.16). One of the most fascinating hilltown–cave settlements is Matera, in southern Italy. It is a medium-sized town composed of two areas: a conventional town on a plateau and cave dwellings developed down a cliff overlooking an impressive valley. The elite buildings (church, municipality, and hotel) are located on the plateau, where a vibrant social life takes place on Main Street; the caves are reserved for dwellings and ancillary workshop spaces, served by pathways with steps developed on the side of the cliff.

Figure 10.15. Hill towns. (Top) Village in Morocco. (Bottom) Matera, Italy.

231

The cultural value and symbolism of high ground is expressed in many ways. Take, for example, the Campidoglio in Rome, an open space where civic uses have been clustered for a long time because of the Campidoglio's preeminent position overlooking the city. When Michelangelo was commissioned to redesign it, he sought its morphological roots and brought utilitarian solutions to highly expressive levels. The staircase connecting the lower level with the Campidoglio became a magnificent physical expression of the topography of the site, and the plaza itself was designed as a trapezoid to accentuate its depth to those arriving from the staircase. In turn, the view of Rome is masterfully framed by the two civic buildings on each side (Figure 10.17).

The wise use of a site is not limited to the use of high ground. Fishing villages offer countless examples of how to make the best use of a site. Cadaques, a fishing village on the Mediterranean coast of Catalonia in Spain, is a classical type with narrow streets lined with dwellings going uphill from the beach (see Figure 10.10). The island of Thera, also in the Mediterranean, is a composite type with a lower harbor village and an upper high-ground village that offers a rich variety of vistas and spatial experiences out of proportion to its small size and poor economy.

Design responses to the morphological conditions of a site can have striking results even in the poorest of environments: the desert. Of course, oases are obvious sites for settlements as well as for limited cultivation and grazing, as in the many oasis towns in the Sahara. Sometimes, however, people ex-

Figure 10.16. Caves in southern Spain.

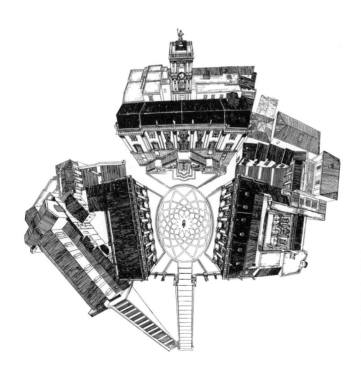

Figure 10.17. Exaltation of high ground. (Top) Capitoline Hill, before Michelangelo's work. (Bottom) Piazza di Campidoglio, 1538. Michelangelo Buonarotti. (Drawings by J. H. Aronson)

233

cavated down from the floor of the desert to create one of the most imaginative types of settlements: A square open space was dug several dozen feet below ground level, and around it layers of caves were excavated from the sides of the main space. The floor of the excavated space could be used for cultivation, while the microclimate of the community was greatly tempered by the surrounding earth. These extraordinary settlements – cave dwellings without hills or cliffs, but with water and protection from the sun in the middle of the desert – were built with primitive technology!

The most outstanding design solutions in the desert, the Arabian and Persian gardens, are paradises in the middle of hell. Within walls erected to protect the gardens from the desert, the Middle Eastern and Mediterranean cultures created their own world with water canals, trees and flowers, birds and tamed animals, gazebos and verandahs – the Garden of Eden repeated one thousand and one times, from the deserts of India to the arid zones of Spain, and duplicated across southern Europe and Latin America. They were designed on a large scale for palaces and on a small scale for simple dwellings, demonstrating that all members of the society had a common cultural identity. They were the sites of such civilized behavior as ritual cleansing with water, and they were places of respite for the weary travelers. These gardens were (and are) such powerful cultural patterns that they are often found in nonarid climates. The Palace of the Alhambra, near Granada in Spain, for instance, is built on high ground in a fertile area and includes a number of interior courts designed as symbolic gardens (Figure 10.18).

The contrast between those traditional settlements and today's is great. It extends beyond the current urbanization of good agricultural land just because it is level and thus cheap to build on, the pollution of water resources, and the brutal simplification of earth forms. Today, there is a pervasive lack of community consciousness regarding the earth – the need, as well as the convenience, of locating settlements according to site morphology. Most of all, there is a lack of social and professional imagination: Apartment buildings are not as seductive as hill towns, and the ubiquitous "landscaped" areas are pitiful compared with the powerful and poetic Persian gardens.

CLIMATE

As in the case of other morphological factors, traditional settlements worked with the local climate, not against it; each

culture found a way of turning climatic liabilities into assets.
In the process, their designs were raised to highly expressive
levels and often became cultural elements with symbolic
meaning. In addition, their concern with microclimate fostered protoscientific observations; the laws of Indies, which
provided the planning guidelines for the establishment of
settlements all over America, included careful public health
considerations such as orientation of buildings and streets in
relation to the sun and the prevailing winds.

The aim was, in every case, the creation of suitable mi-
croclimates within the settlement and within dwellings and
other buildings. Thus, climate and design interacted on various scales, permitting coherent solutions at the community
level as well as at private levels. A few typologies became
institutionalized across regions with similar climates, and
they in turn influenced local cultures through the lifestyles
they fostered. To provide some examples, I will briefly discuss design solutions in hot and dry, hot and humid, cold,
and rainy climates.

Hot and dry climates, in which temperatures are very
high during the day and very low at night, are typical of
desert regions. The traditional design solution is a combination of massive solid walls plus interior courts with
water and vegetation – the gardens in the desert that we
just mentioned. The massive walls absorb heat during the
day, keeping the rooms cool, and release heat during the
night, warming up the spaces. In this way, they perform a
sophisticated daily heat storage function with very simple
technology. In addition, streets are made narrow to keep
out the sun, and often main market streets are shaded with
awnings or trellises, which give the light in these urban
spaces an almost magical quality (Figure 10.19). Some designs actually create breezes through rooms, as in the famous vertical windscoops of Hyderabad with their
magnificent profiles on the roofs of buildings.

Hot and humid climates are typical of tropical regions.
They are characterized by hot days and nights aggravated by
permanent high humidity – which negates much of the effect
of the human transpiration system – plus heavy rainy seasons.
The traditional solution is based on very light walls; a high
percentage of their surface is open for ventilation, so that
rooms can capture the slightest breezes – the only relief for
the human body. Louvers, trellises, balconies, and verandahs
are typical of tropical countries.

In cold climates, design solutions are intended to pre-

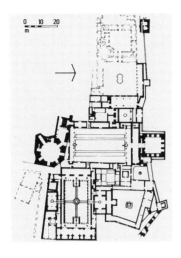

Figure 10.18. The Garden
of Eden on earth. (Left)
The Alhambra Palace,
Granada, 1250–1500. Plan.
(Thames and Hudson Ltd.)
(Right) Court of Myrtles,
with Hall of Ambassadors
at end. (Dr. Jonathan
Drachman) (Bottom)
Generalife Gardens. (Dr.
Jonathan Drachman)

serve heat and to draw as much additional heat as possible from outside sources. As a result, settlements and buildings are very compact, closed to the winter winds, and open to the winter sun. Compact forms (see Chapter 6) minimize the surface-to-volume ratio thus reducing heat loss. Rooms are clustered around fireplaces and kitchens, and fenestration opens to the sunny orientation. In many rural areas, villagers combined several objectives into one, by building stables on the ground floor and their living quarters on the second floor; in this way, the heat of the

Figure 10.19. Covered streets, Fez, Morocco. (Top) Covered retail street. (Bottom) Covered market.

animals rose to the living area, while the animals were protected from predators.

In rainy climates, design solutions exist mainly at the community level, since rain is a problem only after one leaves one's house. Arcades, covered walkways or markets, overhangs, and similar devices not only protect pedestrians but create powerful urban images. The arcades of so many European and Latin American towns are both a civilized response to rainfall and a visual device for framing streets and unifying plazas; the many variations of street arcades indicate the richness with which this idea was developed on both sides of the Atlantic (Figure 10.20). In a particular case, pedestrians were even protected from water when crossing streets: In Pompei's famous crosswalks, stone walkways were installed between sidewalks with two deep cuts to permit carts to pass through.

Each of these design elements acquired important symbolic value and became a central component of its culture. The very image of a culture's lifestyles owes much to its design responses to climate: The Englishman seated by his fireplace at home or relaxing in a shady verandah in India are vivid examples.

In today's industrial cities, and even in many Third World countries where cultural imitation is practiced, all this has been brutally simplified with considerable loss of lifestyle and identity. Money and technology – that deadly combination – have made air-conditioning universal, and in the process have homogenized cultures and regions in the same bland mixture of consumerist fashion for export. This simplistic approach has many other shortcomings: Air-conditioning is energy wasteful, is highly vulnerable to breakdown, and is in need of continuous maintenance; moreover, it is a cause of poor health, because the human body cannot rapidly adjust to the sharp changes in temperature that one experiences on going from an air-conditioned room into the environment, and vice versa. This is one more factor contributing to the destruction of cultural elements and lifestyles and to the unnecessary separation of human beings from the real environment. And yet even in industrialized metropolises, we might experience on a hot day a claustrophobic ride in a badly ventilated subway, followed by a dash across a steamy, busy street and into a gigantic lobby of a skyscraper chilled by air-conditioning to arctic levels. In the winter, rain and snow make pedestrians miserable. I am not advocating an anti-

Figure 10.20 (*facing page*). Arcaded streets. (Top left and right) Zafra, Spain. (Middle left) Jujuy, Argentina. (Middle right) Santiago de Compostela. (Bottom) Garrovillas, Spain (Bernard Rudofsky)

technology approach, but a right-technology approach. Community design must reduce its reliance on purely technological solutions and learn how to work with morphological factors again.

CHAPTER II

PLURALISTIC FORM OF TRADITIONAL COMMUNITIES

Or combination and interface

COMMUNITY FORM AS COMBINATORIAL FORM

An urban community is the product of many wills joined together to achieve common goals. Regardless of internal conflicts, which always exist in a social group, a community should be – and always was in the past – a pluralistic enterprise reflected in a pluralistic form. This pluralistic form is the veritable footprint of the society that inhabits the community.

The physical form of a community is one of the highest cultural expressions of the society, and as such it translates social structure, lifestyle, and values into buildings and spaces, into the physical vessel in which the community lives and evolves. This correlation between physical form and society is well known to archaeologists and anthropologists, who take the spatial organization of settlements and their ancillary artifacts as a point of departure in studying cultures. Whether a settlement is a work of social art or a chaotic heap depends to a large degree on the society's cultural values. Thus, it is very important for community designers to be aware that settlements should be the product not of individual wills, but of communities striving toward agreed-upon objectives.

The pluralistic nature of community form is a basic concept in community design, for two reasons. First, it makes the designer an interpreter and catalyst of the community, as well as of the morphological factors that shape the community. Second, it makes the designer an agent of change when anti-community values threaten the destruction or debasement of a community. Community design cannot be passive or oblivious to the complex range of social and morphological demands. It must be in a position to collect and distill many factors as well as to challenge questionable cultural tendencies. It should attend primarily to the systematic forces that underlie urban form and not only to the final outcome itself, which is often elusive and beyond control.

Yet after laying some much needed theoretical groundwork, we are left with some very pragmatic questions. How did traditional settlements organize their community forms, forms that we admire so much for their aesthetic values? Can we transfer their "métier" into our present practice? In the professionalization of community design, one suspects some tools and approaches were lost.

Most cities, towns, and villages are fundamentally urban patterns, that is, combinations of urban typologies, as discussed in Chapter 3. In small settlements, urban elements combined in simple patterns; in cities, additional elements were woven into the tapestry of built forms and open spaces. But in all cases, the forms of settlements were based on patterns that combined urban typologies – some repetitive, some unique; some continuous, some discrete.

The successful development of patterns has been based on a very simple but sophisticated concept, common across cultures and regions: Patterns consist of urban elements combined according to laws; these combinatorial laws originate from the nature (capabilities and limitations) of the elements, as well as the requirements of the pattern formed by these elements. To borrow from biology, urban patterns are the result of "design genes," which determine the characteristics of the organization. A successful typology contains an inherent "genetic" design code, which guides the process of combination, the appearance of new elements, and, eventually, the generation of patterns.

Traditional settlements have a rich range of urban typologies and combinatorial laws, each element carrying an inherent design code to guide the aggregation of units. The small size of most traditional settlements allowed them to use a simple but effective process for developing pluralistic forms through combination. (The far larger and complex postindustrial metropolis would require more complex design codes.) For purposes of discussion, three kinds of design codes will be examined. In the first case, the built form, the physical structure of the element is paramount, resulting in codes that guide combination through the structural characteristics of the element. In the second case, the spatial organization is paramount, resulting in codes that guide combination through the spatial characteristics of the element. In the third case, the design codes respond to a mixture of both structural and spatial characteristics. Regardless of approach, the individual building carries the seeds of the pattern, which, in turn, carries constraints on and possibilities for individual buildings.

Structural design codes. Barrel-vault villages on the island of Thera in Greece are an example of a structural design code. The roofs of the houses are stone barrel vaults, which give the villages' roofscapes the texture of a three-dimensional tapestry. The vaults' structural characteristics require solid load-bearing side walls, while end walls can be fairly open. This structural constraint guides the combination of rooms to form dwelling units, and of dwellings to form urban blocks, organized in predictably rectangular grids. In addition, the morphological demands of defense and climate led to a solution in which the living floor starts at the second level, which provides protection and a way to catch fresh breezes, while the first floor is used primarily for storage. Exterior stairs leading to the living floor complete the dwelling typology (Figure 11.1, p. 244).

The vernacular "trulli" villages in Alberobello are another example of a structural design code. Buildings with conical stone roofs required footprints of partly curved masonry walls to support the roofs, which led to community patterns governed by roof structure (Figure 11.1, p. 245).

Sometimes a structural design code is weak or contradictory, and "mutant," ill-formed community patterns spring up, as is often the case today in many downtown areas. There, the objective is to maximize the size of office buildings in order to increase profits. Several parcels are assembled, and the building is made as high as possible (the size being feasible because of air-conditioning and elevators). The "prestige," derived in private offices from "having a window," dictates that windows be installed on all sides, allowing higher rents. Each building demands freedom from party walls, and in order to add the maximum number of floors, a façade setback is often provided, resulting in leftover space by the sidewalk. Thus, the pattern is reduced to a nominal grid where buildings are grouped without structural (or spatial) relationships, and streets are merely functional channels without enclosures, since each façade is discontinuous and set at a different plane. The lack of suitable design codes in office buildings has a negative impact on the pattern of the central city.

In postulating new office typologies, we must realize that

a design code is not, strictly speaking, structural; it is also physical. High-rise frames impose few constraints. In some office types, a decision to extend the amenity of windows to all employees would lead to a reduction in floor size and thus, to the possibility of party walls; this would reconstitute the façade plane along the street. In other types, buildings could be articulated over larger parcels, shaping urban open spaces – with height or density incentives – in the tradition of French places or British crescents. In yet other types, light and view amenities could be provided through atriums within much larger structures; their size would dictate being surrounded by lower buildings, much as in the case of spatial recursion of a building in a space surrounded by buildings (see Figure 3.4). Better urban typologies and patterns demand the participation of the public sector in establishing the parameters for design codes; eventually, this would reduce speculative land values – the biggest obstacle to good community design – to more realistics levels.

Figure 11.1. Structural design codes (Bernard Rudofsky) (Right) Barrel-vault village, Apanomeria, Thera. (Opposite) "Trulli" village, Alberobello, Apulia.

Spatial design codes. In Mayan villages, each "dwelling" is really a small residential precinct surrounded by walls enclosing a number of rooms and interior courtyards. These are a particularly good example of a spatial design code. They are combined with other residential precincts along village roads in a system of walls and gates that define a rich hierarchy of public and private spaces. Included in each residential precinct are buffer and reserve spaces allowing for the growth of each dwelling, thus separating the public and private dynamic processes of the village. Growth and change in the domestic precinct take place independently of that at the community level, which is characterized by the addition or subtraction of whole residential units (Figure 11.2).

Better known examples are the courthouse and the town house (party-wall house), widespread residential types whose

combinations are guided by spatial design codes. In the courthouse, the rooms are located around one (or more) patios, allowing three of the four walls to be demising walls with other courthouses, which results in a compact grid pattern with streets defined by walls and domestic private open spaces within each dwelling (see Figure 3.16, bottom). The town house faces front and back to open spaces (front and back yards) while party walls separate it from other units, resulting in a compact lineal pattern with streets defined by either front yards or front façades; private back yards are behind every house, sometimes served by service alleys. Choices affecting the key design elements of this residential type – lot width, relationship between rooms and domestic open space, privacy level, access, and demising walls – influence the total pattern, which, in turn, establishes constraints on and possibilities for each town house, including orientation (see Figure 3.16, top).

Like structural design codes, spatial design codes are sometimes weak, leading to poor community patterns, such as roadside strip developments. These are highly simplified, purely utilitarian zones whose objective is to attract patrons in automobiles to stores, restaurants, and motels. Buildings are surrounded by parking lots, and huge signs are located at the many curb cuts that interrupt the highway. Traffic hazards, environmental degradation, and a nomadic lifestyle

Figure 11.2. Spatial design codes: Mayan dwelling precinct, Yucatán.

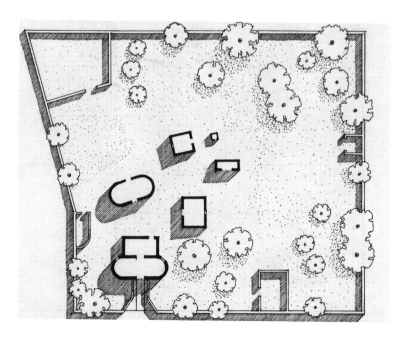

are their by-products. Space, which should have been a critical element in their design, is forgotten. Each business abuts another, but together they do not establish a pattern – they are instead a noncommunity of buildings as a parallel to a noncommunity of people.

As mentioned before, we need to reconsider the design codes of large-scale auto-oriented strips. When businesses catering to automobile patronage are justifiable, they must have a powerful design code to guide their combination along the road. Historical precedents, such as caravanseries, are of limited value; camels and mules can be "stored" more efficiently than cars. Several factors must be considered: the need to enclose turfs and establish landmarks in seemingly infinite parking lots, to denote and distinguish entries, to civilize parking lots through pavement materials and grids of trees over grids of cars, to disaggregate the activities in pavilions within the new "garden with cars," and to humanize pedestrian paths. The public sector has a major role in establishing design codes through new zoning and guidelines for suitable roadside clusters.

Structural/spatial design codes. Sometimes both structural and spatial design codes are followed, as in the Matmata villages in the Sahara, where rooms are built several stories high in rows and laid out in quadrangles around an internal court or plaza. Outside walls form the village's defense wall. Unlike the Thera and Mayan examples, the Matmata settlement is a closed form that, once completed, does not allow further expansion. This is an example of a tight relationship between form and size as discussed in Chapter 6. When the enclosure is completed, the size limit of the village has been reached, and the only alternative is to spawn a new urban form, which is exactly what the Matmatas do: They begin a new sister village (Figure 11.3).

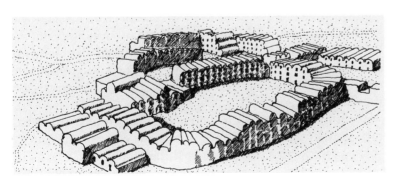

Figure 11.3. Structural/ spatial design codes: Matmata village, Gorfa, Tunisia. Barrel-vault units laid out around a central court.

247

Although this design code places an inflexible limit on growth, it has certain advantages. One is the use of the dwellings' exterior walls for defense – a favorite device of popular builders. The greatest advantage is the combination of individual rooms into a pluralistic form that can stand on its own in the middle of the desert, while creating on a human scale a protected "world" for the community. Furthermore, the inherent need to spawn new villages prohibits growth beyond this very necessary, intimate human scale and creates the potential for a hierarchy of communities – a wise approach for civilizing a desert.

Focusing our comments on size-limiting design codes, we might note that there are many cases that would benefit from a growth limit and a mechanism for spawning new precincts – chief among them the sprawling office parks that merge along highways, in random aggregations without hierarchies, centers, or boundaries. Clearly, one has to question such wholesale dispersion of employment along roads, as has already been discussed. My recommendation to cluster them in exurban centers around public transportation nodes would naturally establish an internal order, hierarchy, and size limit.

There might be cases in which auto-oriented employment areas were acceptable. Combined design codes limiting their size would have to be part of their built typology. The location and size of parking garages would determine the range of pedestrian access to potential office buildings. The location of urban amenities such as restaurants, stores, and health clubs, forming a social and spatial nucleus, would establish a physical core. The definition of open-space buffers would establish the spatial limits of office parks. As in the previous proposals, the public sector would have to ensure the new design codes through zoning and design guidelines – consistent with regional policies justifying such centers.

Combinatorial form. Combinatorial form is based on design control at two levels: the level of urban elements and the level of combinatorial laws. The latter laws establish the relationships among the elements and between the elements and the total pattern, which allow designers to concentrate on urban elements and relationships, and not necessarily on the final form.

Community design can be conceptualized as a combinatorial game, with pieces, moves, specific effects, and general rules within which players make different choices. The game institutionalizes a systematic understanding of urban communities, allowing adjustments, pluralism, and randomness; it also permits designers to focus on patterns as well as to learn from the experiences of earlier stages of development.

Combinatorial design, however, is not a linear process without concern for the totality. As we know, the size of an urban system imposes limitations on urban form, and thresholds force changes in structure, in technology, or even in the spawning of a new system. Large size and thresholds are critical in today's urban areas, whether in the developed or underdeveloped world. As size increases, there must be feedback between the parts and the whole to ensure satisfactory rearrangement. In the process, some elements combine in increasingly larger aggregations – dwellings, buildings, blocks, precincts; others emerge at given size thresholds – highways, mass transit, central areas – changing the nature of the urban pattern (Figure 11.4).

INTERFACE OF ELEMENTS IN PATTERNS

The combinatorial process places urban elements in special relationships with one another and with the totality. In the combinatorial process, elements and combinatorial laws are subject to direct control, but the specific way in which elements interact generates a second wave of effects. Interface between elements, their contact surfaces and areas, and their mutual definitions are key to community design. Individual buildings are often less important than the relationships they form in the urban pattern.

Recalling the three dualities that characterize urban patterns (see Chapter 3), it is clear that interaction plays a prime role. In the case of unbuilt space–built form, one defines the other in a gestalt that is a three-dimensional interface. Continuous–discrete events define each other through scale. In the case of repetitive–unique events, one defines the other through contrast. In each duality, elements are defined relatively against their opposite: open space defines buildings, and vice versa; a building is unique compared with the surrounding buildings; and so on.

Unbuilt space–built form interface. The interface of urban elements played a major role in traditional settlements, being responsible for the creation of some of the most successful man-made environments. Starting with the duality of unbuilt space–built form, the interface between exterior spaces and buildings constitutes one of the highest priorities for community design, since some of the most basic urban typologies emerge from it.

There are two broad "families" of urban space, each leading to radically different environments, relationships with buildings, and use. The first family, that of streets and plazas, includes all urban spaces defined by buildings and closely interfacing with building façades. These spaces are used for pedestrian, as well as vehicular, movement and social activities: This is the "tidal zone" of urban areas, to borrow an ecological term. In this intermediate zone of streets and plazas, riders become pedestrians, private and public worlds meet, and myriad activities occur (see Figures 10.11 and 10.12).

The second family, that of parks, includes open, smaller-scale versions of the natural world domesticated for recreational use – the "lungs" of settlements. Here urban size plays

Figure 11.4. Urban thresholds: Port Authority Bus Terminal and related access–exit highways. (Port Authority of New York and New Jersey)

an important role: Small settlements surrounded by fields have no need for parks. Small towns and villages have only streets and plazas. But larger cities need – and invented – parks, a threshold element determined by size.

The relationship between unbuilt space and built form is very different in the two families of open space. In the case of streets and plazas, there is a much closer interaction between building and open space, a "nearness" that shapes façade details; the use of open space can be very active and is based on human beings relating to one another. In the case of parks, there is a rather detached interaction between building and open space, a broad spatial definition based on views from a distance. The use of open space is generally more passive, based as it is on human beings relating to nature.

Design hybrids have characteristics of both families. For example, wide urban boulevards with generous tree-lined gardens are clearly defined by building façades along which pedestrians promenade and vehicles circulate, but include green areas suitable for the kinds of recreation found in parks. They may be virtually linear parks. Some public parks in large cities were enjoyed for many decades as the place to promenade on Sundays. Promenading was a social function that urbanites conducted in established routes through parks such as the Bois de Boulogne in Paris or Central Park in New York. This ceremonial function, one of great symbolic value, is another victim of the cultural trend away from community-based interaction.

Many urban typologies emerge from this interdefinition between unbuilt space and built form. In the first place, urban spaces are almost always defined by vertical closures, indicating the critical role of building mass and façade in defining urban space. Urban spaces can also have horizontal closures – roofs – as do the open markets of Fez or Marrakesh, which constitute veritable community halls (see Figure 10.19). Furthermore, views can be framed by streets, closed in by plazas, or open as in some parks. Proportion and scale offer a wide range of combinations, from narrow alleys at the domestic level to wide boulevards at the urban level. Spatial tendencies vary from the concentric and even static space of self-contained medieval plazas to the dynamic and even processional space of baroque creations such as the place at Nancy.

In summary, what is the contemporary experience in designing the critical interface between buildings and urban spaces? Downtown streets are being destroyed by façade setbacks and leftover so-called plazas in front of office towers.

Suburban streets are single-function roads where nobody walks. Urban patterns have been slashed by highways, leaving brutal wounds in the urban tissue, which lack any spatial definition. What values make these highway intrusions possible? Values that are telling expressions of the culture: disregard for centuries of community building and a single-minded concern for higher speed to reduce the commuting burden. Highways certainly must have a role in urban areas, a role in proportion to their size and generated land uses, a role as a new threshold element that must coexist with the existing pattern, a role that should extend to the control of exit ramps, related streets, and parking destinations.

Plazas have traditionally been at the apex of the urban hierarchy. Some years ago, Copley Square in Boston, a historical space defined by Richardson's Trinity Church and McKim, Mead, and White's public library, was "remodeled" to eliminate a street that cut through it, but the space was destroyed by disjointed level changes, meaningless walls, and other obstructions thrown in without sense of order or orientation. It is clear that our culture has forgotten what a plaza is, and many fine urban spaces have been destroyed by senseless redesigns.

In many projects creating a plaza, the needed spatial definition is absent and there is a fear of buildings touching buildings, not unlike the fear of people touching people. There is also an absence of any sense of "center," reflecting perhaps the social experience of the centers of power being removed from most people's awareness and the erosion of cultural allegiance to hollow urban centers. Even in the best architectural efforts, such as Chandigarh, the capital city of Punjab, India, designed by Le Corbusier, there are no urban spaces, but only a vacuum where buildings are located – an inexplicable shortcoming in a culture and climate that demand a wide range of urban spaces (Figure 11.5).

Brasilia, the new capital of Brazil, sums it all up: This is the bureaucratic noncity par excellence where urban spaces have been replaced by highways. It is the noncity where there could never be a popular demonstration in the streets and where politicians and bureaucrats escape to Rio de Janeiro for the weekend.

Some designers faced with widespread urban disintegration change tactics and decide to call "open space" some of the many vacant lots resulting from abandonment and arson. Thus, playgrounds and miniparks appear in the middle of urban deterioration in an attempt to fill the gaps; these are nothing more than false teeth in the gap-toothed grimace of the urban pattern. From the urban jungle to the suburban wasteland, open space is created by default. Office parks, campuses, and tract developments are engulfed by "green areas," which are nothing more than leftover spaces called "open space" – what a contrast to the powerful urban park concepts of Olmstead and Haussman!

Continuous–discrete events interface. One of the difficulties with many large-scale elements is determining their proper adjacency to buildings. Some continuous elements, such as railroad tracks and highways, may require physical separation from buildings. Others, such as open spaces, main streets, major boulevards, and canals, may invite the development of buildings and activities in close proximity. Traditional settlements often placed buildings next to a continuous event, so that they shared walls. For example, dwellings were sometimes built next to defense walls to save construction, but the doors and windows faced the streets – a way to be near and yet far from the defense walls.

Interfacing between continuous and discrete events is even more important in today's industrial city because of the intrusion of continuous events such as highways and commuter rail. The standard approach has been to ignore the interface

Figure 11.5. Urban vacuum and the noncity. Secretariat, Chandigarh, 1958. Le Corbusier. (Tiofoto AB/Lennart Olson)

and simply cut through the urban pattern. But the lessons of traditional settlements have much to teach us. How, for example, are we to deal with the problem of elevated highways cutting through downtown areas?

The approach of being near and yet far, of locating buildings with their backs against the highway and their fronts facing urban spaces with social activity, could be highly promising. In city centers, highways could run in elevated urban "canals," within the back walls of buildings, opening at street intersections to offer views of the city as well as to unveil their presence to urbanites as "viaducts" for the orientation of both drivers and pedestrians. The abutting buildings would be designed to have only one main open façade, the back façade being a service zone. Exit ramps could be built into the viaduct walls, leading to garages developed next to the highway – some in the lower floors of the abutting buildings – eliminating the overload of city streets, while guiding riders directly to these streets. This solution, unlike the underground highway, would offer ventilation, light, and selected views. It would deal with the private automobile as a "public–private system" by providing terminal garages adjacent to the viaduct infrastructure. Special efforts would be required at several levels: at the public level, in the design of the continuous viaduct and the establishment of guidelines for the building types abutting it; at the private level, in the design of specific buildings as variations of the established typology; and at both levels, in the design of the interface.

Establishing a buffer space between highway and urban pattern would also require a creative design approach – one based on a wide right of way within a lower-density urban pattern, which would allow the development of linear parks around the roadway. One of the conditions for the application of this approach would be the appropriateness of dividing the urban area with a linear park, as well as developing community facilities in the park to act as "bridges" between the two sides. The design would provide open space to existing residential areas, as well as space for activities, such as athletics, that would not be unduly affected by the traffic-generated noise; in any case, arborization would reduce the noise transmission. It might be possible to locate in the right of way metropolitan facilities, such as stadiums, without imposing their traffic load on urban streets. Of course, this and other design approaches could be combined: Viaduct "canals" could be located in dense central business areas and linear parks in surrounding residential zones.

254

Repetitive–unique events interface. Finally, the repetitive–unique events interface focuses on the relationship between special buildings and the rest of the urban pattern. The design solutions are based on the approach discussed earlier in reference to traditional settlements: The two elements could be facing each other across urban streets or plazas; they could be separated by parks that might also act as buffers or visual settings; or they could be tightly set against each other, sharing a wall but effectively turned away from one another.

Often the first and third solutions are complementary. Unique buildings tightly inserted within an urban pattern so that they have party walls with surrounding repetitive buildings turn their main façade to urban streets or plazas. This approach was very common in medieval towns, where not even the most impressive cathedral was seen in full view, but rather was unveiled in a process of slow discovery, partial views, surprises and, occasionally, spatial explosion when opening to a plaza (Figure 11.6). The establishment of open space around unique buildings makes them more distant from the community, sometimes even isolated; background perspectives are given more value than close-up views in this case (Figure 11.7).

Among the most troublesome shortcomings of today's urban design are its impoverished responses to this interface. The typical attitude is reflected in Mussolini's opening of the Via della Consolazione to allow an impressive perspective of St. Peter's basilica and piazza in Rome, an experience that is

Figure 11.6. The surprise of discovery: Rouen Cathedral, as seen by an observer emerging from a side street.

contrary to Bernini's concept of creating a dramatic contrast between the approach through narrow streets and the spatial explosion of the piazza. This single-minded perspective, belying an underlying fascistic attitude, has become standard in many urban large-scale complexes, such as the state capitol in Albany and Lincoln Center in New York. There is certainly room for formal spaces and long perspectives, as is evident from many magnificent urban complexes, from Jefferson's University of Virginia (Figure 11.8, top) to the city of Beijing (Figure 11.8, bottom). But there should also be room for more informal, though not less magnificent, complexes; I am reminded in particular of an exceptional modern work, Alvar Aalto's village hall in Saynatsalo, Finland (Figure 11.9).

THE URBAN WALL AS THE LOCUS OF INTERFACE

Throughout our discussion of the interfacing of urban structures and spaces, building walls have appeared as vertical physical elements that ultimately control this interfacing. What is a wall? The most immediate answer is that a wall is a boundary plane between interior and exterior space. But a wall is more than a plane; it is the area where the interface between interior (buildings) space and exterior (urban) space is determined and developed. Thus, the form and thickness of a wall are determined by both the interior space of buildings and the exterior space of the community. This means that buildings, as "owners" of walls, must respond to forces

Figure 11.7. Buildings with open space: Forbidden City, Beijing. (Daphne Politis)

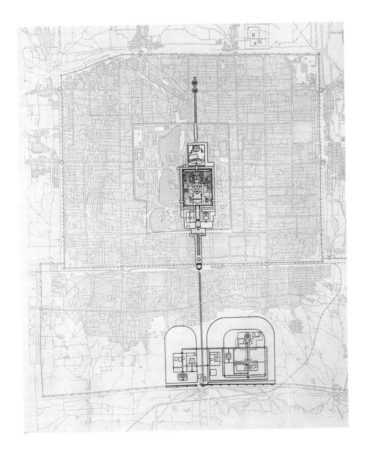

Figure 11.8. Formal precincts and formal cities. (Top) University of Virginia, Charlottesville, 1817–26. Thomas Jefferson. (University of Virginia) (Bottom) Beijing. (Edmund N. Bacon, *Design of Cities,* Viking, 1974)

beyond the specifications of the building program, forces that are imposed by urban space.

However, interior and exterior factors are seldom fully congruent, and they can easily be in conflict to some degree. When this is the case, how should buildings and open spaces be designed? The answer is that the façade walls are really interface zones. The interface wall becomes a spatial wall, a "thick" wall, with the interior plane determined by building factors and the exterior plane by urban factors. Walls such as these can be more than building façades; they can evolve into urban walls, with enormous potential for encouraging interfacing activities and spaces. In effect, the creation of thick walls would allow the development of rooms-in-the-wall, which could be oriented toward the inside of the building or toward the exterior urban space.

The concept of the urban wall has ample historical precedent. Some of the best examples are the large baroque elite buildings in Europe – palaces, churches, halls – whose architects shaped the surrounding urban spaces independently of the design of the main interior spaces. In the resulting thick wall, service rooms, secondary spaces, and even "fillers" were located. Besides responding to the forces of urban space, this design solution is pragmatic and, in general, embodies good common sense; building programs usually specify a limited number of secondary spaces, but in reality users soon discover that more are needed. The thick wall provides ideal spaces in which to expand; additional services and secondary rooms can be provided without affecting the basic layout of

Figure 11.9. Informal precincts: Saynatsalo, village hall, 1950–1. Alvar Aalto. (Frederick Gutheim)

the major spaces. In many Roman buildings, much of the area within the thick wall was assigned to the exterior urban space in the form of small stores and shops.

The interface between buildings and urban spaces can be so intimate as to shape even the details of the thick wall, providing a welcome surprise on a very small scale. In many medieval towns, buildings have deep window spaces that, when complemented with seats on both sides of the jamb, form intimate alcoves – alcoves that on the Iberian Peninsula and in America served as places of courtship, with the girl seated inside behind a decorative grille and the boy standing outside on the street. Similarly, many doorways are deep enough for marginal users, such as vendors, and have steps that are used as informal seats. Among the joys of a good urbanscape are the openings in thick walls, transitional spaces that offer opportunities for occasional use and serve as informal meeting places.

The need to create parks and similar areas of the second family of urban spaces leads to radically different urban façades, mainly because of the large scale and the absence of any intimate contact with people. Whole buildings become "thick walls" on a large urban scale, defining exterior space through their geometry and location. The best examples come from the baroque era, when spatial expansion and the recent invention of urban parks demanded such design solutions. Versailles formed the background for the apparently infinite, domesticated natural realm created for the Sun King; British crescents performed a similar role on the level of urban bourgoisie residences. These buildings were not only the boundary between the urban and the "natural" realms; they were the balcony – as in baroque theaters – from which "nature" could be contemplated (see Figures 10.3b and 10.7).

The contrast with present practices could not be more glaring. The ideology of the Modern movement reduced the concept of wall to only a geometric element, a boundary plane, of paper-thin quality. This problem has been compounded in recent years by a historicism that appropriates forms without their roots, leading to walls that are little more than stage props. This has resulted in buildings without tectonics, in urban design without articulated spaces, and in undifferentiated interior and exterior spaces. The recovery of tectonics in buildings, of urban walls and interface zones, is part of the impending renaissance of the art of architecture, which is now passing through the last stages in the dissolution of the Modern movement and its historicist epilogue.

CHAPTER 12

VISUAL PHENOMENA
AND MOVEMENT

Or orientation, variety, and symbolism

LAYERS OF PERCEPTION: COGNITION AND CULTURE

If there is a single element that most fully characterizes popular community design, it is its visual attraction. Traditional communities have been consistently successful in generating visual images with strong aesthetic appeal – a universal appeal that transcends time and space to elicit positive reactions in observers as different as art critics and tourists. What factors are responsible for this success? Are any of them transferable to our age and place?

These are vital questions. The visual environment is not another marginal choice in a consumers' world; it is an essential quality in our lives that cannot be measured by quantitative economic indices. Poverty is widespread in the world, but there is a quantum difference between the decaying slums of U.S. cities and the proud world of villagers in so many places around the globe. It is true that the difference is rooted not only in visual quality, but also in social cohesiveness, cultural coherence, and cosmological unity. Visual quality is one facet of a true community, representing many other layers of sociocultural integration.

The first line of inquiry into the visual quality of traditional communities should address the way we see, understand, and conceptualize the forms in an urban environment. Human beings relate to the physical world through the visual-psychological processes of perception and cognition. Perception is the act of apprehending through the mind and senses, of observing, of being aware. Cognition is the act or faculty of knowing, of consciously gaining and storing new information in the memory. The physical environment "sends" information to the observer, who then processes it. In some cases the information is new and may add to the knowledge of the observer; in others, it is partly known and may reinforce (or alter) the observer's previous knowledge; in yet others, the information is simply redundant, so well known to the observer that he may even fail to register it. Whether an environment creates pleasure or fear, interest or boredom, reassurance or anxiety depends on how the information is perceived.

Although the perception and cognition of forms involve the reception of a potentially large amount of information from the environment, we do not perceive forms analytically or disjointedly. We tend to perceive them as a summary description first, as a totality, since, as Konrad Lorenz said, "the characteristic quality of the whole can be dependent on the universal interaction of literally all of its parts."[1] Even in a game of chess, an activity requiring highly analytical perception, the chess master perceives the distribution of chess pieces in chunks, resulting in what Hoftstadter called working mental images of the board.[2] However, this does not mean that we perceive a totality once and for all; what makes forms visually successful is precisely that they allow for a continuous and increasingly detailed perception; one discovers "new" events as one looks at an appealing form – a discovery that creates curiosity and pleasure.

This process of staged perception, according to Arnheim, follows the principle of similarity, tending toward connection and fusion of formal components according to their relationships, such as size, location, color, direction, and shape, and starting with the simplest organizations.[3] That is, the lower-order visual "messages" corresponding to patterns are perceived more rapidly than the higher-order visual "messages" of the changes in patterns. There is, then, a sort of priority of perception, in which the structural (nondimensional) characteristics are apprehended first as qualitative events, followed by increasingly specific formal (dimensional) characteristics that quantify events. It is in the responsiveness of urban forms to sequential perception needs that much of the success of popular designs is found.

The relationship between the physical world of urban forms and human beings starts with the visual-psychological processes of perception and cognition, but it does not end there. The way in which our eyes and brain function is a universal process; but what we perceive depends to a large extent on our past experience in our society and culture. People respond to the built environment according to the way they have categorized it, according to the associations they have built on previous experience, and according to the reinforcements they have received.[4] In other words, cognition is culturally bound. The "subjective and cultural relativity of perception and cognition"[5] are key factors in establishing the way we see and understand the world according to the specific cultural and even subcultural group to which we belong.

The cultural factor is critical, because "selective screening of sensory data admits some things while filtering others, so that experience as it is perceived through one set of culturally patterned sensory screens is quite different from experience perceived through another."[6] Culture performs a variety of roles in screening perception; it may act as a filter that admits meaningful information while leaving irrelevant data out, or it can act as an amplifier that increases the strength of signs and symbols by accessing knowledge stored in our memory.[7] It is because of the filtering and amplifying roles of culture that people of different groups perceive the same environment differently.

The influence of groups, personal experience, and memory on one's perception of the environment cannot be overestimated; as Lang put it, "Experience shapes what people pay attention to in the environment."[8] It has been postulated that perception occurs on different levels in a far more complex way than anticipated, beyond staged perception and along a continuum of interpretations. At the most concrete level, we perceive the physical characteristics of forms; at the most symbolic level, forms have culturally bound meanings.[9] A spire with a cross is perceived concretely as a built form against the sky towering above other buildings; symbolically, it represents both a religious organization and the highest aspirations of the community.

The messages of the built environment are aggregated, as mentioned before, into combinations or chunks, which allow us to perceive patterns as wholes, and wholes are assigned symbolic meanings.[10] This enables us to manage more efficiently the considerable flow of visual inputs we receive from the environment, by grouping each isolated bit of information into fewer symbolic wholes, each of which carries far more information than the isolated units. Symbolic wholes can be assimilated into cognitive structures or schemata, becoming links between perception and higher mental processes.[11] For example, the symbolic whole "gray Victorian house" summarizes a large and complex group of information units, enough to convey the image of the object and to impress it on the memory together with ancillary cultural values.

Clearly, the members of different cultures will group information in a different way and invest it with different symbolic values; this is another way of understanding how people of different cultures see things differently.

To what degree can the purely visual aspects be separated from other systematic aspects of the urban environment? How much of our visual experience is inextricably mixed with activities and people in urban spaces? It is difficult – perhaps undesirable – to separate the visual and the organizational aspects of built environments, since the interaction between form and content is critical, though not necessarily deterministic. "In order to be of maximum utility, awareness of the physical form of the environment and knowledge of its activity characteristics should be complementary and reversible."[12] Quite often, an implicit relationship is established between the physical pattern of land uses, population distribution, and movement networks, and the spatial organization of human activities and interrelationships.[13] Some writers have theorized about the importance of the meaning of urban forms, including "the knowledge latent in environmental forms and activities to which people are exposed; the knowledge gained as people learn the characteristics of their environment; and the knowledge upon which are based the plans of action used by people to satisfy their various individual and social purposes."[14] They see meaning as the assimilation and memorization of perceived visual inputs in a cognitive structure and their active use in human behavior, stressing the "congruence between activities and form."[15] The importance of this congruence must be seen within the constraints of cultural and time boundaries.

There is a complex interface between built environment and human behavior. According to Gibson, different environments "afford" different behaviors and aesthetic experiences. These are recognized through perception and cognition, which affect spatial behavior. Cognition, in turn, leads to emotional responses, cognitive schemata, and motivations and needs. Our perception of the results of spatial behavior also affects our cognitive schemata; finally, schemata change and/or reinforce perception.[16]

When we recognize that perception involves more than the assimilation of immediate sensorial inputs, that it leads to knowledge and the organization of our behavior,[17] it becomes clear that perception is an active process integrating the senses, memory, and planned action. The process of perception is a case of "isomorphism," an information-preserving

263

transformation in which two complex structures can be mapped onto one another, so that to each part of one structure there is a corresponding part in the other structure, with the two parts playing similar roles in their respective structures.[18] Isomorphism creates meaning in the mind, and thus increases knowledge, since the potential symbols in forms – initially without any intrinsic meaning – acquire meaning. This interpretation allows us to understand the existence of a cultural boundary between formal systems with and without meanings, as well as its removal through the acquisition of knowledge, vocabulary, and perception of nonfamiliar objects.[19] Thus, the concept of isomorphism implies an active functional relationship between the built environment and the human mind, in which individual senses and culture are intertwined.

THE NEED FOR ORDER AND DIVERSITY

Now that we have a certain understanding of the multiple layers of perception between human beings and the environment, the key question is, what information must an urban form generate in order to satisfy our visual-psychological needs? Several visual, psychological, and perceptual studies have found comparable pairs of dualities at the root of order and the organization of form. The human brain combines information in patterns – logical groups – to assimilate the vast amount of information it receives. The brain also seeks changes in these patterns to avoid monotony.[20] Thus, form is organized by the combination of repetitive patterns and changes in those patterns, in a stable relationship. This condition is what Plato called "unity-in-diversity" and what others called "sameness-in-differentness"[21] and "regularity-in-randomness."[22] The recognition of patterns and of the changes made in patterns in response to our visual-psychological needs is a universal characteristic of perceived order and organization of form.

Opposed yet complementary events must combine in a form to be visually satisfying. Each of the two components of the duality has a specific visual role that reinforces the role of the other. For example, Whitehead found that

a rhythm involves a pattern, and to that extent is always self-identical. But no rhythm can be a mere pattern; for the rhythmical qualities depend equally upon the differences involved in each exhibition of the pattern. The essence of rhythm is the fusion of sameness and novelty; so that the whole never loses the essential

264

unity of the pattern, while the parts exhibit the contrast arising from the novelty of their detail. A mere recurrence kills rhythm as surely as does a mere confusion of details.[23]

The pattern forms the background against which changes are perceived, and the changes add interest to the pattern.

Order, then, is dependent on two elements: a pattern and changes in that pattern. Patterns are linked to so-called laws of structure – which are nonquantitative and dimensionless – while changes in patterns are linked to laws of form – which are quantitative and dimensional.[24] The laws of structure govern events leading to the emergence of patterns of order, for they are a prerequisite of formal quantification; the laws of form assign quantities and dimensions to those events, and measure and name patterns as they emerge and change.[25] Formal order is the result of the congruence between these two laws in satisfying the needs of a purposive system.[26]

Urban forms must provide patterns that yield a sense of order; in an urban environment, order is translated as orientation – that is, an observer's understanding or awareness of the urban structure and of his or her own relative position within it. In terms of perception and cognition processes, orientation is a function of the observer's ability to determine his or her position within a model of the environment, this model being shaped by the observer's cognitive maps.[27] According to several researchers, cognitive maps enable people to collect, code, store, recall, and decode information about the relative location and attributes of the physical environment.[28] They make it possible to recognize where one is, to anticipate what may happen next, to evaluate the consequences of what may happen, and to decide what actions to take.[29] Orientation thus requires a fit between messages received from the environment and evolving cognitive frameworks within the human mind.

The clues to orientation imparted by the environment should be well within the capacity of people who are relatively familiar with the environment to understand. In addition, newcomers – or at least newcomers belonging to the same culture – should be able to interpret them on the basis of previous experiences in similar places. And though these visual clues to orientation should be of sufficient clarity and universality for newcomers, they must not be redundant to local residents.

Orientation is essential for human beings, since, as Hall mentioned, their "feelings about being properly oriented in space run deep. Such knowledge is ultimately linked to survival and sanity. To be disoriented in space is to be psychotic."[30] The ancestral need for orientation was based on the fact that it was essential for daily survival in the natural environment. Today, the psychological need for orientation is still felt, even when there is no direct danger; one of the most frightening experiences is finding oneself lost in a place that one thought one knew or would easily know. Contemporary urban life continuously reinforces the need for orientation, because the potential for danger in many urban areas demands survival skills that some have compared to those needed in the wilderness: Certainty of one's location and a capacity to sort out the path of minimum risk are essential. Many functional routines of urban life also require orientation: Finding the right exit on a highway while one is driving at high speed and locating an address in an unknown suburban area are only two examples.

As a complement to providing patterns and structures of order, urban forms must also weave some differences, some novelty, into the urban tapestry. "Exceptions prove the rule," "Everything changes and everything is the same," "Cultures are unique but human beings are universal" are all aphorisms that refer to the same duality: diversity within unity. Systematically, diversity is linked to complexity, since the greater the differences among the elements of an urban area, the more complex the environment will be and thus the more capable of providing large amounts of usable information – that is, nonredundant information – resulting in greater diversity.[31] It is important to note that diversity is perceived by an observer according to his or her cultural background. Essentially, the perception of diversity is based on detectable variations within an established set of expectations.[32]

Variety is imparted to an environment by sets of similar, but not equal, elements that belong to a common and recognizable typology that are perceived as a rhythm in the pattern. This definition of variety is visually most applicable to cases of formal similarity or homology, but it can be extended to cases of functional similarity or analogy. There is a continuum in the interpretation of variety, with the degree of perceived differentiation being an inverse function of the strength of the underlying pattern. In rows of residential town houses, minor architectural differences often provide sufficient variety within the strong pattern of a common typology and homogeneous use. In contrast, in many old suburbs, major stylistic differences among Victorian, Georgian, and Federal houses are necessary to set these elements off within a weaker pattern that imposes only an order of height, massing, and volumes within a mature landscape (Figure 12.1). In all cases, a pattern imposes a matrix of order – of varying strength – and variation represents the acceptable range of changes within the typology of the pattern – wide enough to be recognized yet narrow enough to maintain the integrity of the pattern typology. Thus, variation is the acceptable and noticeable range of differentiation within an order.

Surprise is a visual phenomenon at the far end of the spectrum from variety. As already mentioned, variety not only is a rhythm within an acceptable range of order, but also confirms the order, by maintaining the observer's interest in

Figure 12.1. Variety in different patterns. (Top) Town houses, Boston. (Bottom) Single-family residences, Newton, Massachusetts.

the pattern. In contrast, surprise violates the expectations created by patterns of order, leading to a rapid realignment of the cognitive structures of the observer (who would otherwise experience disorientation) and subsequently to an experience of pleasure, awe, anxiety, or fear. The degree of surprise felt by the observer is a function of the expectations created by the pattern of order as well as by the "universality" of the departure from expectations. The discovery of slums a short distance from the White House in Washington is certainly a surprise, unpleasant to such a degree that one may be reluctant to accept it and may thus feel slightly disoriented. The discovery of the huge façade of a Gothic cathedral upon leaving a narrow maze of streets, on the other hand, is an experience that transcends pleasure to become one of spiritual upliftment (see Figure 11.6).

If the departure from expectations is a recognizable part of the culture, it may be what we call anticipatory or ritual surprise. Either there is an established ritual "game" that presents the surprising event with some consistency, or there are clues leading to an anticipatory sequence of events that mark a climatic or cyclical break in the pattern. Most traditional settlements use this device with considerable success; the desired effect is not to stun the observer but to make the observer a participant in an urban ritual. The anticipation, delightful surprise, and unparalleled thrill of entering Piazza San Marco through the maze of Venetian alleys or of reaching the main plaza in Merida is not diminished by previous experience; on the contrary, it may even be enhanced by memories of the rich surprise waiting (Figure 12.2).

Some types of differentiation within a pattern are, to paraphrase a dictum, in the eyes of the beholder. One of those is ambiguity, which has been defined as "any visual nuance however slight which gives alternative reactions to the same building or urban group,"[33] resulting in more than one (mutually exclusive) interpretation or meaning. Since ambiguity is the result of the perception of a doubtful or uncertain appearance, it has often been thought to be the effect of a *trompe l'oeil*, such as the gravity-defying false columns of the seventeenth-century mannerist architects. But there may be more systematic types of ambiguity, based on alternative interpretations of culturally bound symbols; for example, Christian churches that combine central and longitudinal typologies provoke not only a tension between the two typologies but also a true ambiguity in the observer.

When exclusionary interpretations appear side by side, we

Figure 12.2. Anticipation
or ritual surprise. (Top)
Street leading to the main
plaza in Merida, Yucatán.
(Bottom) Arcades around
the plaza.

have a case of contrast. Quite often, contrasting qualities, such as light and shadow, built and open spaces, high and low places, enhance one another. Sometimes, however, contrast has a negative effect, such as the dwarfing of Trinity Church in Boston by the nearby John Hancock Building or of the church of the same name in New York by the buildings of Wall Street (Figure 12.3).

The mutually reinforcing duality of order and diversity is necessary to achieve desirable visual qualities in urban form. Since urban form is perceived as a source of information, it is important to find in information theory some confirmation of the need for order and diversity. According to Norbert Wiener,

Messages are themselves a form of pattern and organization. Indeed, it is possible to treat sets of messages as having an entropy like sets of states of the extended world. Just as entropy is a measure of disorganization, the information carried by a set of messages is a measure of organization. In fact it is possible to interpret the information carried by a message as essentially the negative of its entropy.... That is, the more probable the message, the less information it gives. Clichés, for example, are less illuminating than great poems.[34]

Figure 12.3. Negative contrast: Trinity Church, New York City.

The visual messages in a built environment provide orientation, until beyond a certain point they became banal visual clichés. The optimal combination of visual messages includes both redundant (anticipated) messages and informative (new) messages.

The visual environment is a hierarchical one in which each level is assigned a specific visual role. Some visual levels must construct a simple and easily understood order, establishing a continuity of fully anticipated experiences that orient the observer. Other visual levels must construct a more complex and only partially understandable order, establishing a sequence of more or less unanticipated experiences that fulfill the observer's need for diversity. Some familiarity is required to allow the observer into the environment, yet some novelty is also necessary to maintain the observer's interest in learning what is unfamiliar.[35] Without diversity there is monotony; without order there is confusion.

The optimal combination of contrasting visual inputs – the certain and the uncertain, the known and the unknown, the clear and the unclear – has not by any means been scientifically established. I believe that the designer, like the poet or the musician, will establish those combinations without waiting for laboratory guidelines. What is important here is not the provision of rules, but an awareness of the qualities that the visual environment must exhibit – and of the human needs it must fulfill. We must create and re-create the visual world, and in many cases rediscover what we have collectively and historically forgotten.

ORIENTATION AND VARIETY
IN TRADITIONAL SETTLEMENTS

The human desire for order, among human beings, community, and universe, has existed since the time of the first primitive cultures. The remains of Stonehenge, Karnak, and Copan are magnificent examples of an articulation of order translated into community design (Figure 12.4). The desire for order has manifested from time to time as ideal abstractions after which real-world communities might be built; the Italian Renaissance utopian cities are but one example (see Figure 2.9).

Urban order manifests mainly as orientation, or directional order. Here the size of an urban area is a critical variable: Whereas smaller towns can be organized around a single center, larger ones have a hierarchy of subcenters, neighborhood open spaces, and unique elements. In smaller towns the organization is based on a two-dimensional pattern, but in larger cities the pattern is three-dimensional – the third dimension consisting of elements that provide orientation, such as landmark towers easily identified by building type or location (Figure 12.5). Traditional urban "intruders" such as bridges and aqueducts often evolved into tools of order, orientation elements with symbolic value that attracted people and uses by their majestic scale – in contrast to the "intruders" of our age, elevated highways and rail transit, which create wastelands and fail to relate to people and uses.

In medieval towns, a set of orientation landmarks, such as defensive walls, plazas with outstanding civic and religious buildings, and main streets, are always identifiable owing to their larger scale and recognizable form and location (Fig-

Figure 12.4. Ancestral order. (Top) Stonehenge, c. 1500 B.C. (British Tourist Authority) (Bottom) Temple of Amon, Karnak, 1530–1323 B.C. (Dr. Jonathan Drachman) (Opposite) Copan, 600 A.D. (Geoffrey Jellicoe and Susan Jellicoe, *The Landscape of Man,* Thames & Hudson, 1975)

ure 12.6). The orientation landmarks tend to maintain a constant relationship with the total urban organization: Walls encircle the town at the perimeter; the main streets originate at the town gates and lead to the main spaces or buildings, permitting an observer with even minimal experience with this type of town to relate the visual inputs to his or her cognitive mental image and thus to become oriented. The maze of secondary streets and alleys that fill the interstices between the main streets offer diversity of all kinds: surprise, mystery, multiple options, alternative interpretations. An orientation landmark – sometimes a tower or dome visible above the rooftops – is always within a short distance of any place in town, and no area in the maze is more than a few minutes' walk from a visual reference. It is possible for one to be immersed in a surprising, intriguing, and mysterious environment and yet feel safe knowing that one can become reoriented within minutes – an assurance that makes the experience more pleasurable.

Theoretically, there are two main paths to achieving diversity – one of the most difficult tasks of the designer: through emphasis and economy of means.[36] Emphasis is a path of escalation that, passing through an ever-increasing process of selection, risks exaggeration; it is the path found in the picturesque, historicist productions typical of the last stages of decadence in a movement. In contrast, economy of means is the path of providing limited hints or clues, which

the observer must grasp, interpolate or extrapolate, and interpret in order to perceive diversity. This path is based on the establishment of an order of subtle differentiation and of valued symbolism; it is the vigorous design approach of a vital culture.

Popular community design has consistently followed the path of economy of means, choosing emphasis only as an

Figure 12.5. Orientation through vertical elements. (Top) Tower of the Palazzo Vecchio, Florence, seen from a side street. (Bottom) Tower of the Palazzo Vecchio, from the Uffizi. (Opposite) Minarets, seen from a side street, Istanbul.

exception. Because the firmly established rules of the cultural tradition impose an equally strong order, a small degree of diversity is enough to produce highly significant information and perceptual richness.[37] In many cases, the sense of order is so pervasive that variation is like a subtle spice, working subliminally rather than in the full consciousness of the observer. An example is the main façade of Amiens Cathedral. The two towers are different, but the initial perception is one of such balance and equilibrium that it takes most observers some time to realize that the towers are indeed not the same. The main façade, however, impresses one from the start, not as a static composition without mystery – as many perfectly symmetrical buildings do – but as strangely alive, in equilibrium yet not static, balanced yet not inert. The secret lies in the variation the two towers bring to the symmetrical order of the main façade (Figure 12.7).

Nowhere are the subtlety and magic of variety in popular design expressed in all its multiplicity as in the human dwellings of villages and towns throughout the world. In each place and each culture, dwellings belong to a common typology: They are almost the same, but are not quite the same. Every building is slightly different, a result of individual interpretation within the sequential, marginal, and disjointed

process of building a human habitat. There may also be subtle changes in lot size and building height that denote a dwelling's location in the urban structure and thus provide directional orientation – that is, denser or higher buildings in smaller lots indicate the direction toward the town center.

There are many sources of variety. For example, in Florence, dwellings have the same façade plane and materials but slightly different windows and roof lines. In Canterbury, the residential streets have the same façade plane and materials, but different details. In Mykonos, variety is provided by the volumes of the access stairs to each house (Figure 12.8). In Portugal, the outstanding variation is the band of color at the bottom of walls and around openings.

In Zafra (Spain) and Granada (Nicaragua) the residential streets are lined with porticoes; these porticoes are not uniform because each one was built by the owner of the building behind it, and hence has its own height, column spacing, and details. Yet the result is one of both satisfying order and exhilarating variety, the visual expression of a community with concern for the common welfare and for individuality at the same time – a magnificent symbol of urban democracy! A community design that establishes guidelines while allowing the continuous interpretation of the rules, that establishes the major hierarchical levels but does not intrude on the minor ones – this is the ultimate lesson of the popular tradition.

In the United States, there is also a wealth of lessons to be learned from preprofessional residential designs, most prominently the nineteenth-century town houses found in many older cities in the Northeast (see Figures 3.16a and 12.1). That urban pattern was based on an easily identified order of main and secondary streets defining regularly subdivided blocks. Within this pattern, each dwelling developed a slight variation of the common town house typology, which was often not more than a rhythmical change in the aggregate form but which effectively raised the complexity of the visual order and introduced a subtle variety. With limited visual devices – that is, economy of means – these neighborhoods became outstanding urban creations.

The traditional urban settlement is based on patterns in which each variation of the "typical" solution results in a rhythm. This is similar to rug weaving, in which the interpretations and peculiarities of the artisan result in a rhythmical individualization of each part within the rug, as well as among rugs from the same region. It was the machine aesthetics of

Figure 12.6 (*facing page*). Order and variety: the medieval town. (Howard Saalman) (Top) Tübingen plan, 1819–21. (Bottom) Tubingen, view from engraving, late fifteenth century.

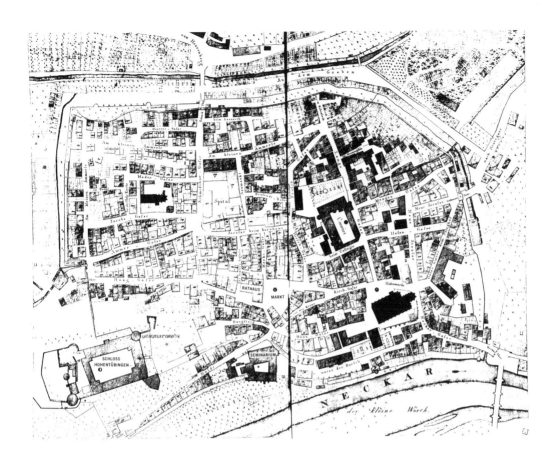

the Modern movement, among other factors, that drastically changed the urban community by enforcing a standard of uniformity upon components.

Disregard for the popular design experience is one of the most damaging effects of the Modern movement, one that influences even those designers who are trying now to emulate popular designs. But I am constantly amazed by the seemingly infinite richness of popular design solutions within the generic idea of a pattern with rhythms. The medieval cathedral (see Chapter 2) typifies the popular design approach: A master established an order on a large scale – the layout of naves, apses, vaults, columns – leaving the specific details to a large number of craftsmen and journeymen, who carved each stone component within the master plan, conferring their individual touch – each column capital is different, for instance (see Figure 2.4).

The basic order of a design can range from overpowering to subtle. The old Palace of Diocletian in Spalato (Yugoslavia) deteriorated into an impressive ruin after the collapse of the Roman Empire; later, a village was built within the framework of the monumental columns and vaults. Urban equivalents of an overpowering order infilled with a variety of elements can be found in different cultures: the main bazaar

Figure 12.7. Subtle variation: Towers of Amiens Cathedral.

in Istanbul is a perfect gridiron network of covered streets within which a varied assortment of shops occurs (Figure 12.9).

The order of the weekly market stalls in plazas throughout Europe is subtle; it is difficult to see how this apparent chaos can be reproduced every week, until one realizes that different trades occupy specific areas and that the pedestrian paths make sense in the context of the surrounding pattern. Those designs in which order slowly emerges from apparent chaos are the ones in which cultural filters play a major role, since the initial understanding of the pattern is apparent only to the hermetic circle of local participants. A good urban example is the lack of orientation, as well as the variety and surprise, that Europeans experience in North African cities such as Fez and Marrakesh (see Figures 6.4, p. 125, top, and 10.19).

As already mentioned, it was the appearance of machine aesthetics, and not simply the application of technology, that imposed patterns of identical – not just similar – units on larger wholes. Composite buildings, apartments, and offices are new large-scale urban components. Individual dwellings and workplaces are often no longer recognizable as units. Given the existence of these composite buildings, a design solution might be to introduce pattern variations on a larger scale, an approach used successfully by the builders of crescents in eighteenth-century England. The principle here is that of introducing a gigantic and ordered exception into the urban pattern, which remains a unique event on a community scale, while the component units (the individual dwellings) are merged in the totality.

This design solution, of course, precludes repetition: Park Crescent in London is a unique event, whereas in Bath there is a sequence of highly distinguishable forms – the crescent and the circus (see Figure 10.7). One need only imagine a crescent repeated several times in succession to envision the monotony and boredom that would debase all the positive qualities of a unique crescent.

Similar approaches can be found in other unique urban forms of the same period: the Place Vendôme or Place de la Concorde in Paris or the complex in Nancy. Each of these forms is organized around highly redundant visual information and is heavily dependent on the aggregation of exactly the same components within a regular geometric totality forming a unified façade. However, when perceived as a large-scale monumental variation and as an orientation landmark within a fairly undifferentiated pattern, its crescents, circuses, and places are seen as magnificent urban events. There is no need for small-scale variation since the whole complex functions as a gigantic variation within the smaller scale and intricate pattern that surrounds it. The strong visual identity generated by its relentless (and elegant) regularity impresses an equally strong mental image on the observer,

Figure 12.8. Variety in popular buildings. (Top) Village near Malaga. Variation of roof lines and wall openings. (Bottom) Zafra, Extremadura. Variation of columns and cornice lines. (Opposite top) Santiago de Compostela. Variation of arcade and roof heights. (Opposite bottom) Churches in Mykonos. Variation of volumes and wall openings.

which in turn reinforces the role of the crescent or the place as an orientation landmark.

This design approach involves a large degree of "invention" of urban types, as elements of urban order and diversity that eventually acquire symbolic value. Often it is not even necessary to develop an "original" urban form to obtain the same results, as in the case of the Rue de Rivoli, a series of apartment houses behind a palatial façade forming a true urban invention: the boulevard (see Figure 2.11, bottom).

In cases such as this, we recognize the detached quality of most urban symbols, which tend to speak to us of intangible values fairly independent of use or activity. What can be the meaning of a series of bourgeois residences tucked behind a palatial façade, if not the social-climbing aspirations of new money in town? Nevertheless, crescents and places and boulevards transcend this and speak of monumental scale, of unique events, of an order that is outstanding among the lesser surroundings; they speak of the climax of urban environments, of hierarchical levels above the individual family dwelling, of symbols within the community. Does it matter so much that nothing besides dwellings are housed behind the palace façade? Not really. The "truth-in-design" concept that holds that a building must express its function has been taken to extremes by the Modern movement. I am saying that one of the roles of buildings and complexes in cities is to create a hierarchy of symbols that give much needed visual-psychological satisfaction.

MONOTONY AND CHAOS: THE MODERN EXPERIENCE

A characteristic of our times is that modern urban design has been oscillating, like a wild pendulum, between the extremes of monotony and confusion. Order and diversity have been misunderstood or forgotten. Perhaps this is the price paid by

Figure 12.9. Pervasive order: Great Bazaar, Istanbul. In heavy lines the two *bedesten*s, multidomed sections with precious goods. (George Mitchell, ed., *Architecture of the Islamic World,* Thames & Hudson Ltd., 1978)

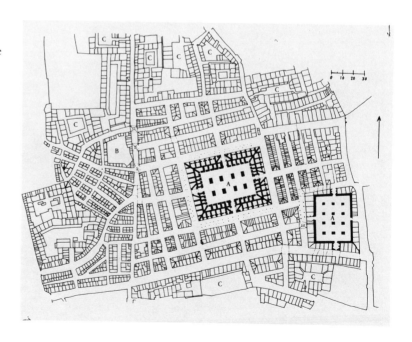

282

a society that has as much technology and affluence as it lacks in common culture and community purpose. Perhaps this is also the price paid by a profession that took over a community responsibility with neither a tradition nor an acquired skill. Ultimately, is it really surprising that there are no community designs in an antiurban society?

Let us pick up again the thread of the influence of the Modern movement, which mainly involved a sweeping simplification of our understanding of the built environment. At the same time that the formal academic conventions of the Beaux Arts were being destroyed and a new aesthetic created, the movement was neglecting basic human psychological needs and ignoring all but the most simplistic visual considerations. Before then, visual needs were not necessarily consciously known, but they were a matter of cultural subconscious reaction – much like the magical use of medicinal herbs in prescientific societies. By drastically simplifying the visual world, the Modern movement somehow echoed the simplification that the Industrial Revolution and the emerging bourgeoisie were forcing on the national states. A blind faith, really a mythical faith, in the machine and in "progress" replaced the richness of traditional societies without providing a viable alternative.

The early visions of the Modern movement were responsible, to a large degree, for the recurrent failures of urban design. The urbanism of Le Corbusier or the Bauhaus is one of absolute dominance of redundant information, extremely low-order visual organization, and absence of diversity at any level, yielding an oppressive feeling of monotony and, ultimately, disorientation. The visual clichés originating in the mechanical repetition of identical elements on all scales and a lack of complexity in visual inputs are typical of a movement characterized by narrowly defined functionalism and obsession with purism and clarity. The Modern world is one of abstract utopias, homogeneous buildings and patterns, and statistical averages. The descendants of the urban proposals of the masters of the Modern movement are the public housing projects built around the world in recent decades (Figure 12.10).

Environmental organization based exclusively on low-level order (monotony), as is typical of modern urbanism, leads, as already mentioned, to sensory deprivation.

All biological systems, particularly those equipped with specialized receptors and complex nervous integration centers, respond primarily to a changing environment. . . . The eye reacts with exceptional speed to a flickering target viewed peripherally and is sometimes surprisingly inattentive to familiar more centrally placed objects. This preference for the new or the changing is an essential mechanism of any system which is to survive for long in the physical world as we know it, for a "steady" environment seldom, if ever, occurs in nature.... What would happen to the physical system if it were confronted with an unchanging [environment]?... The target in view soon becomes perceptually unstable and finally actually disappears from view.... Disappearances are by no means permanent, and the parts of the image which vanish generally return to view within seconds, after which some other part or parts disappear.[38]

Figure 12.10. Modern urbanism: monotony and disorientation. (Below) Le Corbusier, Plan Voisin, Paris, 1925. (Fondation Le Corbusier) (Opposite top) Governor Smith Public Housing, New York, 1948. (New York City Housing Authority) (Opposite bottom) Stuyvesant Town public housing, New York, 1945. (Metropolitan Life Insurance Company)

That is, human beings tend to become sensorially "blind" in monotonous environments, passing through them without perceiving them, like robots who move through, but never really see, space.

Monotony seriously reduces the potential for orientation. Environments must offer subtle gradations of oriented differences – to provide clues of direction and distance – as well as landmarks within the pattern. The value of subtle clues can be found, for example, in comparing a Manhattan-type grid of main avenues and transversal streets with a uniform

284

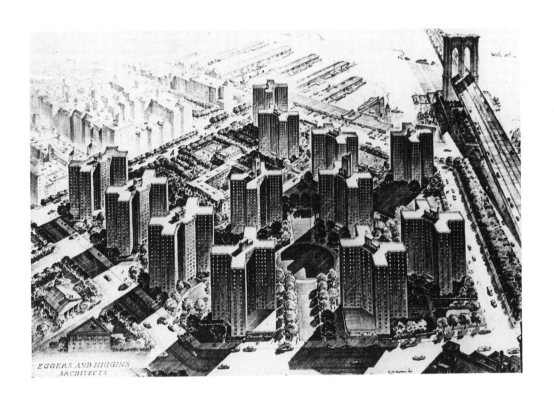

gridiron pattern; the first one is both easily accessible (understandable) and conveys more directional information than the second one.

Monotonous environments restrict behavioral opportunities; they do not challenge human beings; they demand less competence. Although in general the effect of the built environment on people is accommodative and not deterministic, in this case it affects human behavior adversely by restricting its options.[39]

Beyond the urban core, and very important in terms of sheer building square footage, we find what could be loosely called the suburban movement, including conventional tract suburbs and the "inventions" of the 1960s and 1970s: planned unit developments and new towns. The common characteristic of these projects is the repetitive use of a design "solution" to avoid monotony: purposefully winding roads, loops, and cul-de-sacs. Presumably, they are chosen to provide picturesque visual amenities. The result, however, is quite the contrary (Figure 12.11). Winding roads fail to shape any pattern and thus to provide any orientation; it is impossible to develop a cognitive structure of the layout. The only landmarks are the highway and the shopping center, which are invisible from most parts of the project since they seldom have a vertical reference. One explanation for this baffling lack of order is the implicit desire of suburbanites to fence themselves off from strangers; indeed, the few outsiders who venture into suburban tracts must have a good map in hand courtesy of their hosts or they will become hopelessly lost.

Figure 12.11. The disorientation of suburbia.

Is it possible that the perceived disorder and disorientation of suburbia are an expression not only of an antiurban culture, but also of an invisible defense wall?

Another design "solution" found in most suburban projects is contrived variation. There are practically no hierarchical levels, houses are mass built, and yet the developer must continue to fulfill the illusion that each house is unique. Is it not ironic that the desire for individuality is so strong in suburbia, with its mass-produced housing tracts? Attached houses and garden apartments are subject to volumetric articulations that push some units forward and others backward, change pitched roof lines, and expose side walls and jogged fences. Single-family dwellings are often ornamented with superficial disguises, not unlike the costumes at a Mardi Gras party. This sort of design "solution," however, would be dismissed by any sensible master builder because of its lack of sense, misadaptation, and confusion of details.

In recent decades, a movement called (rather mistakenly) "pop architecture" has come into being in order to "explain" a typical U.S. phenomenon: the strip highway development. One after another, buildings and billboards of different form, color, and light arrangements compete for attention; continuous parking lots and the road are the cement that binds this chaos together. The only order is the line of the road, beyond which anarchy reigns, with the result that no structure stands out; each is equally loud (and banal) and, thus, strangely similar to the rest. When searching for a motel or restaurant, a driver can decide where to stop only when he or she recognizes a chain's familiar sign; the slightest bit of orientation is enough to attract one's attention – a fact that is well known to owners of national franchises. There is a continuous flow of visual messages without any perceived link, similar to the random taping of isolated words in several languages; the observer is bombarded with disjointed visual inputs until she or he becomes saturated. Predictability is drastically reduced since there is no understandable rhythm. Why this expression of consumerism has been labeled "popular" is difficult to understand, unless the term refers to its patronage by the so-called popular classes. It is nothing more than an attempt to tap the consumer dollar and to promote fast (and often cheap) consumption, with the easiest option of drive-and-park, a primitive and anticommunity design solution.

The major difference between visual perception today and that in the past is speed; the introduction of radically different speeds in urban areas has created a dichotomy between the

287

fast motorized view and the slow pedestrian view. People in vehicles apprehend only simple patterns and are concerned primarily with functional orientation; the landscapes they perceive are necessarily sweeping and general, a backdrop for the specific signs by which they orient themselves. However, as vehicular speed decreases, and the driver's view becomes closer to that of the pedestrian, there should be an integration of the vehicular with the pedestrian orientation system, through explicit and intelligible visual messages of urban activities, buildings, and people.

Unfortunately, another facet of modern urbanism maintains the visual dichotomy between the city seen from a vehicle and that seen from the sidewalk. Mode segregation is responsible for one of the most unfortunate urban experiences: arrival through a parking lot or garage sequence. Some of the most vital urbanscapes, ranging from Parisian boulevards to American Main Streets, are those that provide for a civilized – and not too controlled – symbiosis of vehicles and people. Urbanites have invented rituals to combine and enjoy each other's views at different speeds. The leisurely parade of horse-drawn carriages now takes the form of automobiles cruising along Main Street. Community design should be concerned with opening choices so that people, whether on foot or in cars, can have a variety of visual experiences. The best might be a purely pedestrian realm with the poetry of San Marco, or it might be a mixed pedestrian and vehicular realm with the illusion of the Champs Elysées.

SYMBOLISM

Ultimately, form reaches the highest level of meaning. Order leads to orientation, and orientation leads to symbolism, in an aesthetic unity of function and spirituality. Physical space becomes social space and eventually acquires symbolic value. Some visual symbols are obscure, even hermetic, recognizable only to members of a culture or to initiated ones, defying outsiders and forming an invisible wall of defense. Others are clear, universal symbols stressing the common experience of humankind and inviting outsiders to share.

Creating visual symbols is one way we translate environmental images into schemata. Some become iconic images such as Lynch cognitive maps.[40] Others become associated images with symbolic meaning.[41] There are many theories of how the environment communicates a whole range of meanings, including symbols. Psychoanalytical theorists be-

lieve in association of images with memories in the uncon-
scious; behavioralists focus on the reinforcing pattern of the
socializing process; and linguists stress the importance of
learning and cultural differences.[42] Still, the implications for
designers remain highly speculative.

To start, order and orientation in cities are closely related to
symbolism. Providing order and orientation is not just a matter of guiding people to functional destinations such as gaso-
line stations; instead, it is a fundamentally different issue of
providing physical guidance within a symbolic hierarchy. The
provision of order and orientation in a symbolic context can be
compared to the creation of a game and of its solution at the
same time. Order and orientation in, say, Florence are based
on the relationship among the Palazzo Vechio, the Uffizi, the
river, and similar urban landmarks (see Figure 12.5). Orientation combines directional references within a landmark, often
a climax, that has symbolic value. The Piazza della Signoria
and the Palazzo Vecchio are not only references, but true
destinations; if the city is considered a "universe," this destination becomes its apex – encompassing spiritual, artistic, and
historic value – as well as a synthesis of the ideals of the
community.

The establishment of an urban order, and thus orientation,
involves an integration of aesthetic and symbolic values. For
instance, the approach to Toledo creates a very specific aesthetic–symbolic unity: From far away the towers of the cathedral appear on the horizon above the town, but as one
comes closer, the cathedral disappears and one must find clues
to the location of the center of this universe. Only as one
becomes very close to it do fragments of the structure sud-
denly emerge at the turn of a street, and, finally, it is possible
to walk around the complex (Figure 12.12). This is consistent
with medieval aesthetics, but for many of the faithful it may
be a symbolic representation of life on earth: One knows
from the beginning the hierarchical relationship between the
sacred and the profane, but one often goes astray and must
search for clues to direct oneself to the heavenly destination,
until at last one is rewarded with the heavenly Jerusalem –
which is what the cathedral stands for on earth. What a magnificent unity of visual pleasure and spiritual symbolism!

Every design component is potentially a bearer of symbols,
and it is only because of the cultural debasement of symbols
and the lack of designers' familiarity with them that current
communities are so impoverished. The Greeks transformed
floors by building platforms as sacred *temenos*; the Egyptians

pushed floors upward to fight the desolate horizontal of the desert, and created pyramids (Figure 12.13). The earth beneath floors has an ancestral association with fertility, abundance, and home and is one of the key relationships between humans and the universe. Roofs were transformed by the Romans, and later by Christian Europeans, into representations of the heavens, through domes and vaults. Churches became scaled versions of the sacred–profane universe that had specific meaning for the faithful and still touches even the most agnostic observer. Walls had always been seen as structures of defense, sometimes physical but always psychological, defining "our" turf versus the undefined, and often hostile, outside world. Few views are more ascetic than and yet so symbolic as the view of the walls of Avila or Angers (see Figure 10.5).

Where there is a wall there must be a door, which makes doors and gates complementary symbols of walls. In effect, doors are interpreted universally as symbols of entry, and have often been lifted to expressive levels as triumphal arches and processional gates – and as forbidden doors (Figure 12.14). This symbolism survives today, albeit in a degraded form, with the concern of institutions and homeowners to have a "main door," even though it may be seldom used if people enter the building from a parking lot or garage. Windows have had a variety of specific meanings, from the high openings where a pope or king appears, to the opening from which a girl talks to her boyfriend. Finally, columns have been the favorite element for developing a system of meaning, a grammar so to speak. Examples are the five Classic orders that appear in buildings from temples to banks. Sometimes, the magnificence of a column has been used in isolation as a favorite urban landmark, the obelisk.

The universality of urban symbols varies. Some symbols are eminently clear because they are so universal, touching common human feelings across cultures; they invite outsiders to share the ideals they represent. The old minaret of the mosque in Seville was transformed into a bell tower for the newer cathedral several centuries after the original construction; yet its religious symbolism remains practically unchanged across centuries and cultures (Figure 12.15). The Spanish conquistadores tended to build Christian churches on top of Indian pagan pyramids, with the result that the native populations preserved the sacredness of the artificial mountain while changing their allegiance from the old to the new religion. The superimposition of the "new sacred" on

Figure 12.12 (*facing page*). Orientation, meaning, and symbolism. (Dr. Jonathan Drachman) (Top) View of Toledo Cathedral from across the river. (Bottom left) Glimpse of the cathedral from a side street. (Bottom right) Arrival at the plaza in front of the cathedral.

top of the "old sacred" is a time-honored tradition in most cultures; this was merely a way of improving upon a recognized hierarchy of beliefs and, thus, upon a commonly understood hierarchy of symbols.

Other symbols are obscure, requiring cultural clues to unlock their meaning. These hermetic symbols are embodied in an isomorphic pattern of forms and system of meaning that admits only those who belong to the culture, or even to a selected group within the culture. For outsiders, the sym-

Figure 12.13. Sacred floors. (Top) Acropolis, Athens, 480–404 B.C. (Bottom) Castillo, Chichén Itzá, A.D. 900–1400.

bols defy understanding and may introduce confusion. Although towers are a basic community design element, their meaning may evade us, as does that of the forest of towers in San Gimignano or Bologna (Figure 12.16). To a twentieth-century observer they are visual images of considerable interest but without meaning; only after discovering that they represented the pluralism and mutual hostility of a number of noble families within the town does the observer begin to understand them. The feelings that they once evoked – the constant threat of attack, the safety of one's own tower, which must be clearly distinguished from the rest, the value attached to the towers of enemies, allies, or neutral families,

Figure 12.14. Gates and doors. (Top) Gate and wall at Avila. (Bottom) Door and wall at Poblet monastery, Catalonia.

the sense of a community fractured from within – all that is lost today.

The mosque in Cordoba is one of the most outstanding complexes in Europe, the prototype of Western Islamic mosques, and a fascinating, mysterious, and magnificent space with its one thousand columns (Figure 12.17). And yet its walls and courts are strangely empty of meaning to us; we cannot understand the message conveyed to the faithful or even to the contemporary people of other faiths who lived in Córdoba while the mosque was the vital heart of the city. Hope, moral teachings, rituals, faith, the meaning of the forbidding walls, the ornate gates, the refreshing fountains are all gone; we can only see the mosque with the eyes of a fellow designer but not enjoy its full symbolic value.

The fact that urban symbols must have meaning for different groups, both insiders and outsiders, is of great importance to designers, especially today, when metropolises are so pluralistic. How does one design with urban symbols in mind when the U.S. city is composed of a wide range of people, from members of wealthy old Anglo families to descendants of European immigrants to poor newcomers from the South, Puerto Rico, Central America, and Mexico? Is there any common cultural element, any common ground? We have found again and again that the U.S. city is experiencing a serious crisis, in which the old urban system is deteriorating and the new system is still unshaped; this is a time of painful transition, of incoherence and internal conflict. People from different cultural traditions are faced with "for-

Figure 12.15. A universal symbol: Giralda Tower, Seville, 1195. First minaret of the Mosque of Seville, later tower of the cathedral.

eign" symbols – few elements have a common value for all urbanites. It is necessary to revise cognitive structures continuously and sometimes to abandon them without replacing them, which erodes people's confidence in their "knowledge" of valid symbols and may cause considerable psychological stress.

There is an urgent need to begin reconstructing visual images with valid meanings, that is, symbols, that are accessible to all members of the urban population if a sense of community orientation and purpose is to be regained. It can be argued, of course, that it would be very difficult for designers to jump ahead and provide symbols for a culture that has not yet been reconstituted. But designers, as instruments of cultural change, can encourage cultural reconstitution. Unfortunately, in a culture permeated with questionable values, designers can be as lost as the rest, as witnessed by the succession of antiurban, consumerist, and novelty-seeking proposals that have filled the professional design journals much as the "season's collections" cover the pages of fashion magazines.

Indeed, what *is* a symbol widely understood today in the U.S. city? The highest towers are skyscrapers built to maximize profits and, in some cases, to satisfy corporations' egos; there is unspeakable luxury in consumption palaces such as Copley Place in Boston, while next door, weeds fill empty lots and burned houses. It is the dollar that is our universal symbol – and for many, it is the only goal. Clearly, other values must be reincorporated into the designer's professional

Figure 12.16. Hermetic symbols: Torre Asinelli and Torre Garisenda, Bologna, 1109–10.

practice, and those who believe in a better society have the responsibility to begin shaping those values even before they are apparent to the rest of society.

The careful orchestration of urban symbols is one of the most sensitive issues we face. On the one hand, it is necessary to reconstruct symbols that are accessible to all of the population; on the other, it is important to retain a hierarchy of symbols, some of them accessible only to members of a subculture in order to increase their sense of belonging to their own group. Furthermore, in creating new visual systems – images, meanings, symbols – it is essential to include parts

Figure 12.17. The eternal building and the forgotten symbol. (Top) Mosque of Córdoba, east façade, 987. (Bottom) Interior, 785.

of the older (understandable) visual system in order to provide a transitional bridge and thus to help people develop a
"new memory." Redundancy may be helpful in forming a
perceptual-cognitive bridge.

The formation of a new memory is indeed a fascinating
phenomenon, of which we have abundant examples but scant
understanding. The issue is how physical built space becomes
social space and, eventually, a symbolic element. In some
cases, the process is bound to a culture: The Greek temple
evolved into a prototypical symbol for banks through a series
of steps that included the rediscovery of the classical orders
as the universal grammar of the Renaissance, their use during
the baroque era to articulate a building hierarchy, and their
neoclassical reuse as a symbol of stability by the most con-
servative institutions of the twentieth century, banks. Sometimes the details of symbols are overlaid with powerful
universal meanings that transcend boundaries: The wooden
spires of New England churches fulfill the same role as the
domes and masonry towers of Latin American churches. It
is here, in what remains of universal symbols, that designers
must search for allegories and allusions to build bridges between the old and the new traditions.

EPILOGUE

An agenda for action

THIS book is, as I said at the beginning, for those who love cities; for those who believe in civilization and want to regain urbanity and choice, regional identity and a sense of community; for those who know that urban areas must be pluralistic forms, the result of community-wide objectives; for those who are working toward more humane communities and are seeking paths of action.

The development of the three major theses of the book – that community designers must regain lost design traditions, acquire insights on the nature of urban systems, and, most important, reverse antiurban cultural trends – could be the basis for both academic and professional strengthening.

The professional education of community designers and, to some degree, architects and city planners must be carefully reconsidered. Architectural history courses should examine the implications of traditional design approaches and solutions for contemporary practice. Social science courses must be focused on the crises of the urban community, recognizing its systematic interrelationships. Sectorial courses on housing or transportation must reach beyond statistical descriptions, highlighting the causes of problems and possible solutions. Studios and workshops must offer genuine professional practice experience that integrates what is learned in other courses and is complemented with advocacy work in the urban community. And seminars should be offered on the cultural and political frameworks of the urban metropolis.

It is often said that planning is process. Community designers should steer the decision-making process toward desired goals, by participating in and influencing the design decisions at different levels in society. Designers must function in communities both as interpreters and as agents of change who challenge antiurban values.

One major objective must be the reconcentration and re-distribution of urban areas. Dispersion, with its waste of energy, pollution, and restriction of choices for lower-income groups, must be reversed, by clustering suburban employment at strategic nodes and higher-density corridors and hence creating the potential for first-rate public transit systems. Land use distribution, density, and public transportation must be planned in an integrated way. However, this objective faces the problem that any metropolitan reorganization of employment centers would affect local property tax revenues, since business uses provide the fiscal base for cities and towns.

One way to implement reconcentration and redistribution would be to create metropolitan authorities empowered to plan key land uses and transportation, as well as to allocate property tax revenues. These tax revenues could be apportioned simply by population and, if redistribution objectives were agreed upon would afford lower-income communities a proportionally higher share. The prospect of higher densities and mass transit would elicit strong opposition from wealthy suburban towns, opposition that could be met only by state legislation similar to that used now to override local zoning and locate low-income housing in suburban areas. The creation of such metropolitan authorities, a fairly radical proposal, should be based on the precedent of several existing metropolitan authorities empowered to plan, manage, and raise revenues for water, sewerage, highway, and mass-transit systems.

Another major objective must be the achievement of heterogeneity and integration, among people, activities, and buildings. Segregation and homogeneity must be challenged across the board. One realistic approach would be to shrink homogenous zones by progressively reducing the size of the urban grain through zoning – by spot zoning, reducing the areas under single-use classification, or by developing packages of mixed uses. In both cases, zoning changes would have to be supported by the local community and enacted by the local government, which would demand considerable political education and action.

A major concern of integration is to make housing choices accessible to less privileged groups. Since housing, in our market economy, is a consumer item increasingly out of reach for most people, it is imperative that integration policies make available social-interest housing in an integrated pattern, throughout the metropolitan area. A major obstacle is the

299

lack of moderately priced land in suburban areas. Some states have had to resort to legislation to force affluent communities to accept a few low-cost units, a process that often involves a lengthy procedure of challenge and approval. The effort demanded today is totally out of proportion with the small number of units involved.

For these reasons, a metropolitan authority whose main responsibility would be to assemble land (paid for, perhaps, with state bonds) where social-interest dwellings could be built in an integrated way is necessary. One of its roles would be to function as a housing "land bank," withdrawing land from real estate speculation to sponsor mixed-income and mixed-race neighborhoods. The metropolitan authority I am proposing must break legal and economic barriers to housing, but it should not give rise to a paternalistic bureaucracy similar to those of housing authorities in some big cities. Its function should be to create the opportunity for social-interest housing in a large number of small parcels intermixed within communities, or in larger integrated neighborhoods – not projects – based, perhaps, on cooperative ownership.

We must also address the preservation of existing neighborhoods threatened by either deterioration or gentrification. The poorer a neighborhood is, the more public support it needs; this should be a key rule of municipal governments. The prevention of deterioration means stopping the damaging cycle of succession and must include a package of programs aimed, in the poorest areas, at reducing the number of absentee landlords and organizing tenants' cooperatives; creating employment through training, the provision of transportation to jobs, and the generation of local building (and other) enterprises; building rehabilitation through local efforts; and developing more community facilities. Typically, line municipal departments make decisions in some of these areas disjointedly and without reinforcing one another. Large city governments may find the creation of geographically based integrated departments (little city halls) a major breakthrough in buttressing and improving their poorest areas. This must go hand in hand with strong local participation, the result of growing community activism and self-awareness.

Other urban neighborhoods, the ethnic, working-class and moderate-income areas, need a different type of assistance. Here, the problem is that of the small private owner: uncertainty and scarce resources to counter deterioration. Public intervention must ensure the survival of the community, reduce individual uncertainty, and mobilize resources and actions.

The integration of urban activities should be based on symbiosis, mixing activities that have common needs along a consumption or production line: from residential housing above retail stores to recapture vitality in central areas, to retail areas adjacent to schools to create protocenters in dispersed exurban areas. Work areas should be closer to residential areas (as long as there is no major negative impact); children should be allowed to see people at work; and artificial "special areas," whether cultural centers or complexes for the elderly, should be distributed within the community.

One approach to achieving a real integration in neighborhoods and communities is to foster a rich nonnested hierarchy of social centers, with different and overlapping catchment areas and boundaries. This must be a major public goal, stressing a strategy of planning public centers such as schools, libraries, and post offices, combined with formulating transportation and land use policies that would offer opportunities for private centers such as stores, churches, and clubs. The public tools of capital budgeting and zoning, as well as interagency coordination, should play critical roles in reaching this goal.

Another major objective is to achieve a range of urban densities, by eroding the pathological extremes of sub-urban and over-urban densities. Reducing over-urban densities involves, among other things, reducing crowding and anonymity at downtown corporate workplaces by imposing size limitations on buildings and offering incentives for designing structures on the human scale. Upgrading suburban densities involves mandating smaller minimum lots and zero line lots, cluster zoning, forming villages along corridors, and reconcentrating outlying centers, whether by converting shopping malls to mixed-use centers with residential units or by reconcentrating office parks near transit stations.

The achievement of a broad range of urban densities in metropolitan areas would require actions at all political levels. Some, such as the upgrading of exurban employment center densities, would be within the domain of the proposed metropolitan authorities, to be coordinated with the provision of mass transit. Others would be the province of local governments, which could prove to be difficult, since exurban towns often reject density increases and question cluster zoning. Such actions must be preceded by political and educational activities on the metropolitan scale and be tied to state fiscal incentives for local municipalities.

One special concern is to reverse the tendency toward megaprojects that destroy the patterns of urban centers. Official city policy must be to foster relatively moderate developments on a scale with the pluralistic nature of the surrounding pattern. This would require controls on the sizes of parcels, buildings, and complexes, together with incentives for developments designed on a human scale and integrated with the street system. Realistic densities and floor area ratios in scale with the street capacity, and limits on parcel sizes, building gross area per elevator core, heights, and distance from work stations to windows, should be part of the zoning and design guidelines in central areas. Incentives should include density or height bonuses for developments that consist of discrete buildings linked to form precincts with the same typology of the surrounding pattern and for those that provide private connections with underground subway stations, bus and taxi shelters, public restrooms, and sidewalk arcades.

Reevaluation of the building types currently being constructed in central cities is part of an assessment of typologies that must take place across metropolitan areas. Obsolete stereotypical buildings can be identified by the environmental problems they generate at the interface between facility and community. Municipalities cannot gain control of the urban infrastructure if they do not have a say in the typology of buildings. Community design guidelines must complement zoning, establishing the rules to be followed by individual architects in the design of each building.

Areas deserving considerable design attention are the zones created at various urban interfaces, such as that between networks and buildings, the "tidal ponds" of urban activities where riders become pedestrians. The new scale of high-speed transportation systems has caused considerable damage to the urban pattern and created a dead interface of highways cutting through communities. Design guidelines can control the traditional interface zones, but we need additional tools in areas with newer, high-speed transportation elements. Here, the public sector may want to control a wider right of way in order to guide the development of buildings abutting it, to establish open space as needed, and to ensure freedom for technological improvements with minimum disturbance to the surrounding pattern.

There are other cases in which the role of public com-

munity designers may have to be extended. The importance
of key "urban walls" in some private buildings, of some
landmark towers, of gates and "doors" within the public
realm, of places of "passage" and "arrival," as well as of
"boundaries" and "bridges" must be recognized. In the same
way that guidelines are set for the preservation of historical
areas, community-wide considerations must guide the design
of other areas of special value in the urban pattern; these are
what we call "landmark areas."

The various actions of community designers must be integrated to ensure orientation and variety. Land use, density,
and other planning variables, including the street network
and the open-space system, should be designed to provide
orientation. In large complex cities, vertical orientation landmarks should be added to the urbanscape. It is equally important that the community design guidelines be flexible to
ensure variety and diversity.

This agenda is extensive and likely to face many obstacles.
Let us summarize the main courses of action. The establishment of metropolitan authorities is essential for dealing with
the regional issues subsumed under growth and development
policies: the location of main centers of employment, the
extension of public transit lines, the banking of land for integrated housing. These authorities should have the power
to override local municipalities in order to zone land in strategic centers and corridors (though not in all the metropolitan
area), to plan main public transportation lines, to acquire land
for housing, and to apportion property tax revenues from
and to the various municipalities. Whether these authorities
derived their power from the state as autonomous agencies,
or were based on county governments, or were extensions
of existing metropolitan authorities, they would represent a
radical change in the administration of major U.S. metropolises. It is very likely that this proposal will generate the
opposition of powerful groups, especially the affluent suburban and exurban municipalities. The civil rights movement
of the 1960s took place mainly in small towns of the rural
South; the 1990s could see another stage of the struggle, this
time fought in metropolitan areas.

On the other hand, the municipal governments of large
cities may have to be selectively decentralized through the
creation of "little city halls," that is, geographically based
departments in the poorest areas that integrate the actions of
the various line functions in order to provide public support.
This approach to halting the deterioration of urban areas and

building sound neighborhoods may face opposition from entrenched political and real estate groups.

Thus, at the same time that I am proposing some selective regionalization of municipal government powers and functions over metropolitan areas, I am also proposing some selective decentralization of large city governments.

The legal instruments used to implement land use plans, zoning bylaws, and ordinances should be the focus of major challenges and reforms at the local level. Changes should include the widespread use of mixed-use packages and/or spot zoning to integrate people and activities, designation of mixed-use areas, coordination with metropolitan authorities in the location and reconcentration of major employment centers, definition of urban density levels and thresholds for urban services, banking of land for public purposes, control of project size, offering of incentives for the construction of better buildings, creation of directional order through land uses and densities, and coordination of programs with municipal agencies.

Many such zoning changes could face strong opposition. One strategy would be to advance along different fronts, progressing faster where there is consensus, while coupling controversial proposals with positions acceptable to local residents and politicians. For example, a policy of reconcentration with higher residential densities should be presented as also preserving open space by avoiding sprawl. Nevertheless, it is apparent that considerable political discussion and activism must take place at the local level.

Community design guidelines must become a standard complement of zoning. They have been used in some major cities, but they have been applied only to major development projects and limited to very basic design parameters. They must be expanded to include typologies and design codes, as well as landmark areas and transportation rights of way. Public-sector elements, such as gates and bridges, must be incorporated into the community design plan as early as possible.

This is an ambitious agenda, which places the responsibility of community design where it belongs, on the public sector as an expression of the political will of the community. (If this were not the case, the problem would be to restore the political will of the community to government.) Though the responsibility of the public sector is expanded, it is also more open ended; there are new areas where the public must act, but its actions must be more flexible, responsive, and adaptive. Pluralism would flourish through public actions that ensure opportunities for everyone to contribute, opportunities that are now often stifled by a few powerful groups that control an increasing share of the decision-making process.

Yet this agenda may not be enough. Purely professional actions must be backed by political actions; purely design objectives must be supported by socioeconomic objectives. The ultimate question, in which design and politics are entangled, is how to distinguish where and when the system should be repaired, and where and when radical rearrangements are necessary. The urban system is showing signs of internal conflict and, probably, of unsolvable problems; it may be necessary to question its basic assumptions. Since the use of propaganda and force to eliminate conflicting subsystems is unacceptable to most of us, the alternative is one of restructuring, probably starting at the grass-roots level.

There is an urgent need for discussions of long-range goals to bring consistency between the proposed actions and the systematic logic of the process of urban change. A major aim should be to challenge the widespread cultural values of an antiurban society – a society that stresses cultural homogeneity, fleeting fashions, consumerism, and degradation of cultural symbols, a society that replaces community interaction with instant communications. This cultural challenge would lead, inevitably, to a sociopolitical challenge of issues at the root of those cultural problems and, eventually, of many of our urban problems. As an example, social and racial discrimination, housing segregation, educational differences, neighborhood deterioration, and sprawl have some common roots in an affluent society stratified along racial and class lines, whose elite groups have abandoned their traditional roles as cultural leaders while maintaining their socioeconomic power.

There is a need to challenge the values of a society based on the class system because that system is undemocratic and inconsistent with the goals of the country, which are supported by the majority of its people. There is also a need to fill the vacuum created by the social elites' abdication of their cultural leadership with a combination of community grassroots leaders and allied professionals, intellectuals, artists, scholars, and scientists. Typically, intellectuals have functioned as courtiers of the social elites, but a growing number of writers, scientists, and artists have taken antiestablishment positions – in most cases on a national level – for example, in favor of civil rights and against the Vietnam War and intervention in Central America. The seeds for filling the cultural vacuum with a democratic and intellectual leadership are there.

The reconstruction of urban communities must stress diversity, as both a social and a visual characteristic, and ensure variety and equality of social groups, so that no one can exert undue dominance. It must stress a rich urban mixture with economic and political balance, an environment that is resilient, enjoyable, and fair. Heterogeneity, interaction, and exchange; competition and cooperation; urbanity and choice; symbolism and spontaneity – all should be there in a wide range of communities, from small towns to large metropolises – a postindustrial society inextricably linked with humane and democratic values.

NOTES

2. TRADITIONS IN COMMUNITY DESIGN

1. See, e.g., Vincent Scully, *American Architecture and Urbanism* (New York: Praeger, 1969), and Sibyl Moholy Nagy, *Native Genius in Anonymous Architecture* (New York: Horizon Press, 1957).

2. Most prominently, see the Bernard Rudofsky trilogy: *Architecture Without Architects* (New York: Museum of Modern Art, 1965), *Streets for People* (Garden City, N.Y.: Doubleday, 1969), and *The Prodigious Builders* (New York: Harcourt Brace Jovanovich, 1977).

3. Robert Redfield, *The Little Community* (Chicago: University of Chicago Press, 1955), and *Peasant Society and Culture* (Chicago: University of Chicago Press, 1961).

4. BELOW THE URBAN SURFACE

1. Brian Berry, "Interdependency of Spatial Structure and Spatial Behavior: A General Field Theory Formulation," *Papers of the Regional Science Association,* 21 (1968): 205–27.

2. Howard T. Odum and Larry L. Peterson, "Relationship of Energy and Complexity in Planning," in Royston Landau (ed.), *Complexity, Architectural Design,* 42, No. 10 (1972): 624–7.

3. Roslyn Lindheim, "Uncoupling Spatial Systems," in *General Systems Yearbook,* Vol. 13 (Ann Arbor, Mich.: Society for General Systems Research, 1968), pp. 99–103.

4. Ibid.

5. Stafford Beer, "Managing Modern Complexity," in Landau (ed.), *Complexity,* pp. 629–32.

6. Melvin Webber, "The Urban Place and the Non-Place Urban Realm," in Melvin Webber (ed.), *Explorations into Urban Structure* (Philadelphia: University of Pennsylvania Press, 1964), pp. 79–153.

7. Britton Harris, "Complexity in the Metropolis," in Landau (ed.), *Complexity,* pp. 637–8.

8. Odum and Peterson, "Relationship."

9. Harris, "Complexity."

10. Nicholas Georgescu-Roegen, *The Entropy Law and the Economic Process* (Cambridge, Mass.: Harvard University Press, 1971).

11. Donald L. Foley, "An Approach to Metropolitan Spatial Structure," in Webber (ed.), *Explorations into Urban Structure,* pp. 21–77.

12. Ibid.
13. Douglas R. Hoftstadter, *Gödel, Escher, Bach: An Eternal Golden Braid* (New York: Vintage Books, 1980).
14. Georgescu-Roegen, *The Entropy Law.*
15. A. Angyal, *Foundations for a Science of Personality* (Cambridge, Mass.: Harvard University Press, 1941).
16. Herbert Simon, "The Architecture of Complexity," in *General Systems Yearbook,* Vol. 10 (Ann Arbor, Mich.: Society for General Systems Research, 1965), pp. 63–76.
17. Lancelot Law Whyte, "On the Frontiers of Science: This Hierarchical Universe," in Landau (ed.), *Complexity,* pp. 611–14.
18. Ibid.
19. Ibid.
20. Ibid.
21. Joseph Needham, *Order and Life* (New Haven, Conn.: Yale University Press, 1936).
22. Whyte, "Frontiers."

5. CITIES IN EVOLUTION

1. J. H. Woodger, *Biological Principles* (London: Routledge & Kegan Paul, 1929).
2. J. Q. Stewart, and W. Warntz, "Physics of Population Distribution," *Journal of Regional Science,* 1 (1958): 99–123.
3. Geoffrey Dutton, "Criteria of Growth in Urban Systems," *Ekistics,* 215 (October 1973): 298–306.
4. Ibid.
5. Peter Cowan, "Studies in the Growth, Change and Ageing of Buildings," *Transactions of the Bartlett Society* (1962–3): 55–84.
6. Kenneth Boulding, *Beyond Economics* (Ann Arbor: University of Michigan Press, 1970).
7. Ibid.
8. D'Arcy W. Thompson, *On Growth and Form* (Cambridge University Press, 1952).
9. Boulding, *Beyond Economics.*
10. Hal. H. Winsborough, "City Growth and City Structure," *Journal of Regional Science,* 4, No. 2 (1962): 35–49.
11. O. D. Duncan, "Population Distribution and Community Structure", *Cold Spring Harbor Symposia on Quantitative Biology,* 22 (1959): 357–71.
12. Donald L. Foley, "An Approach to Metropolitan Spatial Structure," in Melvin Webber (ed.), *Explorations into Urban Structure* (Philadelphia: University of Pennsylvania Press, 1964), pp. 21–77.
13. Nicholas Georgescu-Roegen, *The Entropy Law and the Economic Process* (Cambridge, Mass.: Harvard University Press, 1971).
14. Ibid.
15. Cowan, "Studies."
16. Howard T. Odum, and Larry L. Peterson, "Relationship of Energy and Complexity in Planning," in Royston Landau (ed.), *Complexity, Architectural Design,* 42, No. 10 (1972): 624–7.
17. Cowan, "Studies."

1. Bruce E. Newling, "Urban Growth and Spatial Structure: Mathematical Models and Empirical Evidence," *Geographical Review*, 56, No. 2 (1966): 213–25.
2. Kenneth E. Boulding, *Beyond Economics* (Ann Arbor: University of Michigan Press, 1968).
3. Galileo Galilei, *Discorzi e dimostrazioni matematiche, intorno a due nuove scienze*... (1638). [*Dialogues Concerning Two New Sciences*], trans. H. Crew and A. De Salvio (New York, 1914).
4. Peter Cowan, "Studies in the Growth, Change and Ageing of Buildings," *Transactions of the Bartlett Society* (1962–3): 55–84.
5. P. B. Medawar, *The Uniqueness of the Individual* (London: Methuen, 1957).
6. Cowan, "Studies."
7. S. Brody, *Bioenergetics and Growth* (New York: Reinhold, 1945).
8. J. S. Huxley, *Problems of Relative Growth* (1932) (New York: Dover, 1972).
9. Boulding, *Beyond Economics*.
10. Stephen J. Gould, "Allometry and Size in Ontogeny and Phylogeny," *Biological Reviews*, 41 (1966): 587–640.
11. Geoffrey Dutton, "Criteria of Growth in Urban Systems," *Ekistics*, 215 (October 1973): 298–306.
12. Ranko Bon, "Allometry in the Topological Structure of Architectural Spatial Systems," *Ekistics*, 215 (October 1973): 270–6.
13. Dutton, "Criteria of Growth."
14. Newling, "Urban Growth."
15. Michael J. Woldenberg, "An Allometric Analysis of Urban Land in the United States," *Ekistics*, 215 (October 1973): 282–90.
16. Joseph Needham, *Order and Life* (New Haven, Conn.: Yale University Press, 1936).
17. Leo Schnore, "Some Correlates of Urban Size: A Replication," *American Journal of Sociology*, 69 (September 1963): 185–93.
18. G. M. Neutze, *Economic Policy and the Size of Cities* (Canberra: Australian National University, 1965).
19. Boulding, *Beyond Economics*.

7. LAND USE IN CITIES

1. Simon Gottschalk, *Communities and Alternatives: An Exploration of the Limits of Planning* (New York: Wiley, 1975).
2. Robert Sommers, *Personal Space: The Behavioral Basis of Design* (Englewood Cliffs, N.J.: Prentice Hall, 1969).
3. Edward T. Hall, *The Hidden Dimension*, (Garden City, N.Y.: Doubleday/Anchor Books, 1969).
4. René Jules Dubos, "Man Adapting: His Limitations and Potentialities," in William R. Ewald, Jr. (ed.), *Environment for Man: The Next Fifty Years* (Bloomington: Indiana University Press, 1967), pp. 11–26.
5. Richard Sennett, *The Uses of Disorder: Personal Identity and City Life* (New York: Vintage Books, 1970).
6. Ibid.
7. Ibid.

8. Ibid.
9. Ibid.
10. Ibid.
11. Dubos, "Man Adapting."
12. Sennett, "Uses of Disorder."
13. Jon T. Lang, *Creating Architectural Theory: The Role of Behavioral Sciences in Environmental Design* (New York: Van Nostrand Reinhold, 1987).
14. F. L. Bates, "Position, Role and Status: A Reformulation of Concepts," *Social Forces*, 34 (1956): 313–21.
15. Hall, *The Hidden Dimension*.
16. Sommers, *Personal Space*.
17. Herbert J. Gans, "Planning for People, not Buildings," *Environment and Planning*, 1 (1969): 33–46.
18. Sennett, "Uses of Disorder."
19. S. J. McNaughton and L. L. Wolf, "Dominance and the Niche in Ecological Systems," *Science*, 167 (January 1970): 131–9.
20. Ibid.
21. Ibid.
22. Lang, *Creating Architectural Theory*.
23. Harvey S. Perloff, "A Framework for Dealing with the Urban Environment," in H. Perloff (ed.), *The Quality of the Urban Environment* (Washington, D.C.: Resources for the Future, 1969), pp. 3–25.
24. Eric Lampard, "The History of Cities in the Economically Advanced Areas," in John Friedmann and William Alonso (eds.). *Regional Development and Planning* (Cambridge, Mass. MIT Press, 1964), pp. 321–42.
25. Perloff, "Framework."
26. Kenneth E. Boulding, *Beyond Economics* (Ann Arbor: University of Michigan Press, 1968).
27. Eugene P. Odum, "The Strategy of Ecosystem Development," *Science*, 164 (April 1969): 262–70.
28. Ibid.
29. McNaughton and Wolf, "Dominance."
30. William Michaelson, *Man and His Urban Environment* (Reading, Mass.: Addison-Wesley, 1970).
31. Warren Boeschenstein, "Design of Socially Mixed Housing," *Journal of the American Institute of Planning*, 37, No. 5 (September 1971): 311–18.
32. Ibid.
33. Gottschalk, *Communities and Alternatives*.
34. Ibid.
35. Ibid.
36. Louis Wirth, "Urbanism as a Way of Life," in Paul K. Hatt and Albert J. Reiss, Jr. (eds.), *Cities and Society* (New York: Free Press, 1957), pp. 46–63.
37. Peter Willmott, "Social Research and New Communities," *Journal of the American Institute of Planners*, 33 (November 1967): 387–98.
38. Terence R. Lee, "Urban Neighborhoods as a Socio-Spatial Schema," *Human Relations*, 21 (1968): 241–68.
39. Margaret Willis, "Sociological Aspects of Urban Structure: A Comparison of Residential Groupings Proposed in Planning New Towns," *Town Planning Review*, 39 (1969): 296–306.

40. Lee, "Urban Neighborhoods."
41. Kevin Lynch, *Site Planning* (Cambridge, Mass.: MIT Press, 1971).
42. Christopher Tunnard and Boris Pushkarev, *Man-Made America* (New Haven, Conn.: Yale University Press, 1963).
43. Stanley B. Tankel, "The Importance of Open Space in the Urban Pattern," in Lowdon Wingo (ed.), *Cities and Space* (Baltimore, Md.: Johns Hopkins University and Resources for the Future, 1963), pp. 57–71.
44. Perloff, "Framework."
45. Irving Hoch, "The Three-Dimensional City: Contained Urban Space," in Perloff (ed.), *Quality of the Urban Environment*, pp. 73–135.

8. DENSITY IN COMMUNITIES

1. U.S. Bureau of the Census, Statistical Abstract of the U.S.: 1970 Census of the Population.
2. Jean Bastié, "Paris: Baroque Elegance and Agglomeration," in H. Wentworth Eldredge (ed.), *World Capitals* (Garden City, N.Y.: Doubleday/Anchor Press, 1975), pp. 55–89.
3. David A. Crane and Associates, *A Comparative Study of New Towns* (New York Urban Development Corporation, 1970).
4. Edwin S. Mills, *Urban Economics* (Glenview, Ill.: Scott, Foresman, 1972).
5. William Alonso, *Location and Land Use* (Cambridge, Mass.: Harvard University Press, 1964).
6. Irving Hoch, "The Three-Dimensional City: Contained Urban Space," in Harvey S. Perloff (ed.), *The Quality of the Urban Environment* (Washington, D.C.: Resources for the Future, 1969), pp. 73–135.
7. Jon. T. Lang, *Creating Architectural Theory: The Role of Behavioral Sciences in Environmental Design* (New York: Van Nostrand Reinhold, 1987).
8. Robert Campbell, "Romance of Paris Is Fueled by Its Density," *Boston Globe,* 14 August 1984.
9. Kevin Lynch, *Site Planning,* 2d ed. (Cambridge, Mass.: MIT Press, 1971).
10. Ibid.
11. Ibid.
12. Ibid.
13. Donald E. Schmidt, "Crowding in Urban Environments: An Integration of Theory and Research," in John R. Aiello and Andrew Baum (eds.), *Residential Crowding and Design* (New York: Plenum Press, 1979), pp. 41–59.
14. Daniel Stokols, "A Social-Psychological Model of Human Crowding Phenomena," *Journal of the American Institute of Planners,* 38, No. 2 (1972): 72–83.
15. Lang, *Creating Architectural Theory.*
16. Omer R. Galle and Walter R. Gove, "Crowding and Behavior in Chicago, 1940–1970," in Aiello and Baum (eds.), *Residential Crowding,* pp. 23–39.
17. R. S. Schmitt, "Density, Health, and Social Disorganization," *Journal of the American Institute of Planners,* 32, No. 1 (1966): 38–40; idem, "Implications of Density in Hong Kong," ibid., 29, No. 3 (1963):

210–17; idem, "Density, Delinquency, and Crime in Honolulu," *Sociology and Social Research*, 41 (1957): 274–6; Paul Henri Chombart de Lauwe, *Famille et habitation* (Paris: Edition du centre national de la recherche scientific, 1967); H. Winsborough, "The Social Consequences of High Population Density," *Law and Contemporary Problems*, 30, No. 1 (1965); 120–6; R. Mitchell, "Some Social Implications of High Density Housing," *American Sociological Review*, 36 (1971): 18–29.

18. Stokols, "Social-Psychological Model."

19. Omer R. Galle, Walter R. Gove, and J. McPherson, "Population Density and Pathology," *Science*, 176 (1972): 23–30.

20. Galle and Gove, "Crowding and Behavior."

21. D. Schmidt, "Crowding in Urban Environments."

22. Paul R. Hopstock, John R. Aiello, and Andrew Baum, "Residential Crowding Research," in Aiello and Baum (eds.), *Residential Crowding*, pp. 9–21.

23. J. Brehm, *A Theory of Psychological Reactance* (New York: Academic Press, 1966).

24. H. Proshansky, W. Ittelson, and L. Rivkin, *Environmental Psychology* (New York: Holt, 1970).

25. A. W. Wicker, "Undermanning Theory and Research: Implications for the Study of Psychological and Behavioral Effects of Excess Population," *Representative Research in Social Psychology*, 4 (1973): 185–206.

26. S. Saegert, "Crowding: Cognitive Overload and Behavioral Constraint," in W. Preiser (ed.), *Proceedings of the Environmental Research Association*, Vol. 2 (Stroudsburg, Pa.: Dowden, Hutchinson & Ross, 1973), pp. 254–60; Daniel Stokols, "The Experience of Crowding in Primary and Secondary Environments," *Environment and Behavior*, 8 (1976): 49–86.

27. Stokols, "Experience of Crowding."

28. Stokols, "Social Psychological Model."

29. W. Griffitt, and R. Veitch, "Hot and Crowded: Influences of Population Density and Temperature on Interpersonal Affective Behavior," *Journal of Personality and Social Psychology*, 17, No. 1 (1971): 92–8; D. C. Glass, and J. E. Singer, *Urban Stress* (New York: Academic Press, 1972).

30. Lang, *Creating Architectural Theory*.

31. A. Westin, *Privacy and Freedom* (New York: Ballantine, 1970).

32. William H. Michaelson, *Man and His Urban Environment: A Sociological Approach* (Reading, Mass.: Addison-Wesley, 1970).

33. Edward T. Hall, *The Hidden Dimension* (Garden City, N.Y.: Doubleday, 1966).

34. J. A. Desor, "Toward a Psychological Theory of Crowding," *Journal of Personality and Social Psychology*, 21, No. 1 (1972): 79–83.

35. I. Altman, *The Environment and Social Behavior* (Monterey, Calif.: Brooks/Cole, 1975).

36. S. Milgram, "The Experience of Living in Cities," *Science*, 167 (1970).

37. Hall, *The Hidden Dimension*.

38. R. G. Barker, *Ecological Psychology* (Stanford, Calif.: Stanford University Press, 1968); idem, "Explorations in Ecological Psychology," *American Psychologist*, 20 (1965): 1–14.

39. Kenneth Frampton, *Modern Architecture: A Critical History* (New York: Oxford University Press, 1980).

40. Amos Rapoport, *House Form and Culture* (Englewood Cliffs, N.J.: Prentice Hall, 1969).

41. Lang, *Creating Architectural Theory*.

42. Robert Sommers, *Personal Space: The Behavioral Basis of Design* (Englewood Cliffs, N.J.: Prentice Hall, 1969).

43. American Public Health Association, *Planning the Neighborhood* (Chicago, 1960).

9. DISTRIBUTION IN CITIES

1. Ira Lowry, "Seven Models of Urban Development: A Structural Comparison," in Charles Hemmens (ed.), *Urban Development Models,* Special Rep. 97 (Washington, D.C.: Highway Research Board, 1968), pp. 121–63.

2. Walter Isard, *Methods of Regional Analysis: An Introduction to Regional Science* (New York: Technology Press; Wiley, 1960).

3. Lowry, "Seven Models."

4. Hal H. Winsborough, "City Growth and City Structure," *Journal of Regional Science,* 4, No. 2 (1962): 35–49.

5. Melvin M. Webber, "The Urban Place and the Non-place Urban Realm," in M. Webber (ed.), *Explorations into Urban Structure* (Philadelphia: University of Philadelphia Press, 1964), pp. 79–153.

6. Ibid.

7. Melvin M. Webber, "Order in Diversity: Community without Propinquity," in Lowdon Wingo (ed.), *Cities in Space: The Future Use of Urban Land* (Baltimore, Md.: Johns Hopkins University Press, 1962), pp. 23–54.

8. Clarence A. Perry, "The Neighborhood Unit," *Regional Survey of New York and Its Environs,* Vol. 7 (New York: Committee on the Regional Plan and Its Environs, 1929).

9. Norman Pearson, "Planning a Social Unit," in Gwen Bell and Jaqueline Tyrwhitt (ed.), *Human Identity in the Urban Environment* (Harmondsworth: Penguin Books, 1972): pp. 252–61.

10. American Public Health Association, *Planning the Neighborhood* (Chicago, 1960).

11. Jon T. Lang, *Creating Architectural Theory: The Role of Behavioral Sciences in Environmental Design* (New York: Van Nostrand Reinhold, 1987).

12. George Hillery, *Communal Organizations* (Chicago: University of Chicago Press, 1968).

13. Simon S. Gottschalk, *Communities and Alternatives: An Exploration of the Limits of Planning* (New York: Wiley, 1975).

14. Terence L. Lee, "Urban Neighborhood as a Socio-Spatial Schema," *Human Relations,* 21 (1968): 241–67.

15. Suzanne Keller, *The Urban Neighborhood* (New York: Random House, 1968).

16. Ruth Glass (ed.), *The Social Background of a Plan: A Study of Middleborough* (London: Routledge & Kegan Paul, 1948).

17. Peter Willmott, "Social Research and New Communities," *Journal of the American Institute of Planners,* 33, No. 6 (1967): 387–98.

18. University of Bristol, Geography Department, unpublished research.
19. Pearson, "Planning."
20. Christopher Alexander, "The City Is Not a Tree," *Ekistics*, 139 (1966): 344–8.
21. Webber, "Order in Diversity."
22. Ibid.
23. Isard, *Methods*.
24. Brian J. L. Berry, "The Retail Component of the Urban Model," *Journal of the American Institute of Planners*, 31 (1965): 150–5.
25. Ibid.
26. William Alonso, personal communication.

12. VISUAL PHENOMENA AND MOVEMENT

1. Konrad Z. Lorenz, "The Role of Gestalt Perception in Animal and Human Behavior," in Lancelot Law Whyte (ed.), *Aspects of Form* (Bloomington: Indiana University Press, 1966), pp. 157–78.
2. Douglas R. Hoftstadter, *Gödel, Escher, Bach: An Eternal Golden Braid* (New York: Basic Books, 1979).
3. Rudolf Arnheim, "Gestalt Psychology and Artistic Form," in Whyte (ed.), *Aspects of Form*, pp. 196–208.
4. Jon T. Lang, *Creating Architectural Theory: The Role of Behavioral Sciences in Environmental Design* (New York: Van Nostrand Reinhold, 1987).
5. Amos, Rapoport, "Some Observations Regarding Man–Environment Studies," *Art*, 2, No. 1 (1971): 4–15.
6. Edward T. Hall, *The Hidden Dimension* (Garden City, N.Y.: Doubleday/Anchor Books, 1969).
7. Amos Rapoport, and Ron Hawkes, "The Perception of Urban Complexity," *Journal of the American Institute of Planners*, 36, No. 2 (1970): pp. 106–11.
8. Lang, *Creating Architectural Theory*.
9. J. J. Gibson, *The Perception of the Visual World* (Boston: Houghton Mifflin, 1950); idem, *The Senses Considered as Perceptual Systems* (London: Allen & Unwin, 1968).
10. Rapoport and Hawkes, *Perception*.
11. Lang, *Creating Architectural Theory*.
12. Carl Steinitz, "Meaning and the Congruence of Urban Form and Activity," *Journal of the American Institute of Planners*, 34, No. 4 (1968): 233–48.
13. Catherine Bauer-Wurster, "The Form and Structure of the Future Urban Complex," in Lowdon Wingo, Jr. (ed.), *Cities and Space,* (Baltimore, Md.: Johns Hopkins University Press, 1966), pp. 73–101.
14. Steinitz, "Meaning."
15. Ibid.
16. J. J. Gibson, *An Ecological Approach to Visual Perception* (Boston: Houghton Mifflin, 1979).
17. W. R. Gardner, "To Perceive Is to Know," *American Psychologist*, 21 (1966): pp. 11–19.
18. Hofstadter, *Gödel, Escher, Bach*.
19. Ibid.
20. John R. Platt, "Beauty: Pattern and Change," in Donald W. Fiske

and Salvatore R. Madi (eds.), *Functions of Varied Experience* (Homewood, Ill.: Dorsey Press, 1961), pp. 402–30.

21. Hofstadter, *Gödel, Escher, Bach.*

22. Floyd Allport, *Theories of Perception and Concepts of Structure* (New York: Wiley, 1955).

23. A. N. Whitehead, *The Principles of Natural Knowledge* (Cambridge University Press, 1925).

24. Platt, "Beauty."

25. Allport, *Theories of Perception.*

26. Ibid.

27. Romedi Passini, *Wayfinding in Architecture* (New York: Van Nostrand Reinhold, 1984).

28. E. C. Tolman, *Purposive Behavior in Animals and Man* (New York: Century, 1932); Gary T. Moore and Reginald G. Golledge (eds.), *Environmental Knowing: Theories, Research and Methods* (Stroudsburg, Pa.: Dowden, Hutchinson & Ross, 1976).

29. Stephen Kaplan, "Cognitive Maps in Perception and Thought," in Roger M. Downs and David Stea (eds.), *Image and Environment* (Chicago: Aldine, 1973), pp. 63–78.

30. Hall, *Hidden Dimension.*

31. Rapoport and Hawkes, *Perception.*

32. Ibid.

33. Empson, W., *Seven Types of Ambiguity,* 3d ed. (New York: Meridian Books, 1955).

34. Norbert Wiener, *The Human Use of Human Beings* (New York: Avon Books, 1950).

35. D. O. Hebb, *The Organization of Behavior* (New York: Wiley, 1949); "Drives and the CNS," *Psychological Review,* 62, (1955): 243–54.

36. A. Koestler, *The Act of Creation* (New York: Macmillan, 1965).

37. Hall, *Hidden Dimension.*

38. C. R. Evans and D. J. Piggins, "A Comparison of the Behaviour of Geometrical Shapes When Viewed Under Conditions of Steady Fixation, and with Apparatus for Producing a Stabilised Retinal Image," in D. Vernon (ed.), *Experiments with Visual Perception* (Harmondsworth: Penguin Books, 1966), pp. 293–305.

39. Lang, *Creating Architectural Theory.*

40. Kevin Lynch, *The Image of the City* (Cambridge, Mass: MIT Press, 1960).

41. Anselm Strauss, *Images of the American City* (New York: Free Press, 1961).

42. Lang, *Creating Architectural Theory.*

INDEX

317

oasis, 232
obelisk, 28, 28f, 290
object form, 36, 37
obsolescence, 63, 93, 105, 106f,
    107–8, 180, 228; *see also*
    stability
  classification of, 103–5
Odum, Howard T., 74
office building, 55, 58f, 60, 64, 84,
    116, 177, 193, 248; *see also*
    corporation, headquarters;
    park, office; skyscraper;
    workplace
  high-rise, 37, 39, 58, 61–2, 127,
    243, 244
  speculation, 61, 62
Olmstead, Frederick Law, 181f,
    253
open/unbuilt space, 46, 55, 92,
    148, 149–50, 151, 153, 154,
    165, 166, 172, 177, 179, 181f,
    225, 232, 246, 248, 252–3,
    254, 302, 303
  duality with built form, 40–4,
    41f, 70, 114, 242, 249–53,
    256f, 258, 270
  ratio of, 172, 179
opera, 48, 122, 149, 191
order, 271, 272f, 282f, 288–9
  duality with diversity, 264–6,
    267, 270, 271, 276f, 282
  low-level, *see also* monotony
orientation, 265–6, 271, 295
  in building, 127, 177
  in city, 254, 272–3, 274f, 279,
    281, 288–9, 303
  lacking, 127, 177, 268, 279, 283,
    284f, 286–7, 286f
orphanage, 62
Ottoman Empire, 224; *see also*
    Turkey
overdifferentiation, 123
overhang, 238
oversimplification, 135, 149
overspecialization, 82–3, 91, 99,
    108, 123, 134, 144
overstimulation, 170

palace, 17, 44, 48, 114, 212, 218,
    221, 234; *see also specific palace*;
    façade, in Paris
Palace of the Alhambra, 234, 236f
Palazzo Chiericati, 13f

Palazzo Corner Ca'Grande, 56f
Palace of Diocletian, 278
Palazzo Medici–Riccardi, 56f
Palazzo Rucellai, 56f
Palazzo Vecchio, 48f, 274f, 289
Palazzo Vendramin-Calergi, 56f
Palermo, 166
Palladio, Andrea, 13f
Palma Nuova, 28f
Paris, 9, 64, 137f, 166, 178, 212,
    214, 225, 251, 279, 284f, 288
  density of, 158, 159, 164
  growth of, 89f, 90f, 215f, 216,
    218f
  Haussman plan for, 28, 30, 31f
  urban pattern, 48, 137
Paris Cathedral, *see* Notre Dame
    de Paris
park
  industrial, 149, 161, 188
  linear, 251, 254
  office, 161, 188, 193, 248, 253,
    301
  public, 31f, 122, 166, 250–1,
    252–3, 255, 259; *see also* open/
    unbuilt space
Park Crescent, 279
parking, 54, 62, 105, 119, 120,
    122, 126, 135, 153, 164, 165,
    166, 247, 252, 287, 288, 290;
    see also garage
parliament building, 17, 48
parochialism, 196
Parsons, Talcott, 139
Parthenon, 111f
party wall, *see* wall, party
paseo, 225
passage, sense of, 219, 220f
path, 104, 231, 247, 279
patio house, *see* courtyard house
pattern, and perception, 262, 264–
    5; *see also* rhythm; urban
    pattern
pavilion, 114
peasantry, 11, 14, 139, 189, 216,
    227, 228
pedestrianism, 10, 86, 103, 114,
    124f, 126, 180, 225, 238, 247,
    248, 251, 252, 254, 279
  interface with transportation,
    46–8, 47f, 163, 177, 204–5,
    288, 302
peninsula, 214, 259